MW01088916

Innovation and Public Policy

A National Bureau of Economic Research

Conference Report

Innovation and
Public Policy

Edited by   **Austan Goolsbee and Benjamin F. Jones**

The University of Chicago Press

Chicago and London

The University of Chicago Press, Chicago 60637
The University of Chicago Press, Ltd., London
© 2021 by The National Bureau of Economic Research
Published 2021
Printed in the United States of America

30 29 28 27 26 25 24 23 22 21   1 2 3 4 5

ISBN-13: 978-0-226-80545-0 (cloth)
ISBN-13: 978-0-226-80559-7 (e-book)

DOI: https://doi.org/10.7208/chicago/9780226805597.001.0001

Library of Congress Cataloging-in-Publication Data

Names: Goolsbee, Austan, editor. | Jones, Benjamin F., editor.
Title: Innovation and public policy / edited by Austan Goolsbee and
     Benjamin F. Jones.
Other titles: National Bureau of Economic Research conference report.
Description: Chicago : University of Chicago Press, 2021. | Series:
     National Bureau of Economic Research conference report | Includes
     bibliographical references and index.
Identifiers: LCCN 2021021047 | ISBN 9780226805450 (cloth) |
     ISBN 9780226805597 (ebook)
Subjects: LCSH: Technological innovations—Government policy—
     United States. | Technological innovations—Economic aspects—
     United States. | Science and state—United States.
Classification: LCC HC110.T4 I553 2021 | DDC 338.973—dc23
LC record available at https://lccn.loc.gov/2021021047

♾ This paper meets the requirements of ANSI/NISO Z39.48-1992
(Permanence of Paper).

Relation of the Directors to the Work and Publications of the NBER

1. The object of the NBER is to ascertain and present to the economics profession, and to the public more generally, important economic facts and their interpretation in a scientific manner without policy recommendations. The Board of Directors is charged with the responsibility of ensuring that the work of the NBER is carried on in strict conformity with this object.

2. The President shall establish an internal review process to ensure that book manuscripts proposed for publication DO NOT contain policy recommendations. This shall apply both to the proceedings of conferences and to manuscripts by a single author or by one or more co-authors but shall not apply to authors of comments at NBER conferences who are not NBER affiliates.

3. No book manuscript reporting research shall be published by the NBER until the President has sent to each member of the Board a notice that a manuscript is recommended for publication and that in the President's opinion it is suitable for publication in accordance with the above principles of the NBER. Such notification will include a table of contents and an abstract or summary of the manuscript's content, a list of contributors if applicable, and a response form for use by Directors who desire a copy of the manuscript for review. Each manuscript shall contain a summary drawing attention to the nature and treatment of the problem studied and the main conclusions reached.

4. No volume shall be published until forty-five days have elapsed from the above notification of intention to publish it. During this period a copy shall be sent to any Director requesting it, and if any Director objects to publication on the grounds that the manuscript contains policy recommendations, the objection will be presented to the author(s) or editor(s). In case of dispute, all members of the Board shall be notified, and the President shall appoint an ad hoc committee of the Board to decide the matter; thirty days additional shall be granted for this purpose.

5. The President shall present annually to the Board a report describing the internal manuscript review process, any objections made by Directors before publication or by anyone after publication, any disputes about such matters, and how they were handled.

6. Publications of the NBER issued for informational purposes concerning the work of the Bureau, or issued to inform the public of the activities at the Bureau, including but not limited to the NBER Digest and Reporter, shall be consistent with the object stated in paragraph 1. They shall contain a specific disclaimer noting that they have not passed through the review procedures required in this resolution. The Executive Committee of the Board is charged with the review of all such publications from time to time.

7. NBER working papers and manuscripts distributed on the Bureau's web site are not deemed to be publications for the purpose of this resolution, but they shall be consistent with the object stated in paragraph 1. Working papers shall contain a specific disclaimer noting that they have not passed through the review procedures required in this resolution. The NBER's web site shall contain a similar disclaimer. The President shall establish an internal review process to ensure that the working papers and the web site do not contain policy recommendations, and shall report annually to the Board on this process and any concerns raised in connection with it.

8. Unless otherwise determined by the Board or exempted by the terms of paragraphs 6 and 7, a copy of this resolution shall be printed in each NBER publication as described in paragraph 2 above.

Contents

Preface

Innovation is widely recognized as a central force for raising standards of living. Yet innovative activity is riddled with market failures that can limit private investment. These market failures invite public policy to play a potentially critical role in promoting innovative effort. Indeed, such policies might be among the most important things governments can do to foster key social goals over the long run, including improved human health and rising socioeconomic prosperity. The purpose of this volume is to take stock of recent research that advances our understanding of innovation and the specific roles that public policy can play.

This project was generously funded by the Ewing Marion Kauffman Foundation through a grant to the National Bureau of Economic Research. The Kauffman Foundation has a long tradition of supporting research on entrepreneurship and innovation, in economics as well as other fields. We are very grateful for their support.

In building this volume, we were fortunate to recruit a set of authors who have made key contributions to innovation-policy research and who have come together here to synthesize the latest insights. The authors have produced a series of excellent chapters, each organizing cutting-edge research streams into coherent frameworks that can inform a large set of policy opportunities. With innovation playing a central role in improving standards of living, the stakes in getting policy right are very large. In the individual chapters, and collectively, the authors have provided a concise and accessible guide.

We also thank Josh Lerner, Jim Poterba, and Scott Stern for suggesting that we undertake this project and supporting the effort throughout. Finally, we thank Chad Zimmerman, our editor at the University of Chicago Press, and Helena Fitz-Patrick at the NBER, who were both extremely helpful in managing the publication process.

Introduction

Austan Goolsbee and Benjamin F. Jones

Innovation is often seen as a central force for increasing economic prosperity and improving health. From the early days of the Industrial Revolution, policy makers have recognized the role of scientific and technological advancement. The British prime minister Benjamin Disraeli once observed, "How much has happened in these fifty years. . . . I am thinking of those revolutions of science which . . . have changed the position and prospects of mankind more than all the conquests and all the codes and all the legislators that ever lived" (Lockyer 1903, 735). Disraeli's observation is the more remarkable for having been made in 1870; it predated most of what we think of as the major innovations of the last 150 years—electricity, automobiles and airplanes, antibiotics and vaccines, agricultural advances, computers, the internet, biotechnology, and many others. Compared to 1870, US income per capita today is 18 times higher, and life expectancy at birth is 35 years longer.[1]

Economists have come to understand the central role of innovation through studies of economic growth (e.g., Solow 1956), industrial productivity (e.g., Griliches 1979), sectoral dynamics (e.g., Schumpeter 1942), and

Austan Goolsbee is the Robert P. Gwinn Professor of Economics at the University of Chicago Booth School of Business and a research associate of the National Bureau of Economic Research.

Benjamin F. Jones is the Gordon and Llura Gund Family Professor of Entrepreneurship and a professor of strategy at Northwestern University, and a research associate of the National Bureau of Economic Research.

For acknowledgments, sources of research support, and disclosure of the authors' material financial relationships, if any, please see https://www.nber.org/books-and-chapters/innovation-and-public-policy/introduction-innovation-and-public-policy.

1. For historical real income per capita, see, for example, Jones (2016). For historical life expectancy, see Hacker (2010).

the broader sweep of economic history (e.g., Mokyr 1990; Rosenberg 1982), among other means. US government policy, meanwhile, has come to promote innovation through a suite of mechanisms from systems of intellectual property embedded in the US Constitution to major postwar institutions such as the National Science Foundation and the Research and Experimentation tax credit. Today, the role of public policy to support innovation—and ultimately economic and public health—has perhaps never been felt so acutely. Writing this chapter in 2020, we are collectively facing the coronavirus pandemic.[2] Innovation—including better tests, therapeutic treatments, and new vaccines—will be essential to overcoming the current devastating consequences the pandemic has imposed for health and prosperity.

This volume collects new insights on innovation policy. The contributions study first-order policy mechanisms and actionable ideas that can better fuel scientific and technological advance. Each analysis is based on the latest empirical evidence, understood within the context of existing policies and institutions.

In this introductory chapter, we present an overview of the new contributions, organized around five subjects. The first subject is the social returns to innovation investment, which is central to the case for public support. The second subject is human capital, which can constrain the nation's innovative capacity. The third subject is scientific grant funding, which occurs mostly outside markets and is closely tied to government financing. The fourth subject is tax policy, which can create incentives for and against innovation investment in the private sector. The final subject is entrepreneurship and ways in which government policy may effectively support new venture creation.

The following sections of this introduction consider each of these subject areas, summarizing key findings and highlighting common themes and potential policy implications. Weighing the evidence in each area suggests numerous policy options that may expand the rate of innovative activity in the economy, with potentially high social returns. In the concluding section, we further summarize key themes.

Why Public Policy for Innovation?

The case for public support of innovation rests on two foundations. The first is that innovation is obviously important for society—that is, for raising standards of living. The second is that markets are likely to underinvest in innovation from a society-wide perspective. While the first point is well established, the second point calls for further examination. The private

---

2. In tandem with this volume, the authors had planned to present their work at a major conference in Washington, DC. Even though that meeting was canceled because of the pandemic, the research collected here provides the same content, in depth, and serves as an up-to-date and accessible resource for innovation researchers and policy makers.

sector invests substantial resources in research and development—about 2 percent of GDP (National Science Foundation 2020). What is the case for public policy to support this private investment or to create large public entities like the NIH and the National Science Foundation?

The answer depends on the social returns to innovation: the broad gains experienced by society from a given advance. If innovation is important to rising standards of living, then these returns may naturally be high. But the case for public policy emerges, more precisely, when the social value created by innovation tends to exceed the value captured by the specific innovator. In this case, where innovation investment creates "positive spillovers" on others, the incentives to invest privately in innovation will be too low.

The most obvious form of such positive spillovers may be those following investments in science and basic research. Vannevar Bush, the founding director of the National Science Foundation, described science as opening an "endless frontier" of progress and the "fund from which the practical applications of knowledge must be drawn" (Bush 1945, 17). Because basic research does not directly produce new products and new services, a private return through market sales of a scientific insight is essentially absent. Yet, to Bush's point, progress in basic research may be essential to many downstream advances, and both anecdotes and broad empirical evidence on such spillovers abound (Ahmadpoor and Jones 2017; Dijkgraaf 2017; Flexner 1939).

To take one example, consider the familiar market innovation of ride-sharing (e.g., Uber and Lyft). These businesses depend on the Global Positioning System (GPS), a network of satellites that allows drivers and riders to locate each other. These satellites, first launched in 1978, depend in turn on many scientific breakthroughs, including Einstein's theory of general relativity, which is used explicitly to adjust the clock signals in GPS satellites, prior to launch. And Einstein's theory of general relativity, developed in 1915, depends critically on the initially obscure work of Bernhard Riemann, who in 1854 developed the necessary mathematical tools. These scientific breakthroughs, coming from basic research in mathematics and physics, ultimately opened doors to transformative marketplace innovations.

More broadly, spillovers may exist among marketplace innovations themselves, and these spillovers may be large. Such spillovers can occur through many channels, including the value downstream users receive from the innovation, the value captured by competitors who imitate the innovation, and the value captured by future innovators who build on the new idea. Apple created the first mass-market smartphone, providing large benefits to consumers; it also facilitated imitative entry by other smartphone makers; and it enabled enormous downstream innovation, creating new applications, technologies, and businesses. Not all spillovers from marketplace innovations are necessarily positive, however. For example, through business stealing, an innovation may provide a high return to the innovating business in part by taking business from competitors, who lose out. Innovators may also crowd onto narrow avenues, duplicating and wasting each other's efforts. Whether or not spillovers are positive on net, and the scale of such spillovers, are empirical questions.

In chapter 1 of this volume, "A Calculation of the Social Returns to Innovation," Benjamin F. Jones and Lawrence H. Summers review the existing literature on the social returns to innovation and consider the social returns at an economy-wide scale. The chapter introduces a new method for calculating such returns that integrates across the many spillover margins and many types of innovation. The method further works to incorporate all innovation costs; it avoids picking winners (like the smartphone) and instead includes the costs of successes and failures, as well as innovation costs that go beyond narrow research and development expenditure. The central finding is that the social returns to innovation, as a whole, appear extremely large. Innovation investment appears to pay for itself many times over, with a conservative estimate suggesting that $1 in investment returns at least $5 in benefits on average. Altogether, integrating across this approach and many previous studies, the empirical evidence is robust and clear. The social returns to innovation appear very large and far in excess of the private returns.

Given the evidence for large positive spillovers, there appear to be substantial market failures in innovation, where markets left to their own devices will underprovide innovation investment. This underinvestment in turn constrains growth in standards of living. The case for public investment and public policy to support innovation follows, and innovation policy emerges as a central sphere for governments to advance socioeconomic prosperity and human health. The next question then concerns the specific means of support, given the rich landscape of potential policy dimensions. The balance of the book investigates central dimensions of policy action.

Human Capital for Innovation

At the root of idea creation is innovative labor. This labor is a pipeline for new ideas and, when in limited supply, a potentially fundamental constraint on the rate of progress. The stock of available human capital in turn depends on specific government policies, including education and immigration policy. Chapters 2 and 3 in this volume consider the opportunity to expand the innovative workforce along these lines.

In chapter 2, "Innovation and Human Capital Policy," John Van Reenen studies the sources of innovative human capital and the potential to expand it. He begins with a fundamental observation about innovative labor supply. Namely, increasing spending on innovation, holding the supply of inventive labor fixed, may result in higher prices for the labor rather than more innovation (Goolsbee 1998). By contrast, expanding the supply of inventive labor can both accelerate innovation and reduce its cost. This suggests the key role that human capital policy can play.

Reviewing many margins to expand the pipeline of talent, Van Reenen examines K–12 education, university education, and broader barriers to entering innovative careers. Here we emphasize two of the chapter's key themes. The first theme is that the pool of potential talent appears much larger than the number of people who enter the innovative workforce. For example, the pool of talent based on third grade mathematics test scores appears large compared to the set of individuals who migrate into technology degrees and patenting (Bell et al. 2019a), and features of the child's environment, including household income, as well as gender and race strongly predict entry into patenting (Aghion et al. 2017; Akcigit, Grigsby, and Nicholas 2017; Bell et al. 2019a). Such findings suggest that the national labor pool has a large number of talented individuals, including from underrepresented groups, who do not find pathways into inventive careers.

The second theme is that specific interventions may help children track into inventive careers. For one, early exposure to inventive careers—including through parent networks and through neighborhood exposure to local technology businesses—sharply predicts whether an individual will eventually patent (Bell et al. 2019a). These exposure factors appear causative and suggest that mentoring and other forms of career exposure not only could expand the inventive labor pool but also may be a relatively powerful means to do so (Bell et al. 2019b). School-level interventions also appear promising. Studies of student tracking into gifted or advanced classrooms, using careful research designs, show short- and long-run advantages in math and science skills, and large increases in college enrollment among underrepresented groups (Card and Giuliano 2016; Cohodes 2020). Ultimately, education and career-exposure policies may draw substantially more talent into the innovative labor force, furthering growth. Because inventive careers are also relatively remunerative, these polices may simultaneously improve income mobility and reduce inequality.

Education-oriented policies can expand inventive labor supply over the longer run. More immediate advantages can come through immigration. In chapter 3, "Immigration Policy Levers for US Innovation and Start-Ups," Sari Pekkala Kerr and William R. Kerr examine the role of immigrants in driving US-based innovation and consider various policy reforms that could accelerate US innovation through the immigration channel. A fundamental observation is that immigrants are especially innovative. In particular, while immigrants account for about 14 percent of the US workforce, they account for approximately one-quarter of all US patents and new ventures and one-third of all Nobel Prizes won in the United States. Overall, immigrants are an enormous source of science, engineering, and innovation talent.

Kerr and Kerr review the US immigrant system in detail and consider numerous margins for expanding innovative labor. Several reforms consider expanding the number of visas, including H-1B visas and green cards, and the introduction of targeted visas, such as new forms of visas for entrepreneurs. Other policy reforms consider reallocations within existing quotas. For example, the green card system could relax its heavily binding country-specific caps, which work against countries like India that provide substantial innovative labor. Relatedly, the lottery system used to allocate H-1B visas can be redesigned to allocate more visas to scarce innovative talent. Although comprehensive immigration reform may be needed for changing the overall rate of immigration, several of Kerr and Kerr's actionable policy ideas may achieve large gains by seemingly small adjustments to current practices.

An important set of ideas further connects immigration policy and the US education system. Indeed, US universities attract large numbers of foreign students into their programs, especially for science and technology degrees, and this pipeline of talent is much larger than the numbers of H-1B and other employment visas available upon graduation. Currently, Optional Practical Training visas allow students to work for a limited time after graduation, but the binding green card and H-1B quotas ultimately cause the United States to lose much of this available talent pool. In addition to potentially broadening extensions to H-1B and green card quotas, targeting green cards to those with science and technology degrees ("stapling" green cards to their diplomas) and implementing related policy ideas may expand inventive labor in the United States in particularly targeted and relatively immediate ways.

Scientific Grant Funding

The US science system depends especially heavily on public support. Institutions like the National Institutes of Health (NIH), the National Science Foundation, the Department of Defense, and the Department of Energy, among many other US government agencies, are lead investors in basic research. This research is performed both in government laboratories and, in greater part, through grant funding to researchers outside government, especially in universities. Overall, the US government is the largest funder of basic research in the United States (National Science Foundation 2020).

In chapter 4, "Scientific Grant Funding," Pierre Azoulay and Danielle Li consider these innovation policy tools. The authors consider the case for grant funding as a policy mechanism, review the history of science-funding institutions, and discuss key principles to guide these types of investment. They also discuss mechanisms to continually improve the efficiency and design of science-funding institutions.

The case for science grant funding emerges in both its social returns and its unpredictable uses. Drawing together recent empirical evidence, Azoulay and Li show that the social returns to basic research appear high on average. Yet the exploratory nature of basic research means both that failure is common and that the range of ultimate applications is hard to predict, with returns occurring largely in unexpected spillovers. The example above, linking the market innovation of Uber back to the physics of Einstein and the mathematics of Riemann, shows just how unexpected these spillovers can be. Given this unpredictability, the authors then consider various types of funding mechanisms, comparing grants, prizes, and patents. The authors discuss why up-front grants may be effective when the applied endpoints are unknown and the returns are largely in the spillovers.

Azoulay and Li further investigate policy choices within scientific grant systems. The fundamental uncertainty of basic research suggests tolerance of failure. It further suggests a portfolio approach to science investment. Rather than pick a small number of relatively safe avenues, and crowding grant dollars into these limited conduits, grant design can look across a wide range of independent research avenues, funding projects that may be individually more risky but produce higher collective rates of success. Azoulay and Li apply these design principles to analyze institutions like the NIH and the Defense Advanced Research Projects Agency (DARPA), and consider application areas like Alzheimer's disease. The authors further analyze specific grant allocation mechanisms (such as peer review design) and the implications for grant management policies once awards are given.

Finally, the authors consider means of achieving continuous improvement in the science grant system. They make the fundamental point that the scientific method itself can be used to analyze science funding. Through randomized controlled trials, as well as natural experiments, there are arrays of opportunities to evaluate and improve grant design, increasing the effectiveness of the system and increasing the social returns science funding provides. The authors consider numerous measurement approaches that can help make regular, rigorous evaluation a practical and highly impactful reality.

Tax Policy

When the social returns to innovation exceed the private return, one policy approach is a "Pigouvian subsidy" to encourage innovative behavior. Such a subsidy can raise the private returns to align with the social returns. One way to implement such policies is through tax rate adjustments that aim specifically at innovation investments and outcomes.

In chapter 5, "Tax Policy for Innovation," Bronwyn H. Hall analyzes how advanced economies use tax codes to encourage innovative activity. She highlights the two most common forms of these direct innovation incentives: R&D tax credits (in 42 countries), which help offset R&D investment costs, and so-called intellectual property (IP) boxes (in 22 countries), which reduce tax rates on income from IP. Policy makers face choices, and challenges, in defining the set of activities that count for these tax incentives. Hall explores the practical differences between policies that subsidize the "input," like the R&D credit, versus the "output," like the IP box, and reviews the various policy designs conceptually, with examples from different countries. The chapter then synthesizes the empirical evidence on the effectiveness of these tax instruments.

A substantial body of work documents that private R&D responds strongly to changes in the R&D tax credit. This finding is consistent across many studies and in many different national environments. Hall further examines the detailed design of the credit in the United States, with business examples, and explains that the true size of the credit is much smaller than the statutory rate appears. The credit also ends up being substantially more generous in the United States for recent start-ups than for established companies.

A smaller, recent body of work examines the effects of IP boxes. This research shows that IP boxes appear to impact the location of patent rights across countries. At the same time, there is little evidence that this policy approach increases R&D investment or innovative output. While more studies are needed on IP boxes, R&D tax credits appear to be a more effective mechanism for increasing private innovative investment.

In chapter 6, "Taxation and Innovation: What Do We Know?," Ufuk Akcigit and Stefanie Stantcheva broaden the tax analysis, presenting a framework for many additional margins on which tax policy can influence innovation. They review recent research on the indirect roles of corporate and personal income taxation (as opposed to the direct, innovation-focused tax policies that the Hall chapter emphasizes). Using data on individual inventors in the United States since 1920 and their associated patents and firms, and similar data internationally since 1975, Akcigit and Stantcheva consider how income taxes affect innovative behavior. Their findings document that state and national income tax rates and corporate tax rates can have significant effects on where inventors and firms choose to locate and how much innovation they achieve. At the same time, the authors find that geographic agglomerations substantially reduce the power of tax policy: innovation becomes less sensitive to tax levels in locations where there is already substantial innovative activity.

Akcigit and Stantcheva further discuss the decline in business dynamism in the United States and the role tax policy can play. The declining entry of new firms, and the increasing dominance of incumbent firms, may suggest an unhealthy innovation environment, especially to the extent that new ventures play outsized roles in radical innovations. This decline in business dynamism may also be a contributing cause to the apparent slowdown in US productivity growth. A key observation for tax policy, then, is whether tax policy inadvertently privileges large, incumbent firms. Akcigit and Stantcheva discuss these important issues from a tax perspective as well as from political economy perspectives, where large firms may influence rule setting to their advantage.

Entrepreneurship Policy

This final section considers public policy intended to foster entrepreneurship. In chapter 7, "Government Incentives for Entrepreneurship," John Lerner begins by observing that a great deal of innovative activity in the economy comes from start-up firms, often backed by venture capital investors, rather than from within large companies. Knowing this, governments all over the world have attempted to encourage entrepreneurship, but with mixed success. Lerner presents a sobering overview of the challenges facing governments, drawing on examples from many countries. One challenge involves location. Policy makers often target innovation investments on fairness criteria—geographic equity, for example, leading to substantial investment in places that have not seen much successful entrepreneurship in the past. This emphasis can put new-venture policy in tension with powerful agglomeration economies that make innovation investments more successful in already thriving locations, and studies suggest that returns to public investment are much higher in places with substantial existing private venture activity. Another challenge involves timing, noting the boom-bust patterns that are prevalent in the venture capital system. Cycles in venture capital funding complicate the timing of government policies, which can end up funding new ventures at exactly the moments when the boom is most precarious. Lerner also highlights human capital challenges, where government officials typically have less expertise in the technology and market environments where they invest, compared to professional early-stage investors.

In light of these challenges, Lerner further considers how governments can raise the effectiveness of their entrepreneurship policies. The chapter emphasizes two design principles and some practical examples. The first design principle is independence. The goal here is to insulate investment decisions from political pressures—following a similar model of policy independence as that seen with central banks. The second design principle is private sector matching. By requiring matching funds from the private sector, government policies can leverage the expertise of venture capitalists. At root, these principles can help ensure that public investment achieves high expected returns. These lessons can prove useful at the local, state, and national government levels.

Conclusion

Innovation plays a central role in advancing economic growth and socio-economic prosperity. Higher productivity leads to higher per-capita income, including higher wages, and makes nations and their workers more successful on the world stage. Scientific and technological advances can lead to longer and healthier lives. And innovations can be critical to overcoming specific and high-stakes challenges, from the coronavirus pandemic to climate change.

This book collects new evidence and new ideas concerning innovation policy. It considers the case for public investment in innovation and reviews numerous levers by which policy can advance innovative activity. The chapters consider mechanisms for expanding the pool of innovative labor, encouraging scientific breakthroughs, increasing corporate R&D investment, and accelerating new venture creation. From R&D tax credits to research grants to the immigration system, the book collects the latest empirical evidence and a range of actionable ideas. The overall picture is a rich menu of public policies that can accelerate scientific and technological advance and reap the rewards that innovation affords.

References

Aghion, Philippe, Ufuk Akcigit, Ari Hyytinen, and Otto Toivanen. 2017. "The Social Origins of Inventors." NBER Working Paper No. 24110. Cambridge, MA: National Bureau of Economic Research.

Ahmadpoor, Mohammad, and Benjamin F. Jones. 2017. "The Dual Frontier: Patented Inventions and Prior Scientific Advance." *Science* 357: 583–87.

Akcigit, Ufuk, John Grigsby, and Tom Nicholas. 2017. "The Rise of American Ingenuity: Innovation and Inventors of the Golden Age." NBER Working Paper No. 23047. Cambridge, MA: National Bureau of Economic Research.

Bell, Alexander, Raj Chetty, Xavier Jaravel, Neviana Petkova, and John Van Reenen. 2019a. "Who Becomes an Inventor in America? The Importance of Exposure to Innovation." *Quarterly Journal of Economics* 134 (2): 647–713.

———. 2019b. "Do Tax Cuts Produce More Einsteins? The Impacts of Financial Incentives versus Exposure to Innovation on the Supply of Inventors." *Journal of the European Economics Association* 17 (3): 651–77.

Bush, Vannevar. 1945. *Science: The Endless Frontier*. U.S. Office of Scientific Research and Development. Report to the President on a Program for Postwar Scientific Research. Washington, DC: Government Printing Office.

Card, David, and Laura Giuliano. 2016. "Can Tracking Raise the Test Scores of High-Ability Minority Students?" *American Economic Review* 106 (10): 2783–816.

Cohodes, Sarah. 2020. "The Long-Run Impacts of Specialized Programming for High-Achieving Students." *American Economic Journal: Economic Policy* 12 (1): 127–66.

Cutler, D., A. Deaton, and A. Lleras-Muney. 2006. "The Determinants of Mortality." *Journal of Economic Perspectives* 20: 97–120.

Dijkgraaf, Robbert. 2017. "The World of Tomorrow." In Abraham Flexner, *The Usefulness of Useless Knowledge*, 3–49. Princeton, NJ: Princeton University Press.

Flexner, Abraham. 1939. "The Usefulness of Useless Knowledge." *Harper's Magazine*, October.

Goolsbee, Austan. 1998. "Does Government R&D Policy Mainly Benefit Scientists and Engineers?" *American Economic Review* 88: 298–302.

Griliches, Zvi. 1979. "Issues in Assessing the Contribution of Research and Development to Productivity Growth." *Bell Journal of Economics* 10 (1): 92–116.

Hacker, J. David. 2010. "Decennial Life Tables for the White Population of the United States, 1790–1900." *Historical Methods* 43 (2): 45–79.

Jones, Charles. 2016. "The Facts of Economic Growth." In *Handbook of Macroeconomics*, vol. 2, edited by John B. Taylor and Harald Uhlig, 3–69. Amsterdam: North-Holland.

Lockyer, Norman. 1903. "A Presidential Address ON THE INFLUENCE OF BRAIN-POWER ON HISTORY." *The Lancet* 162 (September): 735.

Mokyr, Joel. 1990. *The Lever of Riches: Technological Creativity and Economic Progress*. New York: Oxford University Press.

National Science Foundation. 2020. "Research and Development: U.S. Trends and International Comparisons." January. https://ncses.nsf.gov/pubs/nsb20203.

Rosenberg, Nathan. 1982. *Inside the Black Box: Technology and Economics*. Cambridge, UK: Cambridge University Press.

Schumpeter, Joseph A. 1942. *Capitalism, Socialism and Democracy*. New York: Harper & Row.

Solow, Robert M. 1956. "A Contribution to the Theory of Economic Growth." *Quarterly Journal of Economics* 70 (1): 65–94.

A Calculation of the Social Returns to Innovation

Benjamin F. Jones and Lawrence H. Summers

1.1 Introduction

Standards of living in advanced economies have risen dramatically over the last two centuries, with US income per capita currently 25 times its level in 1820 (Council of Economic Advisers 2011). Scientific and technological advances, ultimately delivering valuable new products and services, are thought to be critical drivers of these gains (Mokyr 1990; Solow 1956). Innovative advances also appear central to improving human health and life expectancy (e.g., Cutler, Deaton, and Lleras-Muney 2006). Yet measuring the social returns to scientific and technological advances has proven difficult. The challenge lies in the many spillover margins that appear inherent in the innovation process and the diffuse manner by which the fruits of research investments are often realized (e.g., Hall, Mairesse, and Mohnen 2010).

This chapter does three things. First, it introduces a new method for calcu-

Benjamin F. Jones is the Gordon and Llura Gund Family Professor of Entrepreneurship and a Professor of Strategy at Northwestern University, and a research associate of the National Bureau of Economic Research.

Lawrence H. Summers is President Emeritus of Harvard University, the Charles W. Eliot University Professor of the Harvard Kennedy School, and a research associate of the National Bureau of Economic Research.

We thank Pierre Azoulay, Stefan Bechtold, Dietmar Harhoff, John Jankowski, Chad Jones, Monika Schnitzer, Scott Stern, Manuel Trajtenberg, Martin Watzinger, seminar participants at ETH Zurich, the Max Planck Institute for Innovation and Competition, participants at the NBER Role of Innovation and Entrepreneurship in Economic Growth conference, and two anonymous reviewers for helpful comments. We gratefully acknowledge support from the Alfred P. Sloan Foundation under award G-2015-14014 and the AFOSR Minerva award FA9550-19-1-0354. All errors are our own. For acknowledgments, sources of research support, and disclosure of the authors' material financial relationships, if any, please see https://www.nber.org/books-and -chapters/innovation-and-public-policy/calculation-social-returns-innovation.

lating the average social returns to innovation. This method integrates across the many types of spillovers that innovative investments create. Second, the chapter considers how the social returns vary according to potentially important but not commonly addressed features of innovation. These features include the roles of diffusion delays, capital embodiment, learning-by-doing, productivity mismeasurement, health outcomes, and international spillovers. The robust finding is that the social returns to innovative investments appear large. If a narrow set of innovative efforts (such as formal R&D) drive the bulk of productivity gains, then the social returns to these investments are enormous. If a much broader set of innovative efforts drives productivity gains, then the social returns to these broader activities appear merely large. In light of the high social returns, the final part of the chapter discusses the prospects for increased innovative effort to accelerate improvements in standards of living and economic growth.

The existing literature emphasizes that the social gain from a new idea may differ substantially from the private gain captured by the original innovator (e.g., Griliches 1992; Nordhaus 2004). The divergence between private and social returns follows from various spillovers that appear integral to the innovation process. Positive innovation spillovers may include benefits to users (e.g., Trajtenberg 1989), benefits to imitators (e.g., Segerstrom 1991), and intertemporal benefits where new ideas enable additional innovations in the future (e.g., Romer 1990; Scotchmer 1991; Weitzman 1998). One can look to examples like electricity, the computer, or the Human Genome Project—and the new products, businesses, and industries they have spurred—to realize that the private gains to the initial innovators may be small compared to the productivity or health gains that result for society as a whole. However, while such spillovers suggest that the social returns of an innovation may substantially exceed the private returns, other forces may lead innovators toward overinvesting in new ideas. Overinvestment could occur through business stealing (e.g., Aghion and Howitt 1998), research duplication (e.g., Dixit 1988), and/or intertemporal costs where finding new ideas today raises costs for finding new ideas later (e.g., Jones 2009; Kortum 1997).

In light of these spillovers, researchers have long been interested in understanding the social returns to innovation, with an emphasis on formal R&D investment. Case studies of specific technologies (e.g., Griliches 1958; Mansfield et al. 1977; Tewskbury, Crandall, and Crane 1980) have counted up the R&D investments targeting specific products and then examined the benefits from the technologies developed. Other literature uses regressions to examine how firm and industry R&D investment pays off in productivity gains (e.g., Bloom, Schankerman, and Van Reenen 2013; Hall, Mairesse, and Mohnen 2010). These regressions study spillovers by linking a given firm's or industry's productivity to the R&D performed by other firms or industries. Regression methods have also been deployed at the national level to study how aggregate productivity gains are associated with aggregate

R&D investment, including spillovers from R&D in other countries (e.g., Coe and Helpman 1995). Finally, macroeconomic growth models have been calibrated to data, and the social returns to R&D calibrated under various assumptions about functional forms and their parameter values (e.g., Jones and Williams 1998). These varied approaches typically reach broadly similar conclusions: the social returns to R&D are large.

At the same time, each of the above approaches faces methodological difficulties. Case studies of specific technologies raise the question of whether the results generalize to other technologies. This concern is more acute if the case studies tend to "pick winners," which would lead to overstatement of the typical R&D returns. The regression methods often face challenges of causative interpretation. Further, regression methods must delineate the scope of spillovers, and distant spillovers or intertemporal spillovers are largely ignored. For example, these methods do not incorporate the role of basic research and the widespread but typically delayed influences that basic research may have on opening new avenues of commercial application (Ahmadpoor and Jones 2017). Yet it is exactly the innovations with diffuse implications—electricity, the computer, genetics research, machine learning—that may be especially important for society and for understanding the returns to innovation investments.

Given these challenges, this chapter introduces a new and complementary methodology. We present new calculations for the social returns to innovation investment, building on core features of the innovation and growth literature. Our measures emphasize the advantages of examining the path of GDP, which acts to aggregate and net out complicated spillovers involved in the innovation process. The approach offers a seemingly quite general means of estimating the average social returns. Moreover, the simplicity of the method allows us to transparently examine the influence of other, potentially key features that are not typically addressed in studies of the social returns to R&D. These features include embodied versus disembodied technological progress, diffusion rates, learning-by-doing, productivity mismeasurement, health benefits, cross-country spillovers, and other dimensions for assessing the social returns.

The intuition for our approach is straightforward. Modern growth theory, following the work of Robert Solow, tells us under reasonably broad conditions that the growth rate of GDP per person will be equivalent to the growth rate in total factor productivity (Solow 1956). In the absence of this productivity growth, per-capita income will remain constant. In advanced economies, long-run growth in productivity is often interpreted to come from investment in new ideas, which is the basis of modern endogenous growth theory (e.g., Aghion and Howitt 1992; Romer 1990).

Taking this approach seriously, the average returns to innovative investments are determined by linking the aggregate cost of innovation investments to the aggregate production increase that results. Intuitively, by looking at the net value-added gains in the GDP path, one can implicitly net out the spillover margins. By looking at total innovation investment, one includes both research successes and failures. A simple social returns calculation can proceed as follows. Let income per capita be y, innovation investment per capita be x, and the discount rate be r. If a year's worth of innovation investments creates a g percent increase in productivity, then the ratio of benefits to costs is:

$$\rho = \frac{g/r}{x/y}.$$

The key idea here, as in endogenous growth theory, is that by investing a GDP share x/y in innovation today (i.e., once), we permanently raise productivity in the economy by g percent, the present value of which is g/r. Notably, this approach suggests that the average social returns to innovation may be enormous. For example, if we take an R&D investment orientation, with the R&D share of GDP at its usual level in the United States, $x/y \approx 2.7\%$, and let these investments drive productivity growth, then we have $g \approx 1.8\%$.[1] Standard discount rates then imply that $1 of R&D investment today on average creates over $10 of economy-wide benefits in today's dollars.[2] This return is extremely large, but it follows from the basic mechanics of growth, as understood in advanced economies. That is, a permanent gain in living standards from a seemingly small investment in innovation will, by the above logic, tend to suggest enormous returns.

Having established this baseline, "R&D only" analysis, the chapter examines several reasons it may be too high. First, we consider the role of diffusion, where the gains from R&D may pay off slowly, delaying the benefits that are achieved and thus reducing their present value. Second, we consider the role of capital deepening in accounting for some of the productivity gains and, relatedly, we consider the role of capital-embodied technical change, where the value of R&D investments may only be realized through investments in new types of fixed assets. Third, we consider the possibility that productivity growth occurs without formal R&D but due to other kinds of activities, such as new-venture creation or learning-by-doing. In each case, we calibrate adjusted returns. All of these analyses act to reduce the estimated social returns to innovation investments, but we will also argue that under plausible assumptions the returns still appear very high.

The chapter then examines several reasons that, under the above calculation, the (already high) estimates of social returns may be too low. We first

1. We will consider the role of capital deepening and many other extensions to this simple calculation in the body of the chapter.

2. An alternative social returns calculation is the internal rate of return. This is the discount rate at which the benefits and costs are the same. This rate of return is $r^* = g/(x/y)$ for the simple calculation above. Using the same values for g and x/y, we then have $r^* = 67\%$.

consider the role of inflation bias, causing real GDP growth to understate gains due to product improvements and new product introductions. Second, we consider health, which is a main target of R&D investments and may bring large social returns, but where mortality and morbidity are not well accounted for in standard GDP per-capita measures. Third, we consider international diffusion, where economies around the world may also benefit from the innovation investments undertaken in frontier economies.

Finally, the chapter considers the distinction between the average and the marginal social return to innovation investments. Our calculations throughout are explicitly about the average return, which avoids having to assume very specific production functions. However, policy makers may naturally be more interested in the marginal investment returns. That is, policy choices will hinge on whether additionally increasing innovation investment levels will see the same kinds of returns that the average return calculations indicate. We therefore consider how to bridge between marginal and average returns and present specific estimates of the marginal returns.

The rest of the chapter proceeds as follows. In section 1.2, we introduce our methodology and consider baseline calculations of the average social return. In section 1.3, we consider reasons that these baseline calculations may be too high, and then consider reasons the baseline calculation may be too low. In section 1.4, we consider distinctions between the average and the marginal social return and discuss the prospects for increased innovation investment to raise the rate of advance in socioeconomic prosperity. Section 1.5 concludes.[3]

1.2   The Average Social Returns to R&D: A Baseline

In this section we introduce a baseline calculation of the average social returns to innovation investment. This method is meant to achieve three things. First, it acts to integrate across the many spillovers inherent to innovation. Second, it clarifies the basic logic for why the social returns to innovation appear high. Third, it provides a foundation for discussing, and clarifying, a range of additional and potentially first-order issues that bear on the social returns, which we will consider in section 1.3.

1.2.1   Toward the Social Returns to Innovation

The social returns to innovation depend on the cost of innovation and the benefit that results. That the social returns tend to appear high in vari-

---

3. Three appendices provide further context and results. Appendix A details the many types of spillovers that appear inherent to the innovation process and provides examples of each. Appendix B reviews the existing empirical literature that works to confront these spillovers and estimate the social rate of return. Appendix C provides proofs of the formal results in the chapter.

ous analyses[4] speaks to the fact that the costs often appear low yet the gains often appear substantial and durable. In particular, a new idea, method, design, etc., can be created at some up-front cost (i.e., paid once) but then raise productivity more or less forever. For example, calculus, invented in the 17th century, was a permanent advance in mathematics that has been used ever since.

More generally, the productivity gain can be seen to endure even if a specific innovation becomes obsolete—that is, the earlier innovation is replaced by something better. For example, consider a software innovation that raises the productivity of workers by p_1 percent. If this were the last innovation ever produced, it would continue to provide this p_1 percent gain forever. But let's say instead that another software innovation comes along that replaces the original software and raises the productivity of workers by an additional p_2 percent. We can think of this sequence of innovations in two ways. First, we can think of the original innovation as producing a permanent gain of p_1 percent and the second innovation as, at some further innovation cost, producing an additional gain of p_2 percent. In this sense, the gain from the original innovation remains. Alternatively, we might consider the average return to both innovations together. Here we add up the innovation costs and add up the total productivity gains (i.e., without attempting to parse individual contributions), so that the innovation investments have a permanent effect in combination.

This kind of thought experiment lies behind the "case study" approach. Because innovations interact in complex ways, and many small innovations may together advance productivity in a given product line, separating out the marginal returns of each innovation is difficult. The case study method thus often pools the innovation costs and benefits across many related innovations and calculates an average social return to the broader technological advance, rather than the marginal return of each micro-innovation (e.g., Griliches 1958).

The limitation of case studies is one of representativeness, where they are unlikely to describe innovation investment returns in general. In particular, case studies of failures are rare, even though failure in innovation is common (Arrow 1962; Kerr, Nanda, and Rhodes-Kropf 2014). By leaving out failures, case studies may overstate the general social returns to R&D. Yet the advantages of the case study approach may still be had, separately from this limitation, by expanding the boundaries of the exercise. This occurs if one applies the approach to the economy as a whole. By aggregating across all innovation investment, one incorporates not only successful investments but also the "dry holes" of failed investments. Total innovation costs also incorporate the potential wasteful duplication of innovative efforts. On the benefit side, the path of aggregate productivity gains nets out the imitative

4. See appendix B for a review.

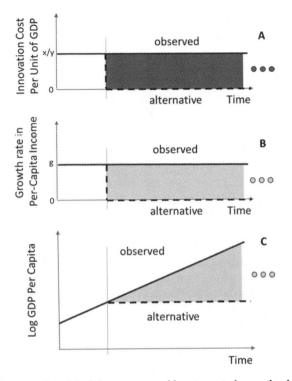

Fig. 1.1   Conceptual model of the economy-wide returns to innovation investment

and business-stealing spillovers between and across firms and industries.[5] The long-run path of productivity gains also accounts for intertemporal spillovers and the benefits of basic research.

1.2.2   The Average Social Returns to Innovation

To develop this idea formally, consider two thought experiments. Both provide a baseline view of the social returns to innovation (which we extend further below). In the first thought experiment, we "turn off" all innovative investments forever and consider the costs and benefits (see figure 1.1). On the innovative investment side, we move from the observed level of innovation investments to no innovation investment (figure 1.1A). On the output side, if productivity advances cease with no further innovation, then we move from the observed level of growth to a state of no further growth (figure 1.1B). Thus, per-capita income remains constant (figure 1.1C). This alternative, no-growth state is also the outcome in modern endogenous

---

5. That is, the path includes "creative destruction" where a new innovation makes an earlier one obsolete. The net gains in valued-added output incorporate this effect.

growth theory (Aghion and Howitt 1992; Romer 1990), but note that the key assumption here is more general than specific endogenous growth models.[6]

The average social returns to the observed level of innovative investments then follow directly. The cost of innovation is the present discounted value of the innovation investments. This is the present value of the rectangle in figure 1.1A. The benefits of innovation are the present value of the discounted gain in per-capita income. This is the present value of the triangle in figure 1.1C. The ratio of the benefits to the costs then gives the social cost-benefit ratio.

As shown in appendix C, the social cost-benefit ratio is extremely simple and intuitive. It is

$$(1) \qquad\qquad \rho = \frac{g/r}{x/y}.$$

The cost, in the denominator, is the ratio of innovation investment expenditure (x) to GDP (y). The benefit, in the numerator, is the growth rate (g) that results, discounted to the present at the discount rate (r). We are suppressing time in this expression to emphasize that the ratio of innovation investment expenditure to GDP and the growth rate of income are approximately constant over time.

This expression, although derived over the entire time path of innovation expenditure and the entire time path of productivity gains, produces an interpretation based on the intuitive nature of innovation gains. Namely, we can think of the cost-benefit ratio as the cost of one year's innovation (x/y) producing a stream of net output gains that are g percent higher. The present value of this permanent output gain is g/r.

As an alternative thought experiment, consider figure 1.2. Here we imagine that we turn off innovation investment for one year only (figure 1.2A) rather than forever (figure 1.1A). Since we do not innovate that year, we see no gain in productivity growth that year (figure 1.2B and 1.2C). However, at the end of the year, we start innovating again. In particular, we undertake exactly the same innovation projects as on the observed path. It should therefore be clear that the economy, with exactly the same innovations, leads to exactly the same productivity levels, only now the innovation costs occur with a one-year delay, and the economy arrives at each productivity level one year later.

In this alternative thought experiment, the present value of the innovation costs on the observed path versus the alternative path is one year's innovation costs, or x/y. The benefits are being g percent richer in each future period, the present value of which is g/r. These are the present values of the

---

6. That is, if there are diminishing returns to capital, then the absence of productivity growth means no growth in per-capita income.

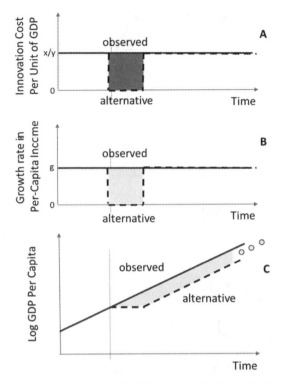

Fig. 1.2 **Alternative conceptual model of the economy-wide returns to innovation investment**

shaded areas in figure 1.2A (costs) and 1.2C (benefits). The social benefit-cost ratio is then, again, exactly as in (1).

Finally, an alternative calculation is to measure the discount rate where the costs and benefits would be equal (i.e., where ρ = 1). This internal rate of return is written

(2)
$$r^* = \frac{gy}{x},$$

providing a social internal rate of return as an alternative measure to the social benefit-cost ratio.

1.2.3   The Average Social Returns: An "R&D Only" Baseline

With the expression (1), we can now calculate a baseline average social return to innovative investments. Taking the US economy, we have $g = 1.8\%$ as the average long-run growth rate. Using total public and private R&D investment to account for innovation investments (x), the long-run average

Table 1.1   Average social returns by social discount rate

Social discount rate (r)	Average social benefit-cost ratio (ρ)
1%	66.7
2%	33.3
3.5%	19.0
5%	13.3
7%	9.5
10%	6.7
67%	1

value of x/y is approximately 2.7 percent.[7] Taking a discount rate of 5 percent, we then have

$$\rho = \frac{.018/.05}{.027} = 13.3 .$$

This says that $1 of R&D investment today produces, on average, a $13.3 benefit in today's dollars. In other words, the baseline calculation suggests that the social returns to R&D are enormous.

An open question here is what discount rate to choose. The lower the discount rate, the greater the innovation benefits. The social discount rates used by governments range from 3.5 percent (United Kingdom) to 7 percent (United States). Some argue that social discount rates should be lower still, and equilibrium real interest rates have been trending downward for decades (Rachel and Summers 2019). US 30-year inflation-protected government bonds point to a 1 percent discount rate on average over the last decade. Using such low discount rates would further amplify the social returns, but even high discount rates suggest the social returns are very large (see table 1.1).

As an alternative calculation, focusing on the internal rate of return, (2), and assuming again that $g = .018$ and $x/y = .027$, we have $r^* = 67\%$. By this standard, the social returns are also enormous. For example, if a private citizen could access an investment with a 67 percent annual rate of return, that individual could become very rich very quickly. Of course, as a social return, this rate of return is not available to an individual investor. But it may be available to society as a whole. The question becomes whether and how society can further invest to take advantage of this high return (see section 1.5).

Overall, this simple baseline calculation based on R&D expenditure sug-

---

7. US R&D expenditure is based on numerous surveys of the National Science Foundation, and includes R&D performed and funded by private businesses with at least five employees, federal and state governments, universities, and nonprofit organizations.

gests that the average social returns to innovation are very large. This result aggregates across failed and successful R&D projects. It also incorporates the manifold spillovers involved in R&D, including intertemporal spillovers. In magnitude, the result reinforces the common finding in the prior literature, surveyed in section 1.2, and comes in at the upper range of existing estimates. We can now adjust this baseline calculation on numerous dimensions to assess whether it may be too large or too small, which is the subject of the balance of the chapter.

1.3   Extending the Baseline

As an overarching framework for what follows, consider the following adjustment to the social return calculation. We write

$$(3) \qquad\qquad \rho = \beta \frac{g/r}{x/y},$$

where the new term, β, provides for an upward or downward adjustment to the social return. In this section, we first consider forces that make β less than one, so that the baseline calculation in table 1.1 is too high. We will then consider forces that make β greater than one, so that the baseline calculation is too low.

1.3.1   Reasons the Baseline Social Returns May Be Too High

1.3.1.1   *Lags*

The above baseline assumes that the payoff from R&D investments occurs immediately. Yet there may be substantive delays in receiving the fruits of R&D investments. Other things equal, the longer the delays until the benefits are realized, the lower the return.

A simple approach to potential delays assumes that R&D investments borne today increase productivity permanently starting D years in the future. This leads to a straightforward correction to the present value of the benefit stream. The calculation is the same as before, but we now must include a discount factor where[8]

$$(4) \qquad\qquad \beta = e^{-\hat{r}D}.$$

To make an explicit adjustment, we can consider various pieces of micro-evidence. For businesses, the literature suggests a relatively short delay between R&D investment and product introduction. Mansfield et al. (1971) find a three-year median delay. Ravenscraft and Scherer (1982) find, in a

---

8. The appropriate discount factor is $\hat{r} = r - g$. This accounts for both the discount rate, r, for future income as well as income growth, g, which expands the income over which today's innovation will ultimately be felt.

survey, that 45 percent of firms report a one- to two-year delay, 40 percent of firms report a two- to five-year delay, and only 5 percent of firms report a delay beyond five years. Pakes and Schankerman (1984) impute a delay of 1.5–2.5 years between R&D investment and first revenues. For firms included in the database Compustat, which focuses on mature firms in mature industries, Argente et al. (2020) estimate a one-year delay between R&D and product introduction.

The first introduction of the product is not, however, the time at which use in the market peaks. Leonard (1971) studies 19 manufacturing industries and finds that the growth continues from the second year up until the ninth year after the R&D investment. In mature consumer sectors, the delays to market peak may be shorter. For example, Argente et al. (2020) find that the new consumer products from publicly traded firms typically hit their sales peak one year after introduction. All told, studies of R&D, product introductions, and product sales suggest quite rapid linkages between up-front costs and peak market payoffs. A total delay of three to six years appears reasonable, and a 10-year delay appears very conservative.

For basic research, the delays are naturally longer. Using regression analysis, Adams (1990) suggests a 20-year lag between academic research and productivity growth in the relevant industry. One can also link specific patents to the underlying scientific research that each patent cites (Ahmadpoor and Jones 2017). Examining all US patents indicates an average delay of six years from the patent application to its direct precursor science publications. To the extent that basic research pays off indirectly (i.e., basic research leads to further research that, eventually, becomes an input to marketplace inventions), citation network analysis suggests that even remote basic research investments begin paying off within 20 years.

Table 1.2 reconsiders the baseline social returns calculations using a range of delays.[9] Aggregating across the different types of research, a middle-of-the-road delay estimate may be 6.5 years, and a conservative estimate would be 10 years.[10] An extremely conservative estimate would be 20 years. Using any of these delays, the average social returns to R&D still

9. We use $\hat{r} = 5\%$ in these calculations of the social benefit-cost ratio. With a growth rate of $g = 1.8\%$, this value for $\hat{r}$ assumes a high discount rate of $r = 6.8\%$. To the extent that appropriate social discount rates are lower than this discount rate, the social benefit-cost ratios in table 1.2 are conservative.

10. The National Science Foundation (2020) reports that 63 percent of recent US R&D spending represents product development (i.e., R&D targeted toward the development or improvement of specific products or processes); 20 percent of spending represents applied research (i.e., research that has a specific practical aim or objective); and the remaining 17 percent of spending represents basic research (i.e., without any particular application in view). Taking a mainstream estimate of a three-year delay for product development R&D, a six-year delay for applied R&D, and a 20-year delay for basic R&D, the average delay (weighted across expenditure on each category) would be 6.5 years. Taking a conservative estimate of a five-year delay for development R&D, a 10-year delay for applied R&D, and a 30-year delay for basic R&D, the average delay would be 10 years.

Table 1.2   **Average social returns for different benefit lags**

Delay in years (D)	Corrective factor (β)	Average social benefit-cost ratio (ρ)	Average social rate of return (r*)
0	1	13.3	67%
3	0.86	11.5	29%
5	0.78	10.4	23%
6.5	0.72	9.6	20%
10	0.61	8.1	16%
20	0.37	4.9	11%

appear very large. Even taking a very conservative 20-year average delay, which is well beyond what the microevidence indicates, one would still see a \$4.9 present value benefit for each \$1 spent on R&D.[11] The internal social rate of return declines relatively sharply from the baseline value of $r* = 67\%$ with extended delays, because high internal rates of return heavily discount the future. With a delay of 20 years, the internal social rate of return falls to 11 percent.

1.3.1.2   Incorporating Capital Investment

The baseline approach assumes that growth relies on the innovative investment x. This approach follows from the standard neoclassical idea that total-factor-productivity gains are necessary to achieve positive steady-state growth. Hence, one might accrue the benefit of growth to R&D. However, this approach implicitly ignores potentially important features, including the contribution of capital investment. Here we will introduce capital investment explicitly into the observed and counterfactual growth scenarios.

One can incorporate the capital investment part of productivity growth— or "capital deepening"—under two different viewpoints. In one viewpoint, technological progress is "disembodied" from capital inputs. In the second viewpoint, new technologies must be embodied in new capital inputs, which bring additional costs. The roles of embodied versus disembodied technical progress have long been debated (Denison 1962; Jorgenson 1966; Jorgenson and Griliches 1967; Solow 1960), but all within the common conceptual viewpoint that the productivity growth must come from somewhere and be located in one place or another. Here we consider the disembodied and embodied perspectives in turn.

Disembodied Productivity Growth. In the disembodied perspective, the productivity gains from innovation are felt independently of capital invest-

---

11. A more sophisticated version of this delay adjustment doesn't just consider a single delay, D, but rather uses the full distribution of delays in the micro literature. In practice, however, the more sophisticated approach leads to similar conclusions.

ment. We can then parse per-capita income gains into two features. First is the direct (disembodied) gain from innovation that occurs holding capital fixed; the second would be the capital deepening that these productivity gains further spark.

In standard neoclassical growth theory, where production is Cobb-Douglas, growth in per-capita income follows as

$$(5) \qquad g_y = \alpha g_k + (1 - \alpha)g_A,$$

where g_y is the growth in per-capita income, g_k is the growth in capital per person (capital deepening), and g_A represents technological progress. The term α is the capital share of income, which empirically is approximately one-third. Thus, if technological progress follows from innovative investments and these gains are felt in a fashion disembodied from capital investments, then we have a straightforward correction to our baseline. Namely,

$$\beta = 1 - \alpha \approx \frac{2}{3}.$$

It is then a simple matter to revise the estimates in table 1.1. Simply multiply the social benefit-cost ratio by two-thirds. The returns to innovative investments with this correction still appear very large. The same is true if one applies this correction to table 1.2, which further accounts for potential delays.

Capital-Embodied Productivity Growth. Alternatively, we may believe that the economic gains from innovative investments are in large part realized through the embodiment of these ideas in new forms of capital. For example, an innovation in microprocessors is useful only if it is built into microprocessors themselves. The same may be true for myriad forms of innovation that are embodied in capital equipment and structures. If so, then the benefits from new ideas (and advances in standards of living) require both the R&D expenditure and the investment in building the new or improved capital inputs.

In short, the costs are more than just the R&D. We can no longer make a clean separation between the innovation and the capital-deepening components, and the natural correction here is to include both investments together. The added piece is the cost of capital deepening. One can proceed empirically here and also consider theoretical bounds on these additional costs.

Empirically, since 1960, the annual net domestic investment of the US private sector has averaged 4.0 percent of GDP. This net investment, which does not include R&D expenditure, incorporates capital deepening. Viewing these costs as necessary to realize the gains of R&D, the total costs to innovative investments would then be viewed as the summation of the R&D investment (2.7 percent) and net domestic investment (4.0 percent), or 6.7 percent of GDP. Thus we could say empirically that

Table 1.3   **Average social returns with capital costs**

Capital costs to realize productivity gains	Corrective factor (β)	Average social benefit-cost ratio (ρ)	Average social rate of return (r^*)
Disembodied technical change			
—	0.66	8.9	44%
Capital-embodied technical change			
Net domestic private investment	0.40	5.3	27%
All capital deepening	0.30	4.0	20%

$$\beta \approx \frac{2.7}{6.7} = 0.40.$$

This "embodied" version of capital deepening thus reduces the social returns to R&D more than a "disembodied" innovation calculation. Nonetheless, given the baseline social returns presented in table 1.1, such a correction still points to extremely high social returns (see table 1.3).[12]

The above calculation can be further adjusted in several senses. First, net investment costs are not just about capital deepening; they also include investment costs that extend the capital stock over a growing population. The US population has grown annually at 1.0 percent on average since 1960, and the US workforce has grown at 1.5 percent annually. This makes the above adjustment conservative—tending to understate the social returns. Second, capital deepening might occur outside the net investment data from domestic businesses, including, for example, through infrastructure or other public investments. While private capital equipment investment may be especially important, other investment costs, if unaccounted for, would make the above adjustment less conservative.

We can generalize as follows. Along the equilibrium growth path of the economy, the deepening component of investment is equivalent to the growth rate in per-capita income times the capital-output ratio. That is,

$$(6) \qquad \frac{i_{deep}}{y} = \frac{k}{y} g,$$

where i_{deep} is the cost of investment that increases capital per worker, and the other terms are defined as above. The ratio of the US capital stock to US GDP has averaged 3.5 since 1960. Thus, capital-deepening costs are approximately 3.5g. This suggests that the capital-deepening cost would, in total, be 3.5 × 1.8 percent, or 6.3 percent of GDP. This correction is larger than the 4.0 percent net domestic investment cost taken from private

---

12. For the capital-deepening component, the issue of lags is substantially less germane. In the embodied-innovation perspective, the costs of the capital investment occur very close to the time of use of these embodied ideas in the economy. Thus, the lag corrections in table 1.2 do not apply to most of the innovation cost under this embodied-innovation perspective.

businesses. Adding in the 2.7 percent of GDP for R&D, the total cost of innovation (idea creation and implementation) rises to 9.0 percent of GDP. This suggests that $\beta \approx 0.3$.

Table 1.3 summarizes these results. The conclusion is that accounting for capital deepening will reduce the social returns to innovation, and that embodied technical change reduces these returns more than disembodied technical change. Nonetheless, the main conclusion is that the social returns to innovation still appear extremely large.

Finally, note that incorporating capital investment doesn't diminish the society-wide gains. Rather it acts to spread the gains over a broader set of investments, beyond R&D. The social returns to capital deepening thus appear much larger than the equilibrium private rate of return to capital investment would suggest. To the extent that embodiment is important, R&D investment and capital investment collectively unlock large social returns. From a policy point of view, supporting R&D and capital deepening together would then be important to attaining the high social returns from innovative investments.

1.3.1.3 Other Innovation Costs

The above analysis links productivity growth in the economy to R&D investment and capital investment. To the extent that innovations come from other types of investment, one would undercount true innovation costs and thus overstate the social returns. Here we consider these possibilities.

One potentially important source of innovation is the effort of entrepreneurs. Most of these businesses are not growth oriented, representing self-employment or permanently small businesses like single-establishment restaurants, nail salons, and so on; however, a small set of new businesses is focused on creating transformative innovations (e.g., Azoulay et al. 2020; Guzman and Stern 2017). While the formal reported R&D of small businesses is not large, the broader activity of growth-oriented new ventures may also be considered as innovative investment.[13] A practical adjustment to account for these innovative startups can include total venture capital investment as an additional innovation cost. Since 1995, total annual venture capital investment in the United States has been as high as $130 billion (2018) but has often been less than $30 billion.[14] On average, total venture

13. Historically, R&D expenditure measures in the United States explicitly did not include the innovative activities of businesses with fewer than five employees. However, beginning in 2016, the National Science Foundation's National Center for Science and Engineering Statistics began collecting data on a nationally representative sample of businesses with one to four employees. This sample, the Business R&D and Innovation Survey—Microbusiness (BRDI-M), estimates that such businesses spent $4.8 billion on R&D in 2016 (see https://www.nsf.gov /statistics/2019/nsf19325/), which amounts to a very small expenditure compared to total R&D expenditure in the United States.

14. Source: Pitchbook/NVCA, https://pitchbook.com/media/press-releases/us-venture -capital-investment-surpasses-130-billion-in-2019-for-second-consecutive-year.

capital investment since 1995 is less than 0.3 percent of GDP. Adding all venture capital investment would therefore raise the costs of innovation investments from 2.7 percent to 3.0 percent of GDP, suggesting $\beta = 0.9$. This adjustment only modestly affects the social returns.

Additional inroads to estimating other innovation costs come from business surveys. Eurostat's Community Innovation Survey asks firms to compare their R&D costs with any additional innovation costs. In the 2016 survey, these numbers are available for 28 countries (Eurostat 2019). Taking these countries as a whole, firms report that R&D expenditures amount to 55 percent of total innovation costs. The non-R&D innovation costs are primarily investment in capital assets, including equipment, machinery, and software. These costs are linked to the adoption and diffusion of the innovations (Brouwer and Kleinknecht 1997; Evangelista et al. 2010) and can thus be seen as a component of the capital-embodied productivity gains analysis in section 1.4.2. Thus, one could take $\beta = 0.55$ to account for these "other costs," or one could use the broader β correction that already encapsulates broad forms of associated capital investment costs, as in table 1.3.[15]

1.3.1.4   Learning-by-Doing and Incidental Innovation

A different challenge to the above estimates comes on the benefit side. To the extent that productivity growth comes from other sources, assigning the productivity growth to explicit R&D investment, new venture investment, and capital investment would overstate the social returns to these investments. What happens if new ideas, or the spark of ideas, come from outside the above processes? Some innovative ideas may emerge from incidental inspirations among workers in the course of ordinary labor activities, rather than through focused investment expenditure. Learning-by-doing is typically seen as productivity improvements that come through accumulated experience and skill in a production process (Arrow 1961; Bessen 2015). Such advances might be seen as essentially "free" sources of productivity gains.

To relate this possibility to the social returns to innovation, consider three perspectives. First, canonical examples of learning-by-doing, like airframe manufacturing (Wright 1936) suggest that these productivity gains can be large. However, these gains typically hinge on and occur after the introduction of a new good or production process. In this sense, learning-by-doing acts as a kind of free innovation process that comes ex post of necessary

---

15. Another cost dimension may be human capital investment. That said, if the most relevant marginal investment for R&D purposes is certain forms of graduate training, this is a very small share of GDP. Moreover, formal R&D costs (which are included in all the above social returns estimates) include wages to R&D workers, thus incorporating the annual cost of this human capital. A different and perhaps more open dimension is skill-biased technical change, which can be thought of as the "human-capital-deepening" analog to physical capital deepening. Here, the embodiment of more ideas in people (via longer education) could be seen as an additional cost to innovation. Such human capital considerations are an interesting and potentially rich dimension for further analysis.

up-front costs, such as the R&D investment in the airframe design or the capital investment in producing the manufacturing machinery and facilities. From this perspective, learning-by-doing is akin to the lag adjustment in section 1.3.1, and one can therefore incorporate learning-by-doing by allowing for lags in the benefits of the up-front innovation investment costs.

Second, there may be "free ideas" that come to individuals, including individuals who do not participate in any measured R&D or investment process. Concretely, an individual may have an idea while driving to work, or while engaged in some work process, concerning things like a new jet engine design, computer application, web service, or medical device. Product users may also be an important source of new concepts (Von Hippel 1976). However, to the extent that the initial idea may appear to come for free (i.e., outside a measured investment process), the implementation of a new computer application, medical device, etc., will presumably bear further development costs and/or investments in fixed assets. If so, then using a broad measure of investment as featured in section 1.4.2 should still capture the total costs for achieving the productivity gain.

Finally, there may be free ideas that require no investment to implement. Returning to the learning-by-doing literature, the so-called Horndal Effect provides an example of productivity gains in a Swedish ironworks that appear to occur without any formal investment (Lundberg 1961). If such gains are actually investment-free, and are responsible for a substantial portion of productivity growth, then the average returns to the measured innovation investments above would be correspondingly lower. It is difficult to assess this possibility in general. The reader can adjust the social returns, however, in a straightforward manner, by choosing β as the share of productivity growth that hinges on actual investment. Taking the broad returns set forth in table 1.3, one could assume that half of productivity gains are achieved without relying on any R&D investment, any new venture investment, or any capital investment, and still the average social returns to these measured innovation investments would be large.

1.3.1.5   Summary

Collectively, we have considered several independent reasons that the baseline social returns calculation may be too high. Analyzing each correction in isolation, the social returns to innovative investments tend to remain high. Analyzing several potential corrections at once, it is still difficult to find a result where the social returns are not high. The most important correction appears to be how we treat capital investment, especially if the results of R&D must be embodied in capital equipment. Incorporating long delays between the up-front investments and the ensuing productivity gains, which can additionally incorporate learning-by-doing, the social benefits still substantially exceed the costs. As we will discuss next, there are also several forces pushing in the other direction, which suggest that the baseline calculation may be too low.

1.3.2 Reasons the Baseline Calculation May Be Too Low

1.3.2.1 *Productivity Growth Mismeasurement*

Calculating the path of real GDP is challenging. Economists have long recognized various problems in inflation statistics—including substitution bias, product improvement, and the introduction of new goods—that undermine the accuracy of inflation indices. Since at least the Stigler commission (Stigler et al. 1961), the economics consensus has been that inflation in consumer and producer prices is overstated, and hence real GDP growth is understated. The Boskin Commission found that the consumer price index overstated inflation rates by 1.10 percent per year, with a "plausible range" of 0.80 percent to 1.60 percent per year (Boskin et al. 1996). The most substantial source of bias found (0.60 percent) was due to the introduction of new goods and quality changes in existing goods—that is, outcomes of innovation itself, so that the benefits of innovation were understated in concrete ways. The Boskin Commission's findings and recommendations led to changes in price measurement approaches, and net of these changes the inflation bias was subsequently estimated to be an approximate 0.65 percent overstatement per year (Gordon 1999), although quality advances and new goods problems remain particularly challenging. The ongoing advance of computing, the internet, and associated digital services has now led many economists to believe that inflation bias may be much worse again today (Brynjolfsson, Collis, and Eggers 2019; Goolsbee and Klenow 2018).

Applying these kinds of biases to gross domestic product overall will substantially increase the growth rate of the economy. The baseline social return to innovation will consequently increase. The correction is

$$(7) \qquad \beta = 1 + \frac{inflation\ bias}{g}.$$

Table 1.4 considers corrections to the baseline social returns, under various assumptions about inflation bias. Taking the Boskin Commission's central estimate (1.10 percent), which may be the right number historically, we see

Table 1.4   **Average social returns, correcting for inflation bias**

Inflation bias (% per annum)	Corrective factor (β)	Average social benefit-cost ratio (ρ)	Average social rate of return (r^*)
0.00	1	13.3	67%
0.40	1.22	16.3	81%
0.65	1.36	18.1	91%
0.80	1.44	19.3	96%
1.10	1.61	21.5	107%
1.60	1.89	25.2	126%

that $\beta = 1.6$. Even with the more modest Gordon estimate of inflation bias (0.65 percent), the social returns are elevated by more than one-third.

1.3.2.2 Health Outcomes

A large portion of R&D, and related capital investment, is related to improving health and longevity. While health may influence productivity, a common target of health innovation is to extend life. Average life expectancy in the United States has risen considerably, from 47.3 in 1900 to 69.7 in 1960 to 78.5 in 2018, and there has been vast progress against infant mortality.[16] Among the contributing factors to these health improvements, innovations play an important role, including the advent and advance of vaccines, antibiotics, cardiovascular treatments, diagnostic and imaging technologies, surgical methods, and oncology products.

From a social return point of view, one could attempt to incorporate some portion of the health gains in the total benefits of innovation. Alternatively, one could remove health R&D from the cost side to produce an average return to non-health-related innovation. On the cost side, about 20–25 percent of government-financed R&D flows through the National Institutes of Health (NIH). In the private sector, approximately 18 percent of private-sponsored R&D in the United States in 2016 came from pharmaceuticals and medicines alone.[17] A broader collective estimate calculates that total medical- and health-related R&D in the United States rose from \$143 billion to \$182 billion between 2013 and 2017, amounting to approximately 30 percent of total US R&D expenditure.[18] Adjusting R&D to remove health expenditure will cause the baseline social return to (non-health-related) innovation to consequently increase. The correction is

$$(8) \qquad \beta = \frac{x}{x - health\ R\ \&\ D}.$$

Table 1.5 considers corrections for alternative measures of health R&D investment. Taking an estimate where health expenditures are 20 percent of total R&D, the social returns to non-health-related innovation rise by 25 percent. This estimate is somewhat conservative in terms of potentially understating health R&D costs. But it may be nonconservative in that it assumes that these health benefits stand fully outside productivity increases; for example, they support longevity or the health of retired individuals, as opposed to being investments in worker productivity.

Adjusting instead on the benefit side, the most direct correction is to incor-

16. Infant mortality in the United States has fallen from 100 deaths per 1,000 live births (1915) to 26 deaths per 1,000 live births (1960) to 5.6 deaths per 1,000 live births in 2017. As Murphy and Topel (2006) point out, in 1900 in the United States, 18 percent of males did not reach their first birthday, but by 2005 one didn't achieve an 18 percent mortality rate until age 62.
17. Wolfe (2018), table 2.
18. National Science Board (2018); Research America (2018).

Table 1.5   **The average social returns, accounting for health**

Health R&D/ total R&D (%)		Corrective factor (β)	Average social benefit-cost ratio (ρ)	Average social rate of return (r^*)
Social returns for non-health-related innovation				
0		1	13.3	67%
20		1.25	16.7	83%
25		1.33	17.8	89%
30		1.43	19.0	95%

Health consumption share (%)	Health consumption growth rate (%)	Corrective factor (β)	Average social benefit-cost ratio (ρ)	Average social rate of return (r^*)
Social returns including benefits of life extension				
25	1.0	1.19	15.8	79%
30	1.5	1.36	18.1	90%
40	2.0	1.74	23.2	116%
50	2.5	2.39	31.9	159%

porate the value of living longer. This is a difficult calculation to make, even in principle. Economists often rely on the value of a statistical life, which can be based on observed expenditure to reduce the risk of death. Using this method and valuing life at $3 million in 1990 dollars, Nordhaus (2005) finds that rising life expectancy has produced annual gains for individuals that exceed the measured growth in the consumption of goods and services.[19] Murphy and Topel (2006) further find enormous welfare gains in the United States from both increased longevity and higher quality of health while alive. In their estimation, the social benefits from improved health are several times the increased expenditure on health care overall.

Explicitly adjusting the social return calculation is somewhat difficult, however, because one needs not just the change in value from improved health but also a different baseline definition of real consumption that incorporates the value of being alive. That is, real GDP per capita is now higher in every period because of this "health consumption," which we denote h. As we show in appendix C, an appropriate correction to the social return is

(9)
$$\beta = \left(1 + \frac{s_h}{1 - s_h} \frac{g_h}{g}\right),$$

where g_h is the growth rate in health consumption and s_h is the share of health consumption in the augmented GDP measure. This correction shows that

19. Nordhaus uses a somewhat conservative value of life measure, compared to other studies and to US government practice in performing cost-benefit analyses.

adding positive growth in health consumption can only increase the social returns to innovation. The amplification factor is increasing in both the growth rate of this health consumption and in the share of health consumption in augmented GDP. Nordhaus (2005) estimates that $g_h \approx 2\%$ in the later half of the 20th century, and one might take $s_h \approx .25$ as a conservative value. Table 1.5 considers adjustments for various values. These estimates are especially speculative given the challenges of the exercise but suggest that the social returns may go up substantially when accounting for health benefits.

The above returns credit the increase in longevity to innovations and, more particularly, to the broad range of R&D costs borne by society. Of course, several key advances in longevity have come from public health interventions, including the advance of clean water supplies in the early 20th century and antismoking campaigns in the later 20th century. Yet these kinds of efforts were in turn based on research insights—for example, Pasteur's germ theory of disease with regard to the importance of clean water, and widespread research about the harms of smoking. Studying the historical gains in life expectancy and, considering its various potential causes, Cutler, Deaton, and Lleras-Muney (2006, 116) argue that "knowledge, science and technology are the keys to any coherent explanation." At the same time, public health interventions, just like the innovations of safety glass, airbags, and other lifesaving features in automobiles, are rooted in research and coupled with follow-on investment. This perspective further suggests that incorporating capital investment (see section 1.3.1) may be appropriate for assessing social returns.

1.3.2.3   International Spillovers

We have focused on R&D expenditure in the United States. However, the benefits of innovation in one place often spread across borders, both because ideas spill over directly and because ideas are embodied in goods and services that are traded across borders. These international spillovers mean that innovation in the United States brings additional benefits beyond an increase in US standards of living. They also mean that some of the US gains are due to innovations that come from other countries.

To examine these international spillovers, one can broaden the lens to a set of advanced economies. Here we consider the G-7 countries and the Organisation for Economic Co-operation and Development (OECD).[20] While it is difficult to say which country is responsible for what portion of innovative benefits, we can look at the innovation expenditure and per-capita GDP paths in these economies collectively.

The US economy invests relatively heavily in R&D (2.7 percent of GDP).

---

20. The G-7 includes Germany, Japan, Great Britain, France, Italy, Canada, and the United States. The OECD has 35 member countries, including the G-7, non-G-7 members of the European Union, Turkey, Mexico, Israel, and South Korea.

Table 1.6   Average social returns, advanced economies as a whole

	R&D (%GDP)	Net investment (%GDP)	Growth rate per capita (%)	Corrective factor (β)	Average social benefit-cost ratio (ρ)	Average social rate of return (r*)
USA						
Baseline	2.7	—	1.8	—	13.3	67%
Net domestic private inv.	2.7	4.0	1.8	—	5.3	27%
All capital deepening	2.7	6.3	1.8	—	4.0	20%
G-7						
Baseline	2.5	—	2.2	1.32	17.6	88%
Net domestic private inv.	2.5	4.0	2.2	1.26	6.8	34%
All capital deepening	2.5	7.7	2.2	1.08	4.3	22%
OECD						
Baseline	2.2	—	3.5	2.38	31.8	159%
Net domestic private inv.	2.2	4.0	3.5	1.59	8.5	57%
All capital deepening	2.2	12.3	3.5	1.21	4.8	24%

Note: The corrective factor β applied here is the ratio of the social returns to the relevant row for the US economy.

By contrast, total R&D investment as a share of total GDP is somewhat smaller for both the G-7 countries as a whole (2.5 percent of total GDP since 2000) and for the OECD members as a whole (2.2 percent of total GDP since 2000).[21] At the same time, income growth per capita is higher in the G-7 and the OECD than in the US economy. Looking since 2000, per-capita income growth rates across the G-7 averaged 2.2 percent and across the OECD averaged 3.5 percent. Table 1.6 considers the implications for the average social returns.

Because R&D investment has declined compared to the baseline, and per-capita income growth rates have risen, the social returns to R&D investment appear higher. One may further want to include capital deepening as an important aspect in realizing these innovation gains. There is little difference, however, since 2000, in the rates of gross domestic capital formation between the United States and the OECD average. Thus, this additional correction, allowing for the role of capital embodiment, will be similar to that in table 1.3. As in table 1.3, a broader and more conservative way to capture capital deepening is to allow for economy-wide deepening that maintains the overall capital-output ratio. Because output is rising faster on average in the G-7 or OECD, this correction calls for greater net capital investment than in the US economy. We also consider this correction in table 1.6. Net of this greater

21. These numbers are calculated using OECD data (https://data.oecd.org/rd/gross-domestic -spending-on-r-d.htm). R&D investment outside the United States has been increasing among the G-7 and among OECD members over time.

investment cost, we still see an increase in the social returns compared to analyzing the United States alone.

Going further, international spillovers of innovation do not stop at the boundaries of the OECD members. The growth in standards of living in developing countries, including China and India, also benefits from innovations in advanced economies. This is true both for productivity gains and health benefits. These advances will be typically felt with a more substantial delay, as developing countries catch up later in many technologies, but with the OECD representing just 17 percent of the world's population, the potential scale of these spillovers is large. While we do not attempt to calculate spillovers beyond the frontier economies, such broader spillovers suggest that the international spillover corrections in table 1.6 are conservative.

1.3.2.4   Summary

We have examined several reasons that the baseline calculation of the average social returns to innovation investments may be too high or too low. Taking just the conservative corrections, the social benefits of innovation investments appear to exceed their costs, and substantially. Adding in natural corrections in the upward direction—due to inflation bias, health gains, or international spillovers—further increases the social benefit-to-cost ratio. Overall, it appears that a conservative estimate of the average social gain is about $5 in benefit per $1 invested. Considering reasonable amounts of inflation bias or health benefits can easily push the average benefit to $10 or even $20 per $1 invested. These gains are just in terms of the US economy. Incorporating international spillovers extends the benefits further. In sum, analyzing the average returns form a wide variety of perspectives suggests that the social returns are remarkably high.

1.4   The Average Return versus the Marginal Return

The analyses in sections 1.2 and 1.3 are explicitly about the *average* social return to innovation investments. By focusing on the average return, we have gained several advantages. We deployed an aggregate-level analysis that can include all R&D costs, including successes and failures, and integrate across complex spillovers inherent to the innovation process. The method can also be leveraged in a transparent manner to assess forces that are not well addressed in the literature on social returns to R&D. These include issues of capital embodiment, lagged effects, productivity measurement, health benefits, and international spillovers. By focusing on the average returns, we stepped past difficult conceptual and empirical issues in how to assign returns to the various components. Overall, we find that the average social returns to innovative investments appear very large.

At the same time, from a policy perspective, we may be particularly interested in the *marginal* returns. That is, we are interested not just in the average social return to what society already does, but also in the social return to undertaking additional investment in innovation. In this section, we consider the extent to which the average social returns are instructive regarding the marginal social returns. Both micro and macro considerations help inform this question, as follows.

1.4.1   Empirical Studies on the Margin

A direct, empirical argument for high marginal returns comes from existing micro literature on the social returns to formal R&D. These studies mainly investigate how variation in R&D expenditure (i.e., marginal variation) within firms and industries predicts future productivity growth of these firms and industries. These studies tend to find large social returns to increasing formal R&D, both through spillovers across firms within an industry and through technological spillovers on firms in technologically related industries (e.g., Hall, Mairesse, and Mohnen 2010). While these studies use regression methods and face difficulties in interpretation, some papers advance causal identification strategies and find large social returns from marginal increases in R&D expenditure by businesses (Bloom, Schankerman, and Van Reenen 2013).[22] Appendix B reviews this complementary literature. Overall, the social rates of return seen in these firm and industry studies, like the average returns seen in our broader calculations, show that the social returns appear very high.

1.4.2   Microreasoning on the Margin

Two related conceptual perspectives can help explain why one would expect the average social returns and marginal social returns to both be high—and even similarly high. In particular, we can write the social returns as

$$r_{social} = r_{private} + r_{spillovers}$$

for a given project.

Empirically, the calculations indicate that r_{social} appears, on average, much larger than standard private rates of return, $r_{private}$. This implies that $r_{spillovers}$ has a large positive mean. It then follows under many distributional assumptions relating $r_{private}$ and $r_{spillovers}$ that the marginal social returns will remain high. For example, if the spillover from a given project is drawn independently from the private return, or if the spillover is drawn as some multiple of the private return, then the marginal social return would remain in excess of the marginal private return. To the extent that most of the social returns are in the spillovers (as suggested by our calculations), it is then natural that the average and the marginal social returns will both be high.

---

22. See also Azoulay, Zivin, and Li (2019) for a causal empirical analysis that finds high returns to increased NIH funding.

A related point follows from the inherent uncertainty in innovation. As Arrow emphasized, it is typically unclear at the start whether a new R&D project is likely to bear fruit (Arrow 1962). Even when one gets close to market applications, failure is a regular occurrence. For example, most entrepreneurial ventures fail (Kerr and Nanda 2009), and those who bet on new ventures—venture capitalists—have substantial trouble predicting which investments will succeed. Kerr, Nanda, and Rhodes-Kropf (2014) studied a prominent venture capital firm and found that the partners' initial scoring of investment opportunities was almost entirely nonpredictive of the future returns to each startup.

This uncertainly is presumably even more acute for basic research, where failure appears very common and the ultimate applications of ideas are hard to predict. For example, a basic research insight like Einstein's general relativity turned out to be an essential tool underlying the Global Positioning System (GPS), which in turn is essential to many technology applications, including new business models like Uber and Lyft (Ahmadpoor and Jones 2017). Similarly, basic research insights into extremophile bacteria in Yellowstone National Park provided the essential gene replication technologies that underpin the biotechnology industry (see Azoulay and Li, chapter 4 in this volume). The connections between basic research and its ultimate applications appear broad, deep, and hard to predict (Ahmadpoor and Jones 2017; Azoulay, Graff Zivin, and Li 2019).

Overall, the uncertain nature of innovation suggests that it is difficult to know the marginal return to an R&D investment, especially for basic research, applied research with uncertain endpoints, or bets on transformative business models. This uncertainty makes it difficult for investors (private or public) to credibly assess the expected returns to such innovation projects. If we are unable to predict the returns of such projects, then the marginal returns to additional investment in such projects may not be too different from the average return of the investments undertaken.

1.4.3   Macroreasoning on the Margin

A final and more explicit approach to assessing the marginal return to innovation is to use growth models. While the average return generalizes across a wide class of growth models, specific calculations of the marginal return will be model dependent. Here we consider the marginal returns by considering the two primary types of innovation models that feature prominently in the endogenous growth literature.

The original approach to endogenous growth theory emphasizes that the rate of advance increases linearly in the level of R&D effort (Aghion and Howitt 1992; Romer 1990). In particular, assume for simplicity that

$$(10) \qquad\qquad g_A = \gamma L_R,$$

where L_R is the number of R&D workers. Intuitively, this leads to the following result, which we show formally in appendix C.

LEMMA 1: *For the knowledge production function (10), the marginal social return to R&D is*

$$(11) \qquad \rho_{marginal} = \frac{g \, / \, r}{x \, / \, y}.$$

That is, the marginal return to additional R&D effort is the same as its average return. This result is intuitive and follows because there are no diminishing returns to R&D effort. When an extra unit of effort at R&D creates a linear increase in the growth rate, the marginal return is identical to the average return. Thus, under classic, Romer-style endogenous growth models, the marginal return to additional R&D, which may be the relevant policy question, appears large and exactly in line with the calculations featured in prior sections of this chapter.

At the same time, there are strong empirical arguments in the growth literature that call for an alternative model of how innovative inputs map onto productivity growth. Namely, empirical evidence points to growing research effort as a requirement to drive a constant growth rate in productivity (Bloom et al. 2020; Jones 1995, 2009; Kortum 1997). The macro facts suggest a relationship of the form

$$(12) \qquad g_A = \delta A(t)^{\theta - 1} L_R(t)^{\sigma},$$

which generalizes (10) on two dimensions. First, it allows for varying degrees of intertemporal spillovers: as the level of productivity, $A(t)$, advances with time, further growth may become easier or harder according to the parameter θ. Second, this generalization allows for varying degrees of diminishing returns to R&D effort at a point in time, via the parameter σ. This model produces the steady-state solution where $g_A = [\sigma / (1 - \theta)]n$ and n is the growth rate in effort applied to R&D.[23]

This empirically grounded knowledge production function leads to the following generalization of the marginal social return to innovation investments, which we show formally in appendix C.

LEMMA 2: *For the generalized knowledge production function in (12), the marginal social return to R&D is*

$$(13) \qquad \rho_{marginal} = \frac{\sigma}{1 + (\sigma - \theta)(g \, / \, r)} \frac{g \, / \, r}{x \, / \, y}.$$

---

23. The steady-state solution requires that $\theta < 1$, which means that the degree of positive intertemporal spillovers cannot be too large.

Table 1.7   **Marginal social returns**

Intertemporal spillovers (θ)	Implied effort elasticity (σ)	Marginal return factor (β)	Marginal social benefit-cost ratio (ρ)	Marginal social internal rate of return (r^*)
−0.75	1.58	0.86	11.4	101%
−0.5	1.35	0.81	10.8	87%
−0.25	1.13	0.75	10.0	73%
0	0.90	0.68	9.0	58%
0.25	0.68	0.59	7.8	45%
0.5	0.45	0.46	6.1	30%
0.75	0.23	0.28	3.7	16%

That is, the marginal return to additional R&D effort is a multiplicative factor of the average return we have calculated in sections 1.2 and 1.3. Connecting to our prior notation, we define this multiplicative factor as $\beta_{marginal}$, where

$$(14) \qquad \beta_{marginal} = \frac{\sigma}{1 + (\sigma - \theta)(g/r)}.$$

This result has several straightforward properties. First, it reproduces the Romer-style marginal return when $\sigma \to 1$ and $\theta \to 1$. Second, other things equal, increasing the degree of intertemporal spillovers (increasing θ) raises the marginal return. Third, other things equal, steeper diminishing returns to research effort (reducing σ) tend to lower the marginal return.[24]

We can take one step further and calibrate the marginal returns. The marginal return depends on several empirically measured variables (g, r, x, y, which we have used to determine the average return) and two unknown parameters (σ, θ). Thus we appear to have two parameters to calibrate. However, keeping in mind that the steady-state growth rate in this model is given by $g_A = [\sigma/(1 - \theta)]n$, we can write

$$(15) \qquad \sigma = \frac{g}{n}(1 - \theta),$$

where we also observe the R&D effort growth rate n. Thus, we have in effect only one parameter to choose.[25]

Table 1.7 presents calibrations of $\beta_{marginal}$ as well as the marginal social return. We use the values for g and r as in section 1.2 and use $n = 2\%$, which

24. This result requires $\theta < 1$ and $g < r$ as conditions for the existence of steady-state growth. Note also that it is possible that the marginal return exceeds the average return. This can occur, for example, if there are increasing returns to research effort at a point in time ($\sigma > 1$) and the intertemporal spillovers are not too small.

25. If we believe we have good information about the degree of intertemporal spillovers, θ, then we can infer σ. Or conversely we could infer θ if we believe we have evidence on σ.

is the growth rate of the US labor force since 1960. We then consider different ranges of intertemporal spillovers from substantially negative ($\theta = -0.75$) to substantially positive ($\theta = +0.75$).

Table 1.7 suggests that the marginal social returns to additional R&D tend to be high. They diminish when there are steep diminishing returns to additional R&D. That is, as additional R&D effort becomes increasingly duplicative of existing R&D, or more broadly additional R&D workers at a point in time are increasingly ineffective, the marginal returns drop.[26]

The literature does not provide clear empirical guidance on the degree of intertemporal spillovers (θ). In models where we "fish out" the pond of ideas or, more generally, the innovative search process becomes more costly as we advance, we expect $\theta < 0$ (Jones 2009; Kortum 1997). However, to the extent that new ideas or tools (e.g., calculus, computers) become fruitful inputs into innovative search, we might expect $\theta < 0$ (Weitzman 1998). Using a model of economic growth and population growth over the very long run, Kremer (1993) provides analysis that suggests a value of θ in the 0.1 to 0.4 range, which would suggest large marginal returns to additional innovative effort, but it's not clear that such values apply in the modern era.

Embedded in the possibility of diminishing returns at the macro level are two underlying notions. First, there may be limited additional innovative lines to pursue, given the stock of current knowledge. Second, there may be limited additional innovative talent in the population. However, micro-evidence appears inconsistent with these constraints. As discussed above, studies of the returns to marginal increases in R&D by firms or in basic research at the NIH point to high marginal returns (Azoulay, Graff Zivin, and Li 2019; Bloom, Schankerman, and Van Reenen 2013). These findings are inconsistent with substantial "idea constraints" in those settings. Regarding "people constraints," there appear to be large opportunities to expand the innovative talent pool in the United States. Expansions in innovative labor could occur through immigration channels (see Kerr and Kerr, chapter 3 in this volume) and through education and early childhood policies (see Van Reenen, chapter 2 in this volume). Key constraints on innovative human capital appear through limited exposure to these career pathways, not in available talent (Azoulay et al. forthcoming; Bell et al. 2019a, 2019b). Immigration, education, and career-exposure policies suggest substantial

---

26. An interesting feature of this calibration is that more positive intertemporal spillovers make the marginal returns to additional innovation decline. While positive intertemporal spillovers seem directly to be an advantage to the social returns, the calibration here requires that large positive intertemporal spillovers be offset by increased diminishing returns (or vice versa). This is required to match observed growth rates. An implication is that, even if one thinks there are steep diminishing returns to additional effort, the marginal social returns to additional effort can still tend to be high. For example, taking $\sigma = 0.23$ (see table 1.7), one is assuming that increasing the investment in innovation by 100 percent would increase innovative output by only 17 percent. Yet the internal social rate of return is still 16 percent per annum (see table 1.7); large, positive intertemporal spillovers make this additional effort still highly valuable.

short-run and long-run potential to cultivate additional innovative capacity and accelerate improvements in standards of living.

1.5   Conclusion

This chapter considers estimates of the social returns to investments in innovation. We have introduced a transparent method that incorporates both innovative successes and failures, while also incorporating manifold externalities at work in the innovation process, including imitation, business stealing, congestion, and intertemporal spillovers. The approach can further engage a range of first-order issues that are often not considered in assessing the social returns. These dimensions include the role of capital investment, diffusion delays, productivity mismeasurement, and health outcomes, among others.

Overall, we find that the average social returns to innovation investments appear very large. If formal R&D and new venture creation drive the bulk of productivity gains, then the social returns to these investments appear enormous. If a much broader set of investments, including capital embodiment, is needed to fulfill these productivity gains, then the social returns to these broader activities still appear large. Even under very conservative assumptions, it is difficult to find an average return below $4 per $1 spent. Accounting for health benefits, inflation bias, or international spillovers can bring the social returns to over $20 per $1 spent, with internal rates of return approaching 100 percent.

We further consider how these average returns may relate to the marginal return of additional investment in innovation. Using various perspectives, motivated by the micro and macro literatures on innovation, there are good reasons to believe that the marginal returns are also high. The implication is that the potential returns to policies that support further innovation investment are high. Innovation investments can credibly raise economic growth rates and extend lives, paying for their costs many times over. And because the social returns exceed the private returns, public policy has a central role, and opportunity, in unleashing these gains.

The analysis also points to key areas for future work. This chapter's methodology calculates the overall social returns to innovation investments, pulling together wide-ranging measurement considerations. At the same time, it leaves open the question of what specific innovative activities are especially fruitful. For example, basic research, applied research, and more incremental product development likely bring different returns. Specific sectors also bear further investigation. For example, this chapter provides basic assessment on the health line, but both the importance of health outcomes and the scale of health R&D call for much more expansive analysis. This chapter also considers how the social returns to R&D investment may be realized by embodying new knowledge through capital deepening, linking innovation returns with other investment dimensions and raising additional avenues for research and policy consideration. Given high social returns to the collected suite of innovation activities, a broad expansion in innovative activities is likely to raise standards of living farther and faster. Future work assessing and pinning down the major drivers of these returns will help tailor policy choices to achieve yet higher social benefit.

Appendix A
Spillovers and the Social Returns to Innovation

The society-wide gains from an innovation may differ substantially from the private gains to the innovator. The difference comes from the many potential "spillovers" that can follow from the creation and introduction of new ideas. In this appendix, we discuss the range of these potential spillovers, which in turn make the measurement of the social return to innovation challenging.

Imitative Spillovers

The innovative investments made by one firm may not only raise the investing firm's productivity, but also raise the productivity of other firms. In particular, other firms can imitate the advance (e.g., Segerstrom 1991). For example, consider computer manufacturers. When a more advanced microprocessor, memory chip, or monitor is created, competing firms will see and learn from these innovations and improve their own products. These "imitative" knowledge spillovers increase the social returns to innovation, even as imitation by competitors may reduce the private return to the original innovator. Beyond product innovations, process innovations—such as Henry Ford's assembly line, Geoff Hinton's artificial intelligence algorithms, or the World Health Organization's surgical checklist—can also be learned and imitated by others, extending the benefits far beyond the original innovator.

User Spillovers

An important, second potential spillover is the benefit that accrues to users (e.g., Trajtenberg 1989). For example, more advanced computing machinery will presumably increase the productivity of the downstream firms that purchase and deploy the machines. This user benefit is not likely to be fully captured by the upstream innovator; in particular, the users who buy the product presumably expect a benefit in excess of the product's price. User spillovers can occur between firms in a vertical supply relationship. They can also occur for the end user—the consumer—creating consumer surplus that is not captured by the innovating firm. The downstream benefits may be especially large when the upstream producers are competitive and imitate each other's innovations (e.g., Petrin 2002).

Intertemporal Spillovers

A potentially central but difficult-to-estimate spillover is intertemporal in nature, where a given advance may influence the capacity for future advances (e.g., Romer 1990; Scotchmer 1991; Weitzman 1998). This intertemporal element could involve opening research avenues in a given product line; a specific advance in jet engine design, say, may inspire a stream of future jet engine innovations. The spillovers may also be far more general. For example, technologies like electricity, computers, and mobile phones serve as platforms for enormous arrays of future innovations. Taking smartphones as one example, these tools have spurred the innovation of millions of new software applications.[27] Mobile phones have also sparked the creation of transformative business models, including mobile payments and the ride-sharing industry.

When the intertemporal spillovers on future innovation are broad, it becomes difficult to measure the social returns to the original innovation. With general purpose technologies like mobile phones, the internet, computers, lasers, and electricity, it is difficult even to enumerate the full set of future applications that build on them. A question like "what is the social return to the internet?" is difficult to answer because the applications are so varied.

This difficulty is also acute with basic research. By definition, basic research is not directed at specific marketplace innovations. Rather, it is intended to advance understanding and introduce new ideas on which future applications may build. Essentially, the marketplace returns to basic research are *all* in the intertemporal spillovers. And although basic research is an uncertain exercise riddled with failure, it also produces insights that are ultimately essential to marketplace innovations and socioeconomic prosperity. For example, without basic research breakthroughs in genetics—from Mendelian inheritance to Watson and Crick's structure of DNA to Kary Mullis's polymerase chain reaction—there would be no biotechnology industry, and many of our most advanced medical treatments would not exist. Advances in mathematics, chemistry, solid-state physics, material science, and statistics, to name just a few fields, underpin substantial marketplace applications (Ahmadpoor and Jones 2017). Asking "what is the social return to learning the structure of DNA?" or "what is the social return to calculus?" is obviously difficult, because, once again, the applications are so varied.

The above discussion suggests that the intertemporal spillovers are largely positive, as an advance can facilitate future advances. But it is also possible

---

27. In 2019, there are 2.47 million apps available on the Android platform and 1.80 million apps available on the Apple platform.

that intertemporal spillovers are negative. The main reason for a negative intertemporal spillover is that we may find discovery of new ideas increasingly difficult. For example, if ideas are fruit on a tree, we may naturally pluck the low-hanging fruit first. Then future innovation will become harder to achieve. There is substantial micro- and macroevidence along these lines, where innovation requires more effort with time (Bloom et al. 2020; Jones 1995, 2009). But it remains an open question whether the intertemporal spillovers are on net positive or negative.

Business Stealing

Returning to firms, additional issues could limit the social return to innovation. In particular, in a competitive context it is possible that the social returns are actually below the private return. This effect comes from "business stealing," where the advance of one firm may come in part by stealing business from other firms (e.g., Aghion and Howitt 1998). Concretely, consider a small innovation that allows a firm to produce a piece of machinery at a slightly lower cost than all the other firms in a competitive market. This innovating firm may then grow to take over the market and see an enormous private return, but the social return may actually be very small. More generally, any time a firm or industry grows at the expense of other firms and industries, looking narrowly at the private R&D returns to the advancing firm or industry will tend, other things equal, toward overstating the social returns.

Duplication

A final kind of negative spillover comes within the R&D process itself, when research teams duplicate each other's efforts (e.g., Dixit 1988). For example, many firms may simultaneously seek to create the same new technology. Similarly, multiple teams conducting basic research may race toward the same experimental result. Because research teams do not internalize their effects on the other teams, there may be too much entry on a given research line.

Appendix B

Empirical Estimates of the Social Returns to R&D: Existing Literature

This appendix reviews existing approaches to calculating the social returns to R&D. We review technology case studies, firm- and industry-level studies, and country-level studies. This literature use a variety of methods and provides a series of informative findings. The typical finding is that the social returns appear very large. At the same time, each approach has methodological limitations.

Technology Case Studies

The "case study" approach compares R&D costs with their associated benefits for specific technologies and sectors. Griliches (1958), in a seminal contribution, considered the development of hybrid corn in the United States. The R&D costs targeting hybrid corn are counted up over several decades. The benefits are calculated as the increased corn output that results, net of increased input costs. Both the R&D costs and the production benefits are summed up at a point in time using an assumed discount rate. In Griliches's central estimate, the social returns appear very large: $1 of R&D costs provides a $7 net present value benefit.[28]

Other case studies have examined numerous agriculture innovations (e.g., Evenson 2001) and small sets of industrial innovations—including mechanical, chemical, electronic, and consumer product innovations (Mansfield et al. 1977; Tewksbury, Crandall, and Crane 1980). Bresnahan (1986) studied mainframe computers in financial services. Trajtenberg (1989) studied CT scanners and their benefits for health care. While estimates vary, these studies typically show large social returns. For example, studies of public agricultural research suggest social returns typically above 40 percent (Evenson 2001). The findings across 37 industrial innovations studied in Mansfield et al. (1977) and Tewksbury, Crandall, and Crane (1980) suggest a median social rate of return of 71 percent.

The primary challenge for case studies is whether they generalize. Hybrid corn, mainframe computers, and CT scanners were successful innovations. Case studies of failures are rare, even though failure in innovation is common (Arrow 1962; Kerr, Nanda, and Rhodes-Kropf 2014). By leaving out failures, case studies may overstate the general social returns to R&D. On the other hand, case studies focus on narrow innovations or applications. The social returns for far-reaching innovations—electricity, lasers, computers, gene sequencing—are very hard to calculate and yet may have the highest social returns of all. Thus, whether the case study evidence overstates or understates the average social returns is unclear.

Firm and Industry Analyses

A separate literature uses regression methods to study the social returns to R&D. In these regressions, the dependent variable is typically the output

---

28. Griliches argues that this estimate is conservative. He uses a high discount rate (10 percent) and other conservative assumptions to argue that the social returns are at least $7 per $1 spent. This equates to an internal rate of return of at least 35–40 percent.

or productivity of the firm or industry. The explanatory variables are R&D expenditures. At the firm level, a private return is estimated by looking at how a firm's own R&D expenditure predicts that firm's output or productivity growth. Social returns are incorporated by further examining how the focal firm or industry's output growth depends on the R&D investments by *other* firms or industries. This cross-firm or cross-industry spillover is estimated in the regression context by including "outside R&D" as a separate predictor of a given firm or industry's outcome.

Regression approaches often find substantial social returns. Hall, Mairesse, and Mohnen (2010) review the regression evidence and suggest that private returns to R&D are most likely in the 20–30 percent range. Estimates of the cross-firm or -industry spillovers tend to be additionally positive, but these estimates vary considerably across studies and are often imprecise. For example, some studies have suggested that large returns can be captured from outsider R&D (Griffith, Redding, and Van Reenen 2004; Griliches and Lichtenberg 1984), while others have suggested that there can be little or no return from outsider R&D (Bernstein and Mohnen 1998; Bernstein and Nadiri 1989; Wolff and Nadiri 1993).

The regression approach embodies a number of assumptions. First, to interpret a regression coefficient as a rate of return, one must assume specific production functions relating R&D to productivity growth. Second, one must make assumptions about lags, since the output growth today may depend not just on last year's R&D expenditure, but on R&D projects begun in prior years. In practice, regression methods typically assume a very rapid payoff of R&D. Third, one must make assumptions about the scope of spillovers, where firms or industries that are nearer in technology may have more spillover potential. Hall, Mairesse, and Mohnen (2010) review the various assumptions authors have used about these dimensions, and the variety of assumptions may help explain variant results.

The regression results also do not imply causation. A positive correlation between R&D expenditures and firm output could be due to reverse causation or omitted variables. Firms with high output growth may choose to do substantial R&D, so that the causation runs backward. And good technology prospects may cause all firms to do more R&D and also see output increases; the apparent spillover from "outside R&D" may then be a spurious association driven by common technology opportunities. Thus, interpreting private or social returns from simple regressions is not straightforward.

In light of these issues, two studies are notable for attempting to causatively estimate the social returns. Bloom, Schankerman, and Van Reenen (2013) use changes in federal and state-level R&D tax incentives, which change the R&D costs of firms. These authors show that R&D expenditures go up when a firm's tax costs go down. The resulting change in R&D investment in turn drives greater firm growth and greater spillovers on other firms.

Bloom, Schankerman, and Van Reenen (2013) estimate a private return of 21 percent and a social return of 55 percent.[29]

A limitation for all regression models of spillovers is that they must take a stand on the boundary of spillovers. Anything "further outside" the outside R&D measures is, by construction, ignored. One omission is basic research, including that conducted in universities and government laboratories. These R&D investments are left out of industry studies but may have important effects. Azoulay, Graff Zivin, and Li (2019) tackle basic research spillovers in the context of biomedical innovation. Using shocks to National Institutes of Health funding allows this study to make a causative interpretation. They find that an additional $10 million dollars in NIH funding leads to 2.7 additional private-sector patents. By imputing market values to these patents, the authors calculate a commercial return of at least $2 per $1 spent by the NIH. The social returns, which would require assessing the net health advantages of these innovations, would presumably be higher. An additional important finding is that half of the patents come in disease areas outside the target of the NIH funding, which points to the broad scope of basic research spillovers.

Country-Level Analyses

Regression models can also be conducted at the national level. Here the dependent variable is national total factor productivity, and the R&D input is the total R&D expenditure within the country. Cross-country spillovers are examined by including other countries' R&D as a separate explanatory variable. Coe and Helpman (1995) study 22 high-income countries. They find a strong positive relationship between R&D expenditure and productivity growth at the national level. Taking the association as causative, the own rate of return to R&D averaged 123 percent in G-7 countries and averaged 85 percent in 15 other high-income countries. Cross-country spillovers also appear substantial, adding another 30 percent to the returns. Several studies consider alternative regression specifications to Coe and Helpman (1995) and alternative national-scale settings or sets of countries. The nations' returns to R&D always appear positive in these studies, but the magnitudes vary considerably, with some studies finding very large returns (e.g., Kao,

29. An important feature of this study is that it confronts two dimensions of R&D spillovers. The effect of "outside R&D" is in principal a mixture of two forces above. First, there may be knowledge spillovers, where technology advances in one firm are absorbed by other firms, raising these other firms' productivity. Second, there may be business stealing, where the gains by one firm may come at the expense of other firms' business. Bloom, Schankerman, and Van Reenen (2013) distinguish these channels by separately considering firms that are close together in technology space (allowing knowledge spillovers) and firms that are close together in product space (allowing business stealing). The finding that the social returns are 55 percent nets out both channels, suggesting that knowledge spillovers dominate.

Chiang, and Chen 1999) and others finding more modest returns (Nadiri and Kim 1996; Westmore 2013).

An important advantage of aggregation to the national level is that it can include all R&D (including basic research expenditure) and net out R&D spillovers across firms and industries, including knowledge spillovers and business-stealing effects. The "own return" in a national regression is thus conceptually much closer to a social return than the narrower technology-, firm-, or industry-level analyses. The cross country aspect of Coe and Helpman (1995) and ensuing studies adds a further dimension of spillover, where the benefits of innovations extend beyond national boundaries.

The disadvantage of country-level regression approaches are similar to above, especially with regard to causative identification. One may be particularly concerned at the national level about spurious associations that disrupt interpretation. For example, R&D investment is responsive to business cycles, leading to reverse causation problems (Aghion et al. 2012; Ouyang 2011). More broadly, omitted variables may bias the correlations.

An alternative macroeconomic approach is model driven. Here authors use specific growth models to calculate the marginal return of additional R&D spending. Jones and Williams (1998) take this approach and show under fairly broad theoretical conditions that private returns to R&D seen in the micro literature will tend to understate the social returns. They conclude that optimal R&D investment is two to four times greater than observed investment. Many ensuing studies build specific endogenous growth models and calibrate them to micro- and macroevidence (e.g., Grossman, Steger, and Trimborn 2016; Jones and Williams 2000; Sener 2008). This work arrives at the similar broad conclusion where the marginal social returns to additional R&D are high and that advanced economies underinvest in R&D.

Summary

Using different methods and data, the existing literature suggests that the social returns to R&D are high. At the same time, the scope of spillovers considered is often limited, especially with studies focused on specific technologies, firms, and industries. Intertemporal spillovers, which may play out in diffuse ways and with long delays, are typically ignored. And each of the above methods has specific limitations. Despite these differences and limitations, the diverse approaches seen across the literature reach similar conclusions: the social returns appear very high. The complementary calculation in this chapter, which addresses several limitations, further indicates that high social returns to innovation investments appear robust.

Appendix C

Formal Results

Baseline Average Social Returns

Here we derive the baseline estimate for the social rate of return to aggregate investment in innovation. The average social returns are calculated by comparing the observed growth path with the counterfactual growth path that would emerge in the absence of innovation investments. We will look at the benefits in terms of per-capita income. For the observed growth case, we see the path of GDP per capita, $y(t)$, and the path of innovation investment per capita, $x(t)$. For the counterfactual case, we have an alternate path of GDP per capita, $\hat{y}(t)$, given an alternate path of investment, $\hat{x}(t)$.

The social returns, $\rho(t)$, are calculated by comparing the ratio of the net present value of the benefits, $B(t)$, to the net present value of the costs, $C(t)$. Namely,

$$\rho(t) = \frac{B(t)}{C(t)}.$$

Let's say the counterfactual path begins at some time t_0. Then, comparing the observed and counterfactual investment paths, the present value of the innovation benefits is

$$B(t_0) = \int_{t_0}^{\infty} [y(t) - \hat{y}(t)]e^{-r(t-t_0)}dt$$

and the present value of innovation costs is

$$C(t_0) = \int_{t_0}^{\infty} [x(t) - \hat{x}(t)]e^{-r(t-t_0)}dt.$$

To proceed to our baseline estimate, we first must define a counterfactual of interest. In particular, we want to consider the average return to all innovation investment, aggregating across the many spillovers associated with this process. As a thought experiment, we can do this by "turning off" innovation at time t_0. Thus, by definition, we write $\hat{x}(t) = x(t)$ for $t < t_0$, and we write $\hat{x}(t) = 0$ for $t \geq t_0$.

The remaining question concerns the counterfactual path of income per capita. For a simple baseline, we write $\hat{y}(t) = y(t)$ for $t < t_0$, and we write $\hat{y}(t) = y(t_0)$ for $t \geq t_0$. That is, we assume that per-capita income stops growing in the absence of further innovation investments. This baseline counterfactual path embeds a set of assumptions, and relaxing those assumptions is the subject of section 1.4. But note that, while simplistic, this counterfactual path is broadly consistent with neoclassical growth theory, where (1) following Solow, growth in per-capita income requires gains in productivity, and

(2) following endogenous growth theory, gains in productivity come from explicit investments in innovation.

For simplicity, take the stylized facts of a balanced growth path, where the observed path of $y(t)$ grows at a constant rate g, and measured innovation investment (i.e., R&D) is an approximately constant share of GDP, and thus also grows at rate g. The present value of the benefits of innovation are then

$$B(t_0) - y(t_0)\left[\frac{1}{r-g} - \frac{1}{r}\right]$$

and the present value of the costs of innovation are

$$C(t_0) = x(t_0)\left[\frac{1}{r-g}\right].$$

It then follows that the social benefit-cost ratio (the amount of benefit per unit of cost) is

$$\rho = \frac{g/r}{x/y},$$

where we have dropped the time notation, t_0, given that we are looking at a balanced growth path, where $x(t)/y(t)$ is constant. Alternatively, one can describe the social rate of return, r^*. This is the discount rate for which the benefits would equal the costs ($\rho = 1$). That is,

$$r^* = \frac{gy}{x}.$$

Discrete Time Analog

As an alternative derivation, we can consider a discrete time analog. Here innovation is not "turned off" forever but rather for just one period. This approach may better clarify that our counterfactual path doesn't change the intertemporal spillovers from innovation, as this counterfactual preserves the exact same path of productivity gains, but with a one-period delay.

In particular, let there be a series of investments, x_t, that improve productivity, A_t. As a counterfactual, we imagine that in some year t_0, no such investments are made, and thereafter exactly the same investments are made as on the observed path, only one period later. That is, we consider the innovation investment path where $\hat{x}_t = x_t$ for $t < t_0$; $\hat{x}_t = 0$ for $t = t_0$; and $\hat{x}_t = x_{t-1}$ for $t > t_0$. Since these are truly identical investments (i.e., the same innovation projects), we imagine that they must have the same ultimate effect on productivity. Thus it must be, ultimately, that $A_t = A_{t-1}$. Now, in neoclassical growth theory, we have y_t/A_t equal to a constant. This implies that, ultimately, $y_t = y_{t-1}$.

In a simple, "immediate innovation effect" model, we have $\hat{y}_t = y_t$ for $t \leq t_0$; and $\hat{y}_t = y_{t-1}$ for $t > t_0$. We take this as our baseline counterfactual case, commensurate with the baseline approach in discussed section 1.2.

What are the social returns? The net present value of the difference in investment costs along the observed path and counterfactual paths is

$$C_{t_0} = x_{t_0}\left[\frac{r}{r-g}\right].$$

And the net present value of the difference in the benefits along the observed and counterfactual growth paths is

$$B_{t_0} = y_{t_0}\left[\frac{g}{r-g}\right].$$

Then, along a balanced growth path we have, once again,

$$\rho = \frac{g/r}{x/y}.$$

Social Returns with Health Benefits

To incorporate health benefits into the social returns, we first expand the definition of GDP to include a "health consumption" component, which represents the flow value of being alive. Denote this health consumption flow as h, and define "augmented GDP per capita" as y^*, which includes this health consumption. That is,

$$y^* = y + h.$$

Similarly, denote the growth rate of augmented GDP per capita as g^*. Based on the above definition of augmented GDP per capita, it follows that

$$g^* = g(1 - s_h) + g_h s_h,$$

where $s_h = (h/y)^*$ is the share of health consumption in augmented GDP, and g_h is the growth rate of h.

The true social returns to innovation will then be

$$\rho^* = \frac{g^*/r}{x/y^*},$$

which makes two adjustments compared to the baseline calculation of the social returns to innovation. First, the relevant benefit measure is based on g^*, which incorporates progress in health. Second, the relevant cost measure is still total innovation expenditure, x, but it is now viewed as a share of the augmented GDP per capita measure, y^*.

Using the expressions for y^* and g^*, the health-augmented social rate of return to innovation can be written as

$$\rho^* = \left(1 + \frac{s_h}{1 - s_h}\frac{g_h}{g}\right)\frac{g/r}{x/y}$$

as presented in the text.

Proof of Lemmas

LEMMA 1: *For the knowledge production function (10), the marginal social rate of return to R&D is* $\rho_{marginal} = (g/r)/(x/y)$.

PROOF: The output path of the economy is $Y(t) = A(t)L_Y(t)$, with workers paid a competitive wage $w(t) = A(t)$. The R&D expenditure path is $X(t) = w(t)L_R(t)$. In per-capita terms, income per capita is $y(t) = A(t)$ and R&D expenditure per capita is $x(t) = A(t)[(L_R(t)]/[L(t)]$.

We compare the observed balanced growth path with a counterfactual path in which R&D expenditure per capita is raised by υ percent. Comparing the observed income path, $y(t)$, and the counterfactual income path, $\hat{y}(t)$, the net present value of the benefits of increasing innovation investment is

$$(16) \qquad B(t_0) = \int_{t_0}^{\infty}(\hat{y}(t) - y(t))e^{-r(t-t_0)}dt = \int_{t_0}^{\infty}(\hat{A}(t) - A(t))e^{-r(t-t_0)}dt,$$

where the counterfactual path begins at time t_0. Comparing the observed innovation expenditure path, $x(t)$, with the counterfactual innovation investment path, $\hat{x}(t)$, the net present value of the costs of increasing innovation investment is

$$(17) \quad C(t_0) = \int_{t_0}^{\infty}(\hat{x}(t) - x(t))e^{-r(t-t_0)}dt = (x/y)\int_{t_0}^{\infty}(\hat{A}(t)(1 + \upsilon) - A(t))e^{-r(t-t_0)}dt,$$

where the resource allocation, $[L_R(t)]/[L(t)] = x/y$, is a constant on the observed balanced growth path and is a constant that is proportionally $1 + \upsilon$ higher on the counterfactual growth path (which is also balanced in this case).

To consider the social returns to R&D, we can then integrate these expressions. Using the Romer-style knowledge production function, (10), we have[30]

$$A(t) = A(t_0)e^{\gamma L_R(t-t_0)}$$

$$\hat{A}(t) = A(t_0)e^{\gamma(1+\upsilon)L_R(t-t_0)}$$

for the observed and counterfactual paths of productivity. The net benefits from increased innovation investment are then

---

30. Recall that the Romer-style growth models require constant population for a balanced growth path.

$$B(t_0) = \frac{A(t_0)}{r - \gamma L_R}\left[\frac{\upsilon\gamma L_R}{r - (1 + \upsilon)\gamma L_R}\right]$$

and the net costs from increased innovation investment are

$$C(t_0) = \frac{1}{x/y}\left[\frac{A(t_0)}{r - \gamma L_R}\right]\left[\frac{\upsilon r}{r - (1 + \upsilon)\gamma L_R}\right].$$

The social return to any adjustment of size υ is then

$$\rho_\upsilon = \frac{B(t_0)}{C(t_0)} = \frac{\gamma L_R/r}{x/y},$$

where we note that the steady-state growth rate on the observed path is $g = \gamma L_R$. Thus we have

$$\rho_{marginal} = \frac{g/r}{x/y},$$

which was to be shown.

LEMMA 2: *For the generalized knowledge production function in (12), the marginal social return to R&D is*

$$\rho_{marginal} = \frac{\sigma}{1 + (\sigma - \theta)(g/r)}\frac{g/r}{x/y}.$$

PROOF: Using the same approach as in Lemma 1 will not work here, because in general the counterfactual path $\hat{A}(t)$ is not simply a constant, proportional change in the growth rate, as in the Romer model. However, the counterfactual path still has a closed-form solution. In particular, we now have the generalized knowledge production function (12)

(12) $$\dot{A}(t) = \delta A(t)^\theta L_R(t)^\sigma.$$

This knowledge production function is a separable, nonlinear differential equation. Separating and integrating both sides, we have solutions of the form

(18) $$\int_{-\infty}^{t} \hat{A}(\tau)^{-\theta}d\hat{A}(\tau) = \int_{-\infty}^{t_0} \delta\hat{L}_R(\tau)^\sigma d\tau + \int_{t_0}^{t} \delta\hat{L}_R(\tau)^\sigma d\tau.$$

On the counterfactual path, the number of R&D workers follows

$$\hat{L}_R(t) = \left\{\begin{array}{l} L_R(t), \; t < t_0 \\ (1 + \upsilon)L_R(t), \; t \geq t_0 \end{array}\right\},$$

where $L_R(t) = L_R(t_0)e^{n(t-t_0)}$ grows at a constant exponential rate n. We therefore integrate (18) and solve for the counterfactual productivity path as

(19) $\hat{A}(t) = A(t_0)[1 + (1 + v)^{\sigma}(e^{\sigma n(t-t_0)} - 1)]^{1/(1-\theta)},$

where $A(t_0) = \hat{A}(t_0) = \{[(1 - \theta)\delta L_R(t_0)^{\sigma}]/\sigma n\}^{1/(1-\theta)}.$

The path $\hat{A}(t)$ cannot be integrated easily into a net present value. However, one can still produce an analytic solution for the marginal social return as follows. First, write the social return as

$$\rho_v = \frac{B(t_0)}{C(t_0)} = \frac{\int_{t_0}^{\infty}(\hat{A}(t) - A(t))e^{-r(t-t_0)}dt}{(x/y)\int_{t_0}^{\infty}(\hat{A}(t)(1 + v) - A(t))e^{-r(t-t_0)}dt} = \frac{1}{x/y}\left[\frac{1}{1 + Q(v)}\right],$$

where

$$Q(v) = \frac{\int_{t_0}^{\infty}v\hat{A}(t)e^{-r(t-t_0)}dt}{\int_{t_0}^{\infty}(\hat{A}(t) - A(t))e^{-r(t-t_0)}dt}.$$

We seek the marginal return, where v is small. While the limit $\lim_{v \to 0} Q(v)$ is not defined in the above form, we can instead use L'Hopital's rule to write

(20) $\lim_{v \to 0} Q(v) = \lim_{v \to 0} \dfrac{\int_{t_0}^{\infty}\hat{A}(t)e^{-r(t-t_0)}dt + \int_{t_0}^{\infty}v(\partial\hat{A}(t)/\partial v)e^{-r(t-t_0)}dt}{\int_{t_0}^{\infty}(\partial\hat{A}(t)/\partial v)e^{-r(t-t_0)}dt}.$

The derivative of the path $\hat{A}(t)$ with respect to v, using (19), is

$$\frac{\partial\hat{A}(t)}{\partial v} = \frac{A(t_0)}{1 - \theta}\sigma(1 + v)^{\sigma-1}(e^{\sigma n(t-t_0)} - 1)\left[\hat{A}(t)/A(t_0)\right]^{\theta}.$$

We can then integrate out the expressions in (20), noting that $\lim_{v \to 0}\hat{A}(t) = A(t)$, and take the limit of $Q(v)$ as

$$\lim_{v \to 0} Q(v) = \frac{r - \theta g}{\sigma g}.$$

With some algebra, we can thus write

$$\rho_{marginal} = \frac{\sigma}{1 + (\sigma - \theta)(g/r)}\frac{g/r}{x/y}$$

as was to be shown.

References

Adams, J. D. 1990. "Fundamental Stocks of Knowledge and Productivity Growth." *Journal of Political Economy* 98 (3): 673–702.

Aghion, Philippe, Philippe Askenazy, Nicolas Berman, Gilbert Cette, and Laurent Eymard. 2012. "Credit Constraints and the Cyclicality of R&D Investment: Evidence from France." *Journal of the European Economic Association* 10: 1001–24.

Aghion, Philippe, and Peter Howitt. 1992. "A Model of Growth through Creative Destruction." *Econometrica* 60: 323–51.

———. 1998. *Endogenous Growth Theory.* Cambridge, MA: MIT Press.

Ahmadpoor, M., and B. F. Jones. 2017. "The Dual Frontier: Patented Inventions and Prior Scientific Advance." *Science* 357: 583–87.

Argente, David, Salomé Baslandze, Douglas Hanley, and Sara Moreira. 2020. "Patents to Products: Product Innovation and Firm Dynamics." Federal Reserve Bank of Atlanta Working Paper No. 2020/4.

Arrow, Kenneth. 1961. "The Economic Implications of Learning by Doing," Technical Report No. 101, Stanford Institute for Mathematical Studies in the Social Sciences.

———. 1962. "Economic Welfare and the Allocation of Resources for Invention." In *The Rate and Direction of Inventive Activity: Economic and Social Factors*, a conference of the Universities–National Bureau Committee for Economic Research and the Committee on Economic Growth of the Social Science Research Council, 609–25. Princeton, NJ: Princeton University Press.

Azoulay, Pierre, Benjamin F. Jones, J. Daniel Kim, and Javier Miranda. 2020. "Age and High-Growth Entrepreneurship." *American Economic Review: Insights* 2: 65–82.

———. Forthcoming. "Immigration and Entrepreneurship in the United States." *American Economic Review: Insights.*

Azoulay, Pierre, Josh Graff Zivin, and Danielle Li. 2019. "Public R&D Investments and Private-Sector Patenting: Evidence from NIH Funding Rules." *Review of Economic Studies* 86: 117–52.

Bell, Alexander, Raj Chetty, Xavier Jaravel, Neviana Petkova, and John Van Reenen. 2019a. "Who Becomes an Inventor in America? The Importance of Exposure to Innovation." *Quarterly Journal of Economics* 134 (2): 647–713.

———. 2019b. "Do Tax Cuts Produce More Einsteins? The Impacts of Financial Incentives vs. Exposure to Innovation on the Supply of Inventors." *Journal of the European Economic Association* 17 (3): 651–77.

Bernstein, J. I., and P. Mohnen. 1998. "International R&D Spillovers between U.S. and Japanese R&D Intensive Sectors." *Journal of International Economics* 44: 315–38.

Bernstein, J. I., and M. I. Nadiri. 1989. "Research and Development and Intra-industry Spillovers: An Empirical Application of Dynamic Duality." *Review of Economic Studies* 56: 249–69.

Bessen, James. 2015. *Learning by Doing: The Real Connection between Innovation, Wages, and Wealth.* New Haven, CT: Yale University Press.

Bloom, Nicholas, Charles Jones, John Van Reenen, and Michael Webb. 2020. "Are Ideas Getting Harder to Find?" *American Economic Review* 110: 1104–44.

Bloom, Nicholas, Mark Schankerman, and John Van Reenen, 2013. "Identifying Technology Spillovers and Product Market Rivalry." *Econometrica* 81: 1347–93.

Boskin, Michael, E. Dulberger, R. Gordon, Z. Griliches, and D. Jorgenson. 1996. "Toward a More Accurate Measure of the Cost of Living." Final Report to the Senate Finance Committee.

Bresnahan, Timothy. 1986. "Measuring Spillovers from 'Technical Advance.'" *American Economic Review* 76: 741–55.

Brouwer, E., and K. Kleinknecht. 1997. "Measuring the Unmeasurable: A Country's Non-R&D Expenditure on Product and Service Innovation." *Research Policy* 25: 1235–42.

Brynjolfsson, E., A. Collis, and F. Eggers. 2019. "Using Massive Online Choice

Experiments to Measure Changes in Well-Being." *Proceedings of the National Academy of Sciences* 116: 7250–55.

Coe, D. T., and E. Helpman. 1995. "International R&D Spillovers." *European Economic Review* 39: 859–87.

Council of Economic Advisers. 2011. *The Economic Report of the President.* Washington, DC: U.S. Government Printing Office.

Cutler, D., A. Deaton, and A. Lleras-Muney. 2006. "The Determinants of Mortality." *Journal of Economic Perspectives* 20: 97–120.

Denison, Edward F. 1962. "The Unimportance of the Embodied Question." *American Economic Review* 54 (2): 90–94.

Dixit, Avinash. 1988. "A General Model of R&D Competition and Policy." *RAND Journal of Economics* 19: 317–26.

Eurostat, 2019. *The Community Innovation Survey 2018.* Luxembourg: Eurostat. https://ec.europa.eu/eurostat/web/science-technology-innovation/data/database?node_code=inn.

Evangelista, E., T. Sandven, G. Sirilli, and K. Smith. 2010. "Measuring Innovation in European Industry." *International Journal of the Economics of Business* 5: 311–33.

Evenson, R. 2001. "Economic Impacts of Agricultural Research and Extension." In *Handbook of Agricultural Economics,* edited by Bruce L. Gardner and Gordon C. Rausser, 573–628. Amsterdam: Elsevier.

Goolsbee, Austan, and Peter Klenow. 2018. "Internet Rising, Prices Falling: Measuring Inflation in a World of E-Commerce." *American Economic Review* 108: 488–92.

Gordon, Robert. 1999. "The Boskin Commission Report and Its Aftermath." *Monetary and Economic Studies* 17 (3): 41–68.

Griffith, R., S. Redding, and J. Van Reenen. 2004. "Mapping the Two Faces of R&D: Productivity Growth in a Panel of OECD Manufacturing Industries." *Review of Economics and Statistics* 86 (4): 883–95.

Griliches, Zvi. 1958. "Research Cost and Social Returns: Hybrid Corn and Related Innovations." *Journal of Political Economy* 66: 419–31.

———. 1992. "The Search for R&D Spillovers." *Scandinavian Journal of Economics* 94: S29–S47.

Griliches, Zvi, and Frank Lichtenberg. 1984. "Interindustry Technology Flows and Productivity Growth: A Reexamination." *Review of Economics and Statistics* 66: 324–29.

Grossman, V., T. Steger, and T. Trimborn. 2016. "Quantifying Optimal Growth Policy." *Journal of Public Economic Theory* 18: 451–85.

Guzman, Jorge, and Scott Stern. 2017. "Nowcasting and Placecasting Entrepreneurial Quality and Performance." In *Measuring Entrepreneurial Businesses: Current Knowledge and Challenges,* edited by John Haltiwanger, Erik Hurst, Javier Miranda, and Antoinette Schoar, 11–62. Chicago: University of Chicago Press.

Hall, Bronwyn H., Jacques Mairesse, and Pierre Mohnen. 2010. "Measuring the Returns to R&D." In *Handbook of the Economics of Innovation,* vol. 1, edited by Bronwyn H. Hall and Nathan Rosenberg, 1033–82. Amsterdam: North-Holland.

Jones, Benjamin F. 2009. "The Burden of Knowledge and the 'Death of the Renaissance Man': Is Innovation Getting Harder?" *Review of Economic Studies* 7: 283–317.

Jones, Charles. 1995. "R&D-Based Models of Economic Growth." *Journal of Political Economy* 103: 759–84.

Jones, Charles, and John Williams. 1998. "Measuring the Social Rate of Return to R&D." *Quarterly Journal of Economics* 113 (4): 119–35.

———. 2000. "Too Much of a Good Thing? The Economics of Investment in R&D." *Journal of Economic Growth* 5: 65–85.

Jorgenson, Dale W. 1966. "The Embodiment Hypothesis." *Journal of Political Economy* 74 (1): 1–17.

Jorgenson, Dale W., and Zvi Griliches. 1967. "The Explanation of Productivity Change." *Review of Economic Studies* 34 (3): 249–83.

Kao, C., M. Chiang, and B. Chen. 1999. "International R&D Spillovers: An Application of Estimation and Inference in Panel Cointegration." *Oxford Bulletin of Economics and Statistics* 61: 691–709.

Kerr, William, and Ramana Nanda. 2009. "Democratizing Entry: Banking Deregulations, Financing Constraints, and Entrepreneurship." *Journal of Financial Economics* 94 (1): 124–49.

Kerr, William, Ramana Nanda, and Matthew Rhodes-Kropf. 2014. "Entrepreneurship as Experimentation." *Journal of Economic Perspectives* 28: 25–48.

Kortum, Samuel. 1997. "Research, Patenting, and Technological Change." *Econometrica* 65: 1389–1419.

Kremer, Michael. 1993. "Population Growth and Technological Change: One Million B.C. to 1990." *Quarterly Journal of Economics* 108: 681–716.

Leonard, W. N. 1971. "Research and Development in Industrial Growth." *Journal of Political Economy* 79 (2): 232–56.

Lundberg, Erik. 1961. "Produktivitet och rdntabilitet: Studier i kapitalets betydelse inom svenskt ndringsliv." Stockholm: Studieforb. Naringsliv o. samhalle: Norstedt (distr.).

Mansfield, E., J. Rapoport, A. Romeo, S. Wagner, and G. Beardsley. 1977. "Social and Private Rates of Return from Industrial Innovations." *Quarterly Journal of Economics* 77: 221–40.

Mansfield, E., J. Rapoport, J. Schnee, S. Wagner, and M. Hamburger. 1971. *Research and Innovation in the Modern Corporation*. New York: Norton.

Mokyr, Joel. 1990. *The Lever of Riches: Technological Creativity and Economic Progress*. New York: Oxford University Press.

Murphy, Kevin M., and Robert Topel. 2006. "The Value of Health and Longevity." *Journal of Political Economy* 114: 871–904.

Nadiri, M. I., and S. Kim. 1996. "International R&D Spillovers, Trade and Productivity in Major OECD Countries." NBER Working Paper No. 5801. Cambridge, MA: National Bureau of Economic Research.

National Science Board. 2018. *NSF Science and Engineering Indicators 2018*. https://www.nsf.gov/statistics/2018/nsb20181/.

National Science Foundation. 2020. *Research and Development: U.S. Trends and International Comparisons*. https://ncses.nsf.gov/pubs/nsb20203.

Nordhaus, William. 2004. "Schumpeterian Profits in the American Economy: Theory and Measurement." Cowles Foundation Discussion Paper No. 1457, Yale University. http://ssrn.com/abstract=537242.

———. 2005. "Irving Fisher and the Contribution of Improved Longevity to Living Standards." *American Journal of Economics and Sociology* 64: 367–92.

Ouyang, Min. 2011. "On the Cyclicality of R&D." *Review of Economics and Statistics* 93: 542–53.

Pakes, Ariel, and Mark Schankerman. 1984. "The Rate of Obsolescence of Patents, Research Gestation Lags, and the Private Rate of Return to Research Resources" in *R & D, Patents, and Productivity*, edited by Zvi Griliches, 73–88. Chicago: University of Chicago Press.

Petrin, Amil. 2002. "Quantifying the Benefits of New Products: The Case of the Minivan." *Journal of Political Economy* 110: 705–29.

Rachel, Lukasz, and Lawrence H. Summers. 2019. "On Secular Stagnation in the Industrialized World." NBER Working Paper No. 26198. Cambridge, MA: National Bureau of Economic Research.

Ravenscraft, D., and Michael Scherer. 1982. "The Lag Structure of Returns to Research and Development." *Applied Economics* 14: 603–20.

Research America. 2018. *U.S. Investments in Medical and Health Research and Development, 2013–2017.* https://www.researchamerica.org/sites/default/files/Policy_Advocacy/2013-2017InvestmentReportFall2018.pdf.

Romer, Paul M. 1990. "Endogenous Technological Change." *Journal of Political Economy* 98: S71–S102.

Scotchmer, Suzanne. 1991. "Standing on the Shoulders of Giants: Cumulative Research and the Patent Law." *Journal of Economic Perspectives* 5: 29–41.

Segerstrom, Paul. 1991. "Innovation, Imitation, and Economic Growth." *Journal of Political Economy* 99: 807–27.

Sener, Fuat. 2008. "R&D Policies, Endogenous Growth and Scale Effects." *Journal of Economic Dynamics and Control* 32: 3895–916.

Solow, Robert M. 1956. "A Contribution to the Theory of Economic Growth." *Quarterly Journal of Economics* 70 (1): 65–94.

———. 1960. "Investment and Technical Progress." In *Mathematical Methods in the Social Sciences,* edited by K. J. Arrow, S. Karlin, and P. Suppes, 89–104. Stanford, CA: Stanford University Press.

Stigler, George et al., eds. 1961. *The Price Statistics of the Federal Government: Review, Appraisal, and Recommendations.* New York: National Bureau of Economic Research.

Tewksbury, J. G., M. S. Crandall, and W. E. Crane. 1980. "Measuring the Societal Benefits of Innovation." *Science* 209: 658–62.

Trajtenberg, Manuel. 1989. "The Welfare Analysis of Product Innovations, with an Application to Computed Tomography Scanners." *Journal of Political Economy* 97 (2): 444–79.

Von Hippel, Eric. 1976. "The Dominant Role of Users in the Scientific Instrument Innovation Process." *Research Policy* 5: 212–39.

Weitzman, Martin L. 1998. "Recombinant Growth." *Quarterly Journal of Economics* 113: 331–60.

Westmore, Ben. 2013. "R&D, Patenting and Growth: The Role of Public Policy." OECD Economics Department Working Papers No. 1047. Paris: OECD Publishing. https://doi.org/10.1787/5k46h2rfb4f3-en.

Wolfe, Raymond F. 2018. "Businesses Spent $375 Billion on R&D Performance in the United States in 2016." National Science Foundation, September 25. https://nsf.gov/statistics/2018/nsf18312/.

Wolff, E. N., and M. I. Nadiri. 1993. "Spillover Effects, Linkage Structure, and Research and Development." *Structural Change and Economic Dynamics* 4 (2): 315–31.

Wright, T. P. 1936. "Factors Affecting the Cost of Airplanes." *Journal of the Aeronautical Sciences* 3: 122–28.

Innovation and Human Capital Policy

John Van Reenen

2.1 Introduction

Since the 1970s, productivity growth in the United States has slowed—reflected in falling total GDP growth from 4 percent in the postwar years, to under 3 percent from the mid-1970s, and to under 2 percent since 2000. Average real wage growth has also slowed over this period, especially for less educated workers. Moreover, at the time of writing, the COVID pandemic has damaged growth by more than any other shock in living memory.

For the most economically advanced countries like the United States, innovation is the critical ingredient to long-run productivity growth. For less developed countries, much productivity can come from catching up to leading nations through diffusion of technological know-how. Even in richer nations, many organizations are behind the technological frontier, and interventions such as upgrading management practices (e.g., Bloom and Van Reenen 2007), speeding up adoption, and reducing the misallocation of resources are extremely valuable. Nonetheless, innovation policy design is a key part of any solution for revitalizing America and can lead to large increases in well-being.

John Van Reenen is Ronald Coase School Professor at the London School of Economics, fellow of the Institute for the Digital Economy at the Massachusetts Institute of Technology, and a research associate of the National Bureau of Economic Research.

This builds on work with many coauthors, in particular Nick Bloom and Heidi Williams. I am grateful for comments by Ben Jones, Austan Goolsbee, and an anonymous referee. This research was supported in part by the Sloan Foundation, Schmitt Sciences, the Smith Richardson Foundation, and the Economic and Social Research Council. The content is solely the responsibility of the author and does not necessarily represent the official views of the NBER. For acknowledgments, sources of research support, and disclosure of the author's material financial relationships, if any, please see https://www.nber.org/books-and-chapters /innovation-and-public-policy/innovation-and-human-capital-policy.

The attraction of human capital policies for innovation is that they act directly on the supply side, to increase the number of potential and actual innovators. Romer (2001) emphasized the advantage of supply side policies. Demand side policies such as tax credits and direct government research and development (R&D) grants can be effective in increasing firms' incentives to do more R&D—and there is an impressive body of microeconomic research on this (Akcigit and Stantcheva 2020; Bloom, Williams, and Van Reenen 2019). However, if the supply of R&D workers is very inelastic, then there is a risk that the increase in demand merely drives up the equilibrium cost of R&D without increasing its volume. In other words, the incidence of the subsidy is on innovation prices rather than innovation quantities. This is what Goolsbee (1998) found in aggregate US data—scientists' wages rose substantially with increased federal R&D spending. Microeconomic analysis might miss this, as the wage increase is a general equilibrium effect, absorbed away by the time dummies typically included in standard evaluations. Furthermore, since R&D workers are above median-pay employees, this type of demand side policy could increase inequality as well as providing little in the way of aggregate innovation.

In reality, the elasticity of supply of R&D workers is unlikely to be completely fixed, especially when we consider immigration into the United States (see below). However, in the short run, supply could be relatively hard to expand, so these concerns are real.

A supply side increase in the quantity and quality of R&D workers carries fewer of these risks. Unless the new workers are dramatically less productive than the existing stock or large quantities "leak out" out into noninnovative activities, we would expect a direct increase in innovation. Furthermore, the increase in the supply of R&D workers should reduce the equilibrium cost of R&D—meaning that a successful supply side policy provides a further indirect boost to the amount of innovation as firms face lower R&D costs. The work in this chapter focuses on such human capital supply side policies.

The structure of the chapter is as follows. I provide some background R&D and workforce statistics in section 2.2; in section 2.3, we discuss the rationale for (and evidence on) innovation subsidies; in section 2.4, we discuss the evidence for four types of human capital supply policies. Section 2.5 offers some concluding comments.

2.2   Background: R&D and the Scientific Workforce[1]

In 2015, spending on R&D performed in the United States was just under half a trillion dollars. Figure 2.1 shows R&D spending as a fraction of GDP for major industrialized countries. The United States spends more on R&D than any other, accounting for roughly 28 percent of global R&D spending.

---

1. Most of the data facts in this paper are drawn from National Science Board (2018).

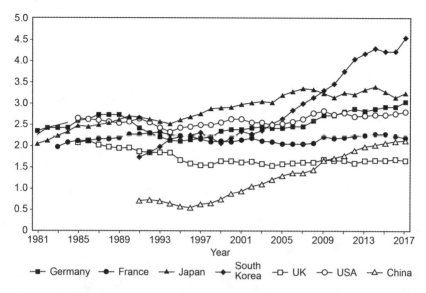

Fig. 2.1   R&D as a proportion of GDP in selected countries, 1981–2017
Source: OECD (2018).

It has maintained an R&D-to-GDP ratio of between 2.5 and 2.7 percent since 1981 (up from 1.3 percent in 1953).

Looking at the time series, however, the situation is less reassuring. China has clearly had a spectacular boom in R&D intensity, but most countries have also enjoyed an increase. Furthermore, the composition of US R&D expenditure has changed significantly: the fraction of government funding has declined precipitously and the share of private-sector funding has risen (see figure 2.2). This matters because the government often supports more basic and higher-risk research than the private sector. Consequently, public R&D will tend to produce the inventions that create the highest knowledge spillovers in the long run. Moreover, there is some evidence that even within private-sector-funded R&D, basic research has declined relative to applied research (e.g., Arora, Belenzon, and Patacconi 2018). The decline in basic research in both public- and private-sector R&D spending may be one reason why the productivity of American R&D appears to have fallen over time, as documented by Bloom et al. (2020).

Colleges and universities are particularly important for basic research (mostly funded by the federal government; they account for just under half of this total). Reflecting that distribution of federal funds across fields, the top agencies supporting federally funded academic R&D are the Department of Health and Human Services, the Department of Defense, and the National Science Foundation.

These statistics focus on R&D spending, but perhaps more germane to

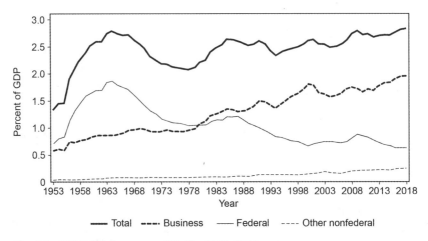

Fig. 2.2   US R&D, by source of funds, 1953–2015

Source: National Science Board (2018).

Notes: R&D spending is categorized by funder rather than performer. Other nonfederal funders include, but are not limited to, higher education, nonfederal government, and other nonprofit organizations.

Table 2.1   Number of researchers per 1,000 employees, selected countries

	United States	China	France	Germany	Korea	Japan	United Kingdom
1981	5.28		3.78	4.65		5.23	5.25
2001	7.29	1.02	6.83	6.63	6.32	9.87	6.57
2018	9.23	2.41	10.9	9.67	15.33	9.88	9.43

Source: OECD, Main Science and Technology Indicators, https://stats.oecd.org/Index.aspx ?DataSetCode=MSTI_PUB#downloaded11.21.20.

Note: US figure is for 2017, as 2018 was not yet published at time of writing.

our focus on innovative human capital is the scientific workforce. Table 2.1 shows that the fraction of all US workers who are researchers has grown consistently since 1981, just like the R&D to GDP ratio. There were about 5.3 researchers per thousand workers in 1981, 7.3 in 2001, and 9.2 in 2017. However, the growth was faster in other advanced economies. France, Germany, and Japan all had lower numbers in 1981, but have overtaken the United States in the most recent years. The most dramatic change over that period has been in South Korea, where the ratio of researchers per thousand employees rose from 6.3 in 2001 to 15.3 today. China's fraction of researchers looks less impressive than its R&D spending in figure 2.1, but it has still more than doubled the researcher proportion since 2001 from 1.0 to 2.4.

Another way of approaching the measurement of science workers is to look at high-skilled visas: J-1 (exchange visitors), H-1B, and L-1 (intracompany transferee). There was an increase from around 150,000 to over 330,000 between 1991 and 2015 for J-1s, the largest category. There was an increase of 52,000 over this same time period in H-1B visas to 175,000. This growth was focused in nonprofit research facilities, universities, and government research labs.

2.3   The Case for Government Promotion of Innovation

Jones and Summers (2021) examine the arguments on why government should support R&D, so we briefly summarize the arguments here (see Bloom, Williams, and Van Reenen 2019 for more detail). In short, theory and evidence imply there are too few innovation workers in America.

The main theoretical argument for government intervention is that there are externalities from R&D as knowledge has characteristics of a public good. The agents who invest their time and resources in innovation expect to see some return, even if it is uncertain. However, many other parts of society will benefit without having to pay much, if any, of this R&D cost. These include firms who imitate the innovation or build on the knowledge created by the inventor's R&D efforts. There are also the consumers (at home and abroad) who enjoy the benefits of the innovation but whose purchase price may be only a tiny fraction of the cost. Indeed, in his *Dictionary of Received Ideas*, Gustave Flaubert (1911) ruefully defined inventors as follows: "All die in the poor house. Someone else profits from their discoveries, it is not fair."

Since the firms and workers engaging in R&D do not capture all of the value of the innovations produced, there will tend to be underinvestment. In other words, the social benefits of R&D will be higher than the private investment in a decentralized market economy. Consequently, there needs to be some government action to promote innovation and bring social and private returns more into line with each other.

There are likely to be many other market failures that mean the level of R&D is suboptimal. For example, Arrow (1962) emphasized financial market failures due to the risk, uncertainty, absence of collateral, and asymmetric information inherent in raising money for innovation (see Hall and Lerner 2010 for empirical evidence). Fundamentally, an inventor wanting to raise finance for her idea will have to convince an external investor of the idea's value. Since the only way to do this is to share more information on the idea, the inventor will be rightly concerned that the information will leak out and be stolen by someone else (such as the financier himself). Hence, R&D will tend to be internally financed within firms, and many good ideas may end up being unrealized.

Another market failure can be traced to product market rivalry. Once we leave the textbook model of perfect competition, an important incentive to innovate is that one firm gains nontrivial market share from another. This "business stealing" motive was germane to Schumpeter's notion of creative destruction and is at the heart of Industrial Organization models and endogenous growth theory, in particular Aghion and Howitt (1992). This means that firms may be in an R&D "arms race" and this can lead to duplicative effort and too much R&D. From a social point of view, a pure reshuffling of market shares is of little value if there is not much fall in quality-adjusted prices. An example would be in parts of the pharmaceutical industry where "me-too" drugs of minor therapeutic improvement can lead to large shifts in market share as doctors and patients want only the best drug (and because of insurance, there is often little sensitivity to price).

A further issue is that the policies that are designed to create incentives to innovate can themselves create other distortions. For example, the intellectual property system generates a temporary monopoly for inventors to overcome the knowledge spillover problem through patents. Of course, these property rights themselves create a consumer loss through higher prices. Further, many patents can be "designed around" and offer little protection. Perhaps most worryingly, the patent system can be abused to create many barriers in order to protect minor increments to knowledge, such as "patent thickets" (see Jaffe and Lerner 2007 for a general discussion).

Given all these complexities, whether the social benefits of R&D exceed the private returns cannot be answered by theory. It is an empirical question. One approach for answering the question is to use case studies. For example, there are many case studies of government interventions that were failures (Lerner 2005), such as the Anglo-French supersonic aircraft Concorde. On the other hand, there are also many examples of major successes, such as jet engines, radar, nuclear power, GPS, and the internet (Janeway 2012; Mazzucato 2013), that began with government funding (often around military spending, with civilian spin-offs an expected spillover benefit). Despite their richness, these historical examples can be hard to assess, although there have been some attempts at more quantitative case studies, beginning with Griliches's (1958) famous hybrid corn analysis. It is still an issue, as Griliches himself emphasized, that it is hard to generalize from case studies, as they are single technologies selected precisely because they appear interesting and successful.

The modern econometric literature on spillovers has tried to look over a wider range of technologies, firms, and industries. One important strand of the literature uses patent citations. The idea is that that a citation is a paper trail indicating that one idea has built upon another (Trajtenberg 1990; Jaffe, Trajtenberg, and Henderson 1993; Griffith, Lee, and Van Reenen 2011). As is well known, however, not all innovations are patented and not all patents are innovations. An alternative approach is to look at the impact of R&D on the productivity not only of the firm who performs the research but also of other firms ("neighbors") who have spillover benefits. The key issue is how to empirically determine who else benefits and who does not—this is a generic problem in social science when thinking about "peer effects" (Manski 1993).

Using panel data on US corporations from 1980 onward, Bloom, Schankerman, and Van Reenen (2013) suggest a methodology based on "distance metrics." The idea is to characterize pairs of firms as close or far apart in technological distance, for example, as proxied by the technological classes where the firms have taken out patents in the past (Jaffe 1986). A firm that is close to another technologically is more likely to benefit from its neighbor's R&D than one that is more distant. A symmetrical argument can be made for business stealing through R&D by characterizing the closeness of multiproduct firms in product market space depending on their sales across their product portfolios.[2] In this case, R&D by a neighboring firm close in product market space is more likely to cause harm. Empirically, the authors show that although both knowledge spillovers and business rivalry effects from R&D are significant, the knowledge spillover effects quantitatively dominate. Note that a strong correlation between changes in a firm's productivity and growth in its neighbors' R&D (even controlling for the firm's own R&D and other factors) is not necessarily causal. Other factors, such as a demand shock or an opening up of scientific opportunities, could drive up both the firm's own productivity and neighbors' R&D. To tackle this question, the authors use innovation policy changes as natural experiments, such as the differential exposure of firms to changes in state and federal R&D tax credits. These policy changes successfully shifted the incentives to perform R&D across firms, generating instrumental variables for the spillover terms and enabling the authors to identify the causal effects of R&D spillovers.

For the US economy as whole, Bloom, Schankerman, and Van Reenen (2013) find that social returns to R&D were about three times higher than private returns between 1980 and 2000. Lucking, Bloom, and Van Reenen (2020) confirm this conclusion using the same methodology, but on more recent data running through 2015.

The finding that on average social returns to R&D exceed private returns (primarily due to knowledge spillovers) even with the level of support the US government provides is the current empirical consensus.

2.4 Human Capital Innovation Policies

There are many possible policies to deal with the innovation deficit. We now turn to consider explicit human capital policies to deal with the problem.

2.4.1 Undergraduates and Postgraduates

The most commonly discussed policy here is to increase the inflow of individuals trained in STEM (science, technology, engineering, and math-

---

2. The distance-based methods can be extended in other dimensions such as geography. Different firms with inventors who are colocated, for example, might be more likely to benefit from each other's R&D activity (e.g., Lychagin et al. 2016).

ematics). The direct way would be to subsidize PhDs and postdocs in these subjects, increasing the generosity of support for training in these fields. Indirectly, training and subsequent careers in these fields could be made more attractive through more grants and support, especially in labs.

More generally, one can imagine support for raising educational attainment at an even younger age (undergraduates and even K through12). There is a huge literature documenting the complementarity between human capital and new technologies ("skill-biased technical change"), so increasing human capital could have a positive effect on technical change (e.g., Autor, Goldin, and Katz 2020; Van Reenen 2011). However, this literature is usually focused on the diffusion of technologies (e.g., adoption of information and communications technology) rather than on pushing forward the technological frontier. For innovation to the economy (rather than to a firm), it is likely that postgraduate qualifications are much more important.

Much macroeconomic analysis has been conducted of the impact of human capital on growth (see, e.g., Sianesi and Van Reenen 2003 for a survey). However, the literature is rather inconclusive because of the difficulty of finding credible instruments at the macro (or industry) level. The large number of other confounders at the aggregate level makes it hard to infer causality. There is a vast literature looking at the impact of schooling on wages, but there is rather a paucity of work looking at more specific interventions on the STEM workforce.

2.4.2   University Expansion

Many papers examine the role of universities in economic prosperity in general and in innovation in particular. A major idea in these papers is that the founding and subsequent expansion in universities increases the supply of workers with STEM qualifications, and that these STEM workers then increase innovation. Geographically, places with strong science-based universities also seem to have substantial private-sector innovation (e.g., Route 128 in Massachusetts or Silicon Valley in California).

Valero and Van Reenen (2019), looking at 50 years of subnational data across more than 100 countries, find that the founding of a university increases local GDP per-capita growth in subsequent years (which also spills over nationally). The Jaffe (1989) paper was a pioneer in this area by documenting that state-level spending on university research in certain industries seems to generate higher local corporate patenting. Acs, Audretsch, and Feldman (1992) use innovation counts instead of patent data and find even stronger effects for spillovers from university research. Related findings of the positive effects of university location on patenting has been found in more recent datasets by Belenzon and Schankerman (2013), Hausman (2018), and Andrews (2020). Furman and MacGarvie (2007) studied how universities with stronger academic research profiles increased the growth of local industrial pharmaceutical labs from 1927 to 1946. They used land grant college funds under the Morrill Acts to generate some exogenous variation in the location of universities to argue that the correlation is causal. In the biotech industry, Zucker, Brewer, and Darby (1998) show that firms tend to locate near universities to take advantage of star scientists.

However, universities may also have other effects on innovation over and above the supply of graduates. First, research by university faculty, sometimes in collaboration with local private-sector firms, could directly increase innovation. The vast literature on clustering has this as one of the mechanisms. Secondly, universities may influence local democratic participation and institutions, which may also have an effect on innovation. If universities have an effect on innovation (or growth) over and above the impact on human capital, then they are not valid instruments for human capital, as this violates the exclusion restriction. Valero and Van Reenen (2019) found that university expansion was associated with more graduates, more innovation, and stronger institutions. Of course, the reduced form effect of universities on innovation is still interesting if it is causal, but the mechanism through which universities raise innovation may not be solely (or even at all) through the human capital channel.

2.4.2.1 Graduate Supply

To make progress in isolating why universities may have an impact on innovation as key suppliers of STEM workers, Toivanen and Väänänen (2016) find that people who grew up around a technical university in Finland had a higher probability of becoming engineers when they reached adulthood. These technical universities rapidly expanded in the 1960s and 1970s in and offered postgraduate engineering. This also led to more patenting: establishing three technical universities caused on average a 20 percent increase in US Patent and Trademark Office patents by Finnish inventors. In a similar vein, Carneiro, Liu, and Salvanes (2018) compare municipalities in Norway where there was an upsurge in government college start-ups in the 1970s to synthetic cohorts of areas where the expansion did not take place. They document evidence for more R&D and a speed up in the rate and direction of technological progress about a decade after the colleges' founding (if they were STEM focused).

Bianchi and Giorcelli (2019) present the most direct test of the role of universities in increasing STEM supply in Italy. The enrollment requirements for STEM majors changed, and this generated a big increase in graduate numbers. In turn, innovation then increased, especially in medicine, chemistry, and information technology. Notably, however, they document that many STEM graduates ended up working in areas such as finance, rather than in the R&D sector. This "leakage" problem is a general one in just increasing the supply side, rather than targeting R&D per se.

2.4.2.2   Research Grants to Academics (and Beyond)

One variety of government programs that seek to encourage innovation is through the direct provision of grant funding (e.g., through the National Institutes of Health, or NIH), either to academic researchers or more widely. Spending public R&D subsidies on universities is intuitive because knowledge spillovers from basic academic research will likely be greater than those from corporate near-market applied research.

The challenge with evaluating whether R&D grants work is that they will tend to target the most promising projects, researchers, and problems. Hence, there could have been positive outcomes even without the grant. Public grants could even crowd out private funding. More optimistically, the grants could also crowd in matched private money (funders certainly try to obtain such "additionality").

Administrative data on US NIH grant applications have been used by Jacob and Lefgren (2011). They implement a "Regression Discontinuity Design" (RDD) that compares applicants that just received a large grant to those that just missed out by using the evaluators' scores given to grant applicants. They find that the grants lead to an increase of about 7 percent (one additional publication over a five-year period). One explanation for the small effect is that those who "just lost" a grant often found alternative sources of funding.

Public R&D grants may affect private firms in several ways. First, academic work can spillover to private firms. Using variation in NIH funding across multiple research areas, Azoulay et al. (2019) find that on average there are an extra 2.7 additional patents filed by private companies following a $10 million increase in academic funding. Second, government-conducted R&D spending (e.g., in labs) can affect private firms. Military R&D spending, for example, is usually driven by exogenous political changes (e.g. Sputnik, the end of the Cold War and 9/11). Moretti, Steinwender, and Van Reenen (2019) use such changes in defense R&D spending and find that there was an elasticity of 0.4 between private and public R&D (i.e., a 4 percent increase in private R&D followed a 10 percent increase in publicly funded R&D). This implies that public R&D *crowds in* private R&D.

Third, government money can be directly given to private firms. Marginal winners and losers from the Department of Energy's Small Business Innovation Research (SBIR) grant applicants are compared by Howell (2017). She finds that early-stage (Phase I) SBIR grants double the chances a winner obtains future venture capital funding (a marker of commercializable innovation potential). They also increase patenting and sales. Howell et al. (2021) find that SBIR grants in the US Air Force also have positive effects on venture capital funding, technology transfer to the military, and patenting, using a Regression Discontinuity Design.

2.4.2.3   *National Labs*

Governments also fund their own R&D labs that may generate more research activity and jobs in the lab's specialist technological area and in its geographical location. Jaffe and Lerner (2001) analyze national labs, such as Stanford's SLAC (National Accelerator Laboratory) and document evidence of spillovers. Helmers and Overman (2017) also document spillovers from Britain's Synchrotron Diamond Light Source. However, this appeared to be primarily through relocation of activity within the UK rather than any aggregate nationwide increase.

2.4.2.4   *Academic Incentives*

How can policies be designed that allow university discoveries to be made in commercializable innovations? The 1980 Bayh-Dole Act changed the ownership of inventions developed with public R&D giving universities more ownership in the intellectual property. Many schools created "technology transfer offices" to support this process and Lach and Schankerman (2008) find that larger ownership of this intellectual property by scientists generated more innovation. Hvide and Jones (2018) look at Norway and find that when academics obtained full innovation rights, they became more likely to launch entrepreneurial start-ups and take out patents. Financial returns for academics seemed to get more ideas out of universities and turned into real products.

2.4.3   Immigration

An important mechanism for increasing human capital is through immigration. The United States historically has a more open immigration policy to other advanced nations. Immigrants account for about 14 percent of the US workforce but make up 17–18 percent of college graduates and 52 percent of STEM doctorates. They also account for about a quarter of all patents and a third of all US Nobel Prizes.

Kerr and Kerr (chapter 3 in this volume) go into more detail on immigration and innovation, and on survey policy options around migration. Much research has found that US immigrants (especially the more high skilled) increase innovation. For example, using state panel data from 1940 to 2000, Hunt and Gauthier-Loiselle (2010) find that increasing the share of immigrant college graduates by one percentage point boosts patenting per person by 9–18 percent. Using changes in policies over H-1B visas, Kerr and Lincoln (2010) find positive effects and argue that these come through the innovation efforts of immigrants themselves. When an inventor dies, this is an exogenous shock to team productivity. Bernstein et al. (2018) find large spillover effects of immigrants on native innovation from such changes (large spillovers are also found by Hunt and Gauthier-Loiselle 2010).

In the early 1920s, the American government introduced immigration quotas with differential degrees of strictness for different countries. Northern Europeans, like Swedes, were less strongly affected than southern Europeans, like Italians. This variation has been exploited to examine how immigration reductions affected innovation. Biographical data in Moser and San (2019) show that these quotas discouraged southern and eastern European scientists from migrating to America. This in turn, depressed US aggregate invention. Negative effects of the quotas are also found in Doran and Yoon (2018). In a similar vein, the arrival in the US in the 1930s of Jewish scientists expelled by the Nazis boosted innovation in American chemistry (Moser, Voena, and Waldinger 2014).

Some work pushes back against this generally positive view of the impact of immigration on innovation. Smaller effects are seen from H-1B visas by Doran, Gelber, and Isen (2015) than Kerr and Lincoln (2010) when lotteries are used to examine the impact. Indeed, Borjas and Doran (2012) argue that publications by US mathematicians actually fell following the fall of the Soviet Union. Their work does not estimate aggregate effects, however. In addition, Moser, Voena, and Waldinger (2014) estimate that most of the effect of immigration on innovation comes from new entry, rather than incumbents. It may also be that be that Borjas and Doran's (2012) findings reflect special features of academic publishing, in particular the sharp short-run constraints on the size of journals and departments.

In summary, my reading of the literature is that there is good evidence demonstrating that immigration, especially skilled immigration, raises innovation. The benefit-cost ratio is particularly high because the cost of educating immigrants has been borne by other countries rather than by American taxpayer subsidies, and, unlike many other supply side policies, the increase in human capital can occur very quickly. However, there are severe political problems with relaxing immigration policy (see Tabellini 2020).

2.4.4 Increasing the Quality of Inventors: Lost Einsteins

2.4.4.1 New Facts on Inventor Backgrounds

There has long been interest in the background of inventors, with statistical analysis of this beginning with Schmookler's (1957) study. More recent work has documented many features of inventors in near population datasets. Bell et al. (2019a) measure inventors by those individuals who are named as inventors on the patent document (both applied and granted patents), not just those who are granted the intellectual property rights (typically the assignees will be the companies that the inventors works for, rather than the individuals themselves). Looking at about 1.2 million inventors since the mid-1990s, they find that many groups are highly underrepresented, such as women, minorities, and those born into low-income families.

Using the inventor data matched to deidentified US IRS data, Bell et al.

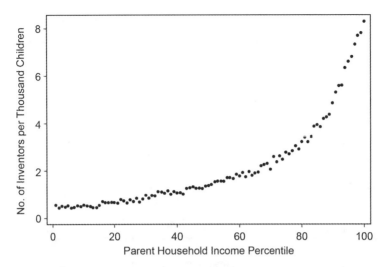

Fig. 2.3 Probability of growing up to be an inventor as a function of parental income

Source: Bell et al (2019a), p. 665; Intergenerational sample. Reprinted by permission of Oxford University Press on behalf of the President and Fellows of Harvard College.

Notes: Sample of children is 1980–1984 birth cohorts. Parent Income is mean household income 1996–2000.

(2019a, 2019b) are able to follow potential inventors across their life cycles. Figure 2.3 shows the fraction of children who grow up to be inventors by the percentile of their parents' income. There is a strong upward-sloping relationship, showing that being born to wealthier parents dramatically increases the likelihood of becoming an inventor later in life. Compared to kids born to parents in the bottom half of the income distribution, those born into the top 1 percent are an order of magnitude more likely to become inventors in the future. This is not due to wealthier children simply producing low-value innovations: conditioning on the top 5 percent of the most highly cited patents produces nearly identical results.

An obvious explanation for the dramatic differences in figure 2.3 could be that kids in poorer families have worse innate abilities than their richer counterparts. For example, if wealthier parents are smarter, their kids are likely to be smarter and, since intelligence and inventiveness are correlated, this could explain the patterns. To examine this hypothesis, Bell et al. (2019a) match math (and English) test score results from third grade and later, which are available for a subsample of the data. There is indeed a strong correlation between third grade math scores[3] and the probability of becoming an

3. Bell et al. (2019a, 2019b) cannot observe math scores before third grade, but it is likely that these partly reflect nurture rather than nature. As the work by Heckman and others has shown, early childhood experience has effects on cognitive and noncognitive outcomes at very young ages.

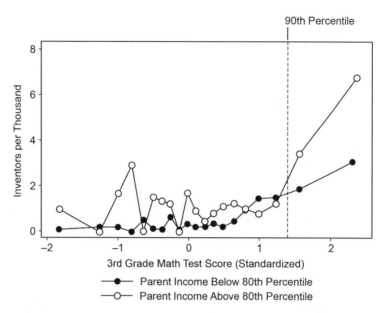

Fig. 2.4   Relationship between math test scores and probability of becoming an inventor

Source: Bell et al (2019a), p. 672; New York City sample. Reprinted by permission of Oxford University Press on behalf of the President and Fellows of Harvard College.

inventor in later life. However, these early test scores account for only under a third of the innovation gap; they cannot account for the vast majority of the innovation-parental income relationship.[4] Figure 2.4 illustrates this by separating the inventor-ability gradient by whether a child was born in the top quintile of the parental income distribution or bottom four quintiles. For both "rich" and "poor" children the probability of growing up to be an inventor rises with math ability and is especially strong for kids in the top 10 percent of the test score distribution. However, even for kids who are in the top 5 percent of talent for math, figure 2.4 shows that those from richer families are far more likely to become inventors.

Interestingly, later test scores become more informative for inventor status: eighth grade math test scores account for just under half of the inventor-parental income gradient. By the time we know which college young people attended (e.g., MIT or Stanford), the role of parental income is tiny. Of course, being born to a poor family means that the chances of going to a top college are very, very low. This suggests that an important part of the transmission mechanism between parental income and later outcomes

---

4. For example, we can statistically "give" the distribution of math test scores of rich kids to poor kids using the DiNardo, Fortin, and Lemieux (1996) reweighting technique.

is through the quality of schooling—something we return to below when discussing policy.

A similar story holds for gender and race (e.g., Cook and Kongcharoen 2010). About 18 percent of inventors born in 1980 were female, up from 7 percent in the 1940 cohort. At this rate of improvement, it would take another 118 years to achieve gender parity. Looking at the New York City data, there is essentially no difference in the third grade math ability distribution for boys and girls (even in the right tail). With regard to race, 1.6 per 1,000 white children who attended New York City public schools become inventors compared to 0.5 per 1,000 Black children. Early ability accounts for only a tenth of these differences.[5]

Rather than ability differences, an alternative explanation for the patterns in figure 2.3 is that it reflects a misallocation of talent. There has been a flourishing of work in recent years suggesting that large amounts of productivity are lost due to such frictions (e.g., Celik 2018; Hsieh and Klenow 2009). Hsieh et al. (2019), for example, estimate that 40 percent of the growth in US GDP per person between 1960 and 2010 is due to reductions in discrimination against women and Black people. Under this view, if disadvantaged groups were given the same opportunities as their similarly talented but more privileged peers, many more of them could have pursued an inventor career and increased the quality and quantity of aggregate human capital. For example, Bell et al. (2019b) estimate a potential quadrupling of aggregate US innovation from reducing such barriers.

Bell et al. (2019a) document that differential exposure rates to inventors in childhood is a very important cause of the lower invention rate of disadvantaged groups. They measure exposure by family environment, proxies for the work network of parents, and innovation rates in the commuting zones where kids grew up. They find a strong association between the probability of growing up to be an inventor and measures of childhood exposure to inventors. Figure 2.5, for example, shows that children growing up in a commuting zone with a high density of inventors are much more likely to become inventors as adults. About 5.5 children in 1,000 in the San Jose, California, commuting zone (which encompasses Silicon Valley) become inventors, compared to about 1 in 1,000 in Brownsville, Texas.

The relationship between place and outcomes appears to be causal. For example, it is not simply the fact that kids who grow up in Silicon Valley are more likely to be inventors; they are more likely to invent in the detailed technology classes (relative to other classes) that the valley specializes in (say, software compared to medical devices). Girls who grow up in places where there is a disproportionate fraction of female compared to male inventors are more likely (than boys are) to grow up to become inventors. Further-

5. Cook (2014) shows that racist violence between 1870 and 1940 led to 1,100 "missing patents," compared to 726 actual patents among African American inventors.

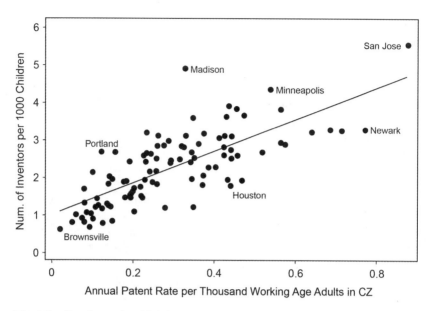

Fig. 2.5   Growing up in a high-innovation area makes it much more likely you will become an inventor as an adult

Source: Bell et al (2019a), p. 691; 100 most populous commuting zones. Reprinted by permission of Oxford University Press on behalf of the President and Fellows of Harvard College.

more, kids who move to high-innovation areas at an earlier age are more likely to become inventors than kids who move at a later age, again suggesting a causal impact of place.

This "exposure-based" view of invention could lead to much larger welfare losses than in the standard talent misallocation models. In Hsieh et al. (2019), for example, barriers to entry into occupations (the R&D sector, in our case) mean a loss of talent. However, since their model is a fully rational Roy sorting model, only the marginal inventors are discouraged from becoming inventors. Great inventors—like Einstein or Marie Curie—will never be put off. In the exposure-based model, however, even very talented people from (say) a poor family may end up not becoming inventors because they are never exposed to the possibility. Bell et al. (2019b) show evidence in favor of this and argue for large welfare losses.

2.4.4.2   Some Policies toward the "Lost Einsteins"

If we took seriously the idea that much talent is being lost because of a lack of exposure to the possibility of becoming an inventor, what are the appropriate policy responses?

A classic set of responses would focus on improving conditions in disadvantaged neighborhoods, particularly in schools. These are justified on their own terms, but the misallocation losses add to the usual equity arguments. It would make sense to target resources on those most likely to benefit, such as disadvantaged kids who show some early promise in STEM. Figure 2.4 shows that being in the top 5 percent of third grade math scores was a strong predictor of future inventor status. This suggests looking into programs that identify early high achievers from underrepresented minorities.

One example is Card and Giuliano (2016), who review the effect of in-school tracking for minorities. They look at one of the largest US school districts, where schools with at least one "gifted/high achiever" (GHA) fourth- (or fifth-) grader had to create a separate GHA classroom. Since most schools only had a handful of gifted kids per grade, most seats in the GHA classroom were filled with nongifted students who were high achievers in the same school grade. They served as upper-track classes for students based on past achievement. Moreover, since schools were already in effect highly segregated by race and income, the program effectively treated a large number of minority students who would typically not be eligible for standard "gifted and talented" interventions.

Card and Giuliano (2016) use a regression discontinuity design to examine the causal effects on students who are tracked since selection is based on a continuous measure of past achievement with a threshold. They find that students significantly improved their math, reading, and science when assigned to a GHA classroom, but these benefits were overwhelmingly concentrated among Black and Hispanic participants. Minorities gained about 0.5 standard deviation units in math and reading scores, a result that persisted until at least the sixth grade (where their data end). These are very substantial gains, comparable in magnitude to "high performance" charter schools evaluated by Angrist, Pathak, and Walters (2013). A concern is that the gains of the participating minorities were at the expense of those who were left behind. To address this, the paper uses a cohort difference-in-differences design comparing schools that tracked to those that did not. They find no evidence of negative (or positive) spillovers from this analysis. The effects do not appear to be coming from teacher quality or peer quality. Rather, the authors suggest that teacher expectations may play a very important role in exposing students to the possibility of greater learning.

Changing to in-school tracking has little financial cost, as there is not an expansion of the number of teachers, classes, or school day. The in-school tracking results from a reallocation of existing resources. This suggests that such interventions could yield very large benefits in terms of growth as well as equity.

Card and Giuliano (2016) look at the short-term outcomes of within-school tracking. By contrast, Cohodes (2020) examines the long-term effects of a similar program in Boston Public Schools' Advanced Work Class (AWC) program. Pupils who do well on third grade test scores are placed in the AWC program and receive a dedicated classroom with high-achieving peers, advanced literacy curricula, and accelerated math in later grades. While the students who participate in AWC tend to be more advantaged than Boston Public School students as a whole, about half of AWC students are Black or Latino, and two-thirds of them receive subsidized school lunch.

Cohodes (2020) estimates the effect of the program using a fuzzy regression discontinuity design by comparing those who scored just above and just below the admissions threshold. There is a large increase in high school graduation for minority students. Perhaps most importantly, AWC boosts college enrollment rates. The program increases college enrollment by 15 percentage points overall, again with gains primarily coming from Black and Latino students. This results in a 65 percent increase in college enrollment for Black and Latino students, most of it at four-year institutions. Using estimated earnings associated with colleges from Chetty et al. (2017) as a measure of college quality, AWC appears to increase college quality by about $1,750 for all students and $8,200 for Black and Latino students, though these differences are not statistically significant.[6]

Bui, Craig, and Imberman (2014) is often seen as a counterexample, as their analysis of a gifted and talented program found no effect. However, the paper does find an effect on science outcome, which may be the critical element for inventors. Furthermore, the paper does not look at heterogeneity of the treatment effect by parental income or minority status.

Another set of targeted policies is around mentorship. Many nonprofit foundations (e.g., the Lemelson Foundation and the Conrad Foundation) run "inventor education" programs targeting disadvantaged children in middle and high schools. Important parts of the program are hands-on experience of problem solving in the local community, and meeting inventors who look like the targeted groups (e.g., women scientists for girls). More generally, one can imagine internship and work exchange programs aimed at young people who would not normally be exposed to high-innovation environments.

Gabriel, Ollard, and Wilkinson (2018) have developed a useful survey of a wide range of "innovation exposure" policies focusing on school-age programs. Although there is a large number of such programs (science competitions being a leading example), they tend to be dominated by students with higher-income parents, boys, and nonminorities. Moreover, the programs

---

6. Although attending an AWC class boosts the average test scores of peers by over 80 percent of a standard deviation, Cohodes (2020) finds little evidence to support peer effects as an explanation for AWC impacts. While AWC teachers have a higher value added, the change is not large enough to account for the gains in college attendance observed here. Instead, it appears that AWC is the beginning of a chain of events that causes participants to stay on track for college throughout high school.

are almost never subject to evaluation. One immediate priority should be devoting resources to researching their impact.

2.5   Conclusions

Innovation is at the heart of growth, and increasing the supply of potential inventors would seem the natural place to start to think about innovation policy. Yet the literature has tended to focus much more on policies that raise the demand for innovation through the tax system or through direct government grants, rather than policies that intervene on the supply side. At one level, this is surprising: if supply is inelastic, then demand side policies may do little to the volume of innovation and may merely increase the wages of R&D scientists. On another level, it is unsurprising: supply side policies will tend to work better in the long run, which makes them harder to empirically evaluate.

In this chapter, we have looked at several different human capital policies for innovation: increasing STEM, immigration reform, university expansion, and exposure policies for the disadvantaged. Clean causal identification of policies is rarer here than in other areas, but there have been some recent and encouraging contributions. In the short run, liberalizing high-skilled immigration is likely to yield a high return. In the longer run, I suggest that exposure policies may produce the greatest effect, but much more work needs to be done in evaluating the effectiveness of such policies.

When considering which policies to adopt, it is important to look carefully at the existing evidence and evaluate its strengths and weaknesses, as I have tried to do in this chapter. However, policy makers will frequently consider many other things rather than just a policy's cost-benefit ratio and how long it takes to see results. First, there is usually a close eye on the *distribution* of the benefits across people and places. "Lost Einstein" policies score well in this respect, as they both improve aggregate innovation and reduce inequality of opportunity. Gruber and Johnson (2019) have emphasized the need to spread innovation subsidies (such as new technology hubs) more widely in the US to embrace "left behind" geographical areas that have the capability to benefit due to existing education and are much cheaper than the high-cost clusters on the coasts. Secondly, rather than the usual economist practice of evaluating one policy at a time, we should consider the multiple interactions between innovation policies. Incorporating these in a growth plan involves building a portfolio of policies to address the most important missions facing Americans, particularly climate change, but also the challenges of improving health and security. Such a plan for growth (e.g., Van Reenen 2020) is likely to be more politically sustainable than a piecemeal approach and in the long run may produce greater gains in human well-being.

References

Acs, Zoltan, David Audretsch, and Marianne Feldman. 1992. "Real Effects of Academic Research: Comment." *American Economic Review* 82: 363–67.

Aghion, Philippe, and Peter Howitt. 1992. "A Model of Growth through Creative Destruction." *Econometrica* 60 (2): 323–51.

Akcigit, Ufuk, and Stefanie Stantcheva. 2020. "Taxation and Innovation: What Do We Know?" NBER Working Paper No. 27109. Cambridge, MA: National Bureau of Economic Research.

Andrews, Michael. 2020. "How Do Institutions of Higher Education Affect Local Invention? Evidence from the Establishment of U.S. Colleges." Mimeo, University of Maryland.

Angrist, Joshua, Parag Pathak, and Christopher Walters. 2013. "What Explains Charter School Effectiveness?" *American Economic Journal: Applied Economics* 5 (4): 1–27.

Arora, Ashish, Sharon Belenzon, and Andrea Patacconi. 2018. "The Decline of Science in Corporate R&D." *Strategic Management Journal* 39 (1): 3–32.

Arrow, Kenneth. 1962. "Economic Welfare and Allocation of Resources for Invention." In National Bureau of Economic Research, *The Rate and Direction of Inventive Activity: Economic and Social Factors*, 609–26. Princeton, NJ: Princeton University Press.

Autor, David, Claudia Goldin, and Lawrence Katz. 2020. "The Race between Education and Technology Revisited." *American Economic Review* 110: 347–51.

Azoulay, Pierre, Joshua S. Graff Zivin, Danielle Li, and Bhaven N. Sampat. 2019. "Public R&D Investments and Private Sector Patenting: Evidence from NIH Funding Rules." *Review of Economic Studies* 86 (1): 117–52.

Belenzon, Sharon, and Mark Schankerman. 2013. "Spreading the Word: Geography, Policy and Knowledge Spillovers." *Review of Economics and Statistics* 95 (3): 884–903.

Bell, Alexander, Raj Chetty, Xavier Jaravel, Neviana Petkova, and John Van Reenen. 2019a. "Who Becomes an Inventor in America? The Importance of Exposure to Innovation." *Quarterly Journal of Economics* 134 (2): 647–713. https://doi.org/10.1093/qje/qjy028.

———. 2019b. "Do Tax Cuts Produce More Einsteins? The Impacts of Financial Incentives vs. Exposure to Innovation on the Supply of Inventors." *Journal of the European Economic Association* 17 (3): 651–77.

Bernstein, Shai, Rebecca Diamond, Timothy McQuade, and Beatriz Pousada. 2018. "The Contribution of High-Skilled Immigrants to Innovation in the United States." Mimeo, Stanford University.

Bianchi, Nicola, and Michela Giorcelli. 2019. "Scientific Education and Innovation: From Technical Diplomas to University STEM Degrees." NBER Working Paper No. 25928. Cambridge, MA: National Bureau of Economic Research.

Bloom, Nicholas, Chad Jones, John Van Reenen, and Michael Webb. 2020. "Are Ideas Becoming Harder to Find?" *American Economic Review* 110 (4): 1104–44.

Bloom, Nicholas, Mark Schankerman, and John Van Reenen. 2013. "Identifying Technology Spillovers and Product Market Rivalry." *Econometrica* 81 (4): 1347–93.

Bloom, Nicholas, and John Van Reenen. 2007. "Measuring and Explaining Management Practices across Firms and Nations." *Quarterly Journal of Economics* 122 (4): 1351–1408.

Bloom, Nicholas, Heidi Williams, and John Van Reenen. 2019. "A Toolkit of Policies to Promote Innovation." *Journal of Economic Perspectives* 33 (3): 163–84.

Borjas, George J., and Kirk B. Doran. 2012. "The Collapse of the Soviet Union and the Productivity of American Mathematicians." *Quarterly Journal of Economics* 127 (3): 1143–1203.

Bui, Sa, Steven Craig, and Scott Imberman. 2014. "Is Gifted Education a Bright Idea? Assessing the Impact of Gifted and Talented Programs on Students." *American Economic Journal: Economic Policy* 6 (3): 30–62.

Card, David, and Laura Giuliano. 2016. "Can Tracking Raise the Test Scores of High-Ability Minority Students?" *American Economic Review* 106 (10): 2783–816.

Carneiro, Pedro, Kai Liu, and Kjell Salvanes. 2018. "The Supply of Skill and Endogenous Technical Change: Evidence from a College Expansion Reform." Discussion Paper Series in Economics 16/2018, Norwegian School of Economics, Department of Economics.

Celik, Murat. 2018. "Does the Cream Always Rise to the Top? The Misallocation of Talent in Innovation." Mimeo, University of Toronto.

Chetty, Raj, John N. Friedman, Emmanuel Saez, Nicholas Turner, and Danny Yagan. 2017. "Mobility Report Cards: The Role of Colleges in Intergenerational Mobility." Human Capital and Economic Opportunity Working Group Working Paper 2017-059.

Cohodes, Sarah. 2020. "The Long-Run Impacts of Specialized Programming for High-Achieving Students." *American Economic Journal: Economic Policy* 12 (1): 127–66.

Cook, Lisa. 2014. "Violence and Economic Activity: Evidence from African American Patents, 1870–1940." *Journal of Economic Growth* 19: 221–57.

Cook, Lisa, and Chaleampong Kongcharoen. 2010. "The Idea Gap in Pink and Black." NBER Working Paper No. 16331. Cambridge, MA: National Bureau of Economic Research.

DiNardo, John, Michelle Fortin, and Thomas Lemieux. 1996. "Labor Market Institutions and the Distribution of Wages: 1973–1992: A Semi-Parametric Approach." *Econometrica* 64 (5): 1001–44.

Doran, Kirk, Alex Gelber, and Adam Isen. 2015. "The Effects of High-Skilled Immigration Policy on Firms: Evidence from H-1B Visa Lotteries." NBER Working Paper No. 20668. Cambridge, MA: National Bureau of Economic Research.

Doran, Kirk, and Chungeun Yoon. 2018. "Immigration and Invention: Evidence from the Quota Acts." Mimeo, University of Notre Dame.

Flaubert, Gustave. 1911. *Le Dictionnaire des idées reçues.* London: Dodo Press.

Furman, Jeffrey, and Megan MacGarvie. 2007. "Academic Science and the Birth of Industrial Research Laboratories in the US Pharmaceutical Industry." *Journal of Economic Behavior and Organization* 63: 756–76.

Gabriel, Madeleine, Juliet Ollard, and Nancy Wilkinson. 2018. "Opportunity Lost: How Inventive Potential Is Squandered and What to Do about It." London: Nesta. https://media.nesta.org.uk/documents/Opportunity-Lost-December-2018.pdf.

Goolsbee, Austan. 1998. "Does Government R&D Policy Mainly Benefit Scientists and Engineers?" *American Economic Review* 88 (2): 298–302.

Griffith, Rachel, Simon Lee, and John Van Reenen. 2011. "Is Distance Dying at Last? Falling Home Bias in Fixed Effects Models of Patent Citations." *Quantitative Economics* 2: 211–49.

Griliches, Zvi. 1958. "Research Costs and Social Returns: Hybrid Corn and Related Innovations." *Journal of Political Economy* 66: 419.

———. 1992. "The Search for R&D Spillovers." *Scandinavian Journal of Economics* 94: 29–47.

Gruber, Jonathan, and Simon Johnson. 2019. *Jump-Starting America: How Breakthrough Science Can Revive Economic Growth and the American Dream.* New York: Public Affairs.

Hall, Bronwyn H., and Josh Lerner. 2010. "The Financing of R&D and Innovation." In *Handbook of the Economics of Innovation*, vol. 1, edited by Bronwyn H. Hall and Nathan Rosenberg, 609–39. Amsterdam: North-Holland.

Hausman, Naomi. 2018. "University Innovation and Local Economic Growth." Mimeo, Hebrew University.

Helmers, Christian, and Henry G. Overman. 2017. "My Precious! The Location and Diffusion of Scientific Research: Evidence from the Synchrotron Diamond Light Source." *Economic Journal* 127 (604): 2006–40.

Howell, Sabrina T. 2017. "Financing Innovation: Evidence from R&D Grants." *American Economic Review* 107 (4): 1136–64.

Howell, Sabrina T., Jason Rathje, John Van Reenen, and Jun Wong. 2021. "OPENing up Military Innovation: An Evaluation of Reforms to the U.S. Air Force SBIR Program." NBER Working Paper No. 28700. Cambridge, MA: National Bureau of Economic Research.

Hsieh, Chiang-Tai, Erik Hurst, Charles I. Jones, and Peter J. Klenow. 2019. "The Allocation of Talent and U.S. Economic Growth." *Econometrica* 87 (5): 1439–74.

Hsieh, Chiang-Tai, and Peter Klenow. 2009. "Misallocation and Manufacturing TFP in China and India." *Quarterly Journal of Economics* 124 (4): 1403–48.

Hunt, Jennifer, and Marjolaine Gauthier-Loiselle. 2010. "How Much Does Immigration Boost Innovation?" *American Economic Journal: Macroeconomics* 2 (2): 31–56.

Hvide, Hans K., and Benjamin F. Jones. 2018. "University Innovation and Professor's Privilege." *American Economic Review* 108 (7): 1860–98.

Jacob, Brian, and Lars Lefgren. 2011. "The Impact of Research Grant Funding on Scientific Productivity." *Journal of Public Economics* 95 (9–10): 1168–77.

Jaffe, Adam. 1986. "Technological Opportunity and Spillovers of R&D: Evidence from Firms' Patents, Profits and Market Value." *American Economic Review* 76: 984–1001.

———. 1989. "Real Effects of Academic Research." *American Economic Review* 79 (5): 957–70.

Jaffe, Adam., and Josh Lerner. 2001. "Reinventing Public R&D: Patent Policy and the Commercialization of National Laboratory Technologies." *RAND Journal of Economics* 32 (1): 167–98.

Jaffe, Adam and Josh Lerner. 2007. *Innovation and Its Discontents*. Princeton, NJ: Princeton University Press.

Jaffe, Adam, Manuel Trajtenberg, and Rebecca Henderson. 1993. "Geographic Localization of Knowledge Spillovers as Evidenced by Patent Citations." *Quarterly Journal of Economics* 108 (3): 577–98.

Janeway, William. 2012. *Doing Capitalism in the Innovation Economy: Markets, Speculation and the State*. Cambridge, UK: Cambridge University Press.

Jones, Benjamin, and Lawrence Summers. 2020. "A Calculation of the Social Returns to Innovation." NBER Working Paper No. 27863. Cambridge, MA: National Bureau of Economic Research.

Jones, Charles. 2016. "The Facts of Economic Growth." In *Handbook of Macroeconomics*, vol. 2, edited by John B. Taylor and Harald Uhlig, 3–69. Amsterdam: North-Holland.

Kerr, William, and William Lincoln. 2010. "The Supply Side of Innovation: H-1B Visa Reforms and U.S. Ethnic Invention." *Journal of Labor Economics* 28 (3): 473–508.

Lach, Saul, and Mark Schankerman. 2008. "Incentives and Invention in Universities." *RAND Journal of Economics* 39 (2): 403–33.

Lychagin, Sergey, Joris Pinkse, Margaret Slade, and John Van Reenen. 2016. "Spillovers in Space: Does Geography Matter?" *Journal of Industrial Economics* 64 (2): 295–335.

Lerner, Josh. 2005. *The Boulevard of Broken Dreams*. Princeton, NJ: Princeton University Press.

Lucking, Brian, Nicholas Bloom, and John Van Reenen. 2020. "Have R&D Spillovers Declined in the 21st Century?" *Fiscal Studies* 40 (4): 561–90.

Manski, Charles. 1993. "Identification of Endogenous Social Effects: The Reflection Problem." *Review of Economic Studies* 60 (3): 531–42.

Mazzucato, Mariana. 2013. *The Entrepreneurial State: Debunking Public vs. Private Sector Myths*. London: Anthem Press.

Moretti, Enrico, Claudia Steinwender, and John Van Reenen. 2019. "The Intellectual Spoils of War? Defense R&D, Productivity and International Technology Spillovers." NBER Working Paper No. 26483. Cambridge, MA: National Bureau of Economic Research.

Moser, Petra, and Shmuel San. 2019. "Immigration, Science, and Invention: Evidence from the 1920s Quota Acts." Mimeo, New York University.

Moser, Petra, Alessandra Voena, and Fabian Waldinger. 2014. "German Jewish Émigrés and US Invention." *American Economic Review* 104 (10): 3222–55.

National Science Board. 2018. *Science & Engineering Indicators 2018*. Alexandria, VA: National Science Board.

OECD. 2018. *OECD Review of National R&D Tax Incentives and Estimates of R&D Tax Subsidy Rates, 2017*. Paris: OECD. https://www.oecd.org/sti/rd-tax-stats-design-subsidy.pdf.

Romer, Paul M. 2001. "Should the Government Subsidize Supply or Demand in the Market for Scientists and Engineers?" *Innovation Policy and the Economy*, vol. 1, edited by Adam Jaffe, Josh Lerner, and Scott Stern, 221–52. Cambridge, MA: MIT Press.

Schmookler, Jacob. 1957. "Inventors Past and Present." *Review of Economics and Statistics* 39 (3): 321–33.

Sianesi, Barbara, and John Van Reenen. 2003. "Education and Economic Growth: A Review of the Literature." *Journal of Economic Surveys* 17 (2): 157–200.

Tabellini, Marco. 2020. "Gifts of the Immigrants, Woes of the Natives: Lessons from the Age of Mass Migration." *Review of Economic Studies* 87 (1): 454–86.

Toivanen, Otto, and Lotta Väänänen. 2016. "Education and Invention." *Review of Economics and Statistics* 98 (2): 382–96.

Trajtenberg, Manuel. 1990. "A Penny for Your Quotes: Patent Citations and the Value of Innovations." *RAND Journal of Economics* 21 (1): 172–87.

Valero, Anna, and John Van Reenen. 2019. "The Economic Impact of Universities: Evidence from Across the Globe." *Economics of Education* 68: 53–67.

Van Reenen, John. 2011. "Wage Inequality, Technology and Trade: 21st Century Evidence." *Labour Economics* 18 (6): 730–41.

Van Reenen, John. 2020. "Innovation Policies to Boost Productivity." Hamilton Policy Proposal 2020-13.

Zucker, Lynne, Michael Brewer, and Marilynn Darby. 1998. "Intellectual Capital and the Birth of US Biotechnology Enterprises." *American Economic Review* 88: 290–306.

Immigration Policy Levers for US Innovation and Start-Ups

Sari Pekkala Kerr and William R. Kerr

3.1 Introduction

US policy makers are always on the hunt for levers that can boost entrepreneurship and innovation. Especially in a time of declining business dynamism (Decker et al. 2014) and an aging workforce, entrepreneurship and innovation raise economic growth, provide jobs, and rebuild government coffers. As America works to rebuild from the devastating effects of the COVID-19 pandemic, these stimulants become ever more important. This chapter reviews potential reforms to the US immigration system that could enhance the contribution of immigrants to the nation's entrepreneurship and innovation.

Policy makers are well aware of high-profile immigrant examples like Tesla and SpaceX founder Elon Musk and Microsoft CEO Satya Nadella, whose images grace the covers of magazines and who are called to testify

Sari Pekkala Kerr is an economist and a senior research scientist at the Wellesley Centers for Women (WCW) at Wellesley College.

William R. Kerr is the D'Arbeloff Professor of Business Administration at Harvard Business School, a Bank of Finland Research Fellow, and a research associate of the National Bureau of Economic Research.

We thank Maggie Dalton and Gorick Ng for excellent research assistance. We thank the National Science Foundation, Smith Richardson Foundation, Harvard Business School, and the Ewing Marion Kauffman Foundation for financial support that made this research possible. The research in this chapter was conducted while the authors were Special Sworn Status researchers of the US Census Bureau. Any opinions and conclusions expressed herein are those of the authors and do not necessarily represent the views of the US Census Bureau. This research was performed at a Federal Statistical Research Data Center under FSRDC Project Number 1731. All results have been reviewed to ensure that no confidential information is disclosed. For acknowledgments, sources of research support, and disclosure of the authors' material financial relationships, if any, please see https://www.nber.org/books-and-chapters /innovation-and-public-policy/immigration-policy-levers-us-innovation-and-startups.

before Congress. They may be less aware, however, of the exceptional depth that lies below these prominent examples. Immigrants account for about a quarter of US start-ups and patents each year, a share that has been increasing for decades. Section 3.2 reviews some recent economic research about immigrant entrepreneurship and innovation and its surprisingly deep influence on the US economy.

Section 3.3 then discusses adjustments to US immigration policy that could boost innovation. We mostly focus on feasible reforms that would operate within the current immigration structure by adjusting the allocation of visas granted for employment-based purposes. The most prominent reform would replace the lottery used for the oversubscribed H-1B visa system with an allocation mechanism that prioritizes specified uses. We also provide a short discussion of comprehensive immigration reform, which could increase the relative share of immigration for employment-based purposes compared to family-reunification purposes.

Section 3.4 considers policies connected to immigrant entrepreneurs. While the United States has visas that cover individuals capable of making substantial business investments, its immigration structure is less accommodating than those of other countries for the admission of business founders lacking existing financial capital (e.g., an immigrant college student on an F-1 student visa who wants to start a company after graduation). We review the approaches of several countries to start-up visas, common traits of recent US legislative proposals, and estimates of the potential economic impact.

Throughout this review, we strictly follow the National Bureau of Economic Research's guideline that papers not advocate a particular policy approach. Our goal is to collect and present economic research on how policy makers can influence US entrepreneurship and innovation outcomes through the immigration process. We thus skip discussion of policies that indirectly influence immigrant entrepreneurship and innovation. An example is the work of Akcigit, Baslandze, and Stantcheva (2016), which shows that top inventors are very sensitive to taxation rates when deciding where to conduct their research. Many of these policies are covered elsewhere in this volume and in Bloom, Van Reenen, and Williams (2019), and these levers often operate in part by making the United States more attractive to skilled immigrants. Similarly, we do not quantify what an overall expansion of US immigration rates would do for entrepreneurship and innovation, as most of the impact would simply come from the larger economy (Clemens 2011).

Our focus is narrower and arguably more useful to policy makers in today's immigration discussions. In America and abroad, recent growth in populism and nationalism has pushed back at many forms of global integration, including skilled- and employment-based migration. Questions about the appropriateness of global linkages will further intensify following the COVID-19 crisis. Yet the combination of a knowledge-intensive economy and a rapidly aging populations in most advanced economies suggests that competition for the world's mobile entrepreneurs and innovators will increase in the decades ahead. Understanding what policy margins could be adjusted is an important foundation for thinking through future national strategies for immigration and the best mechanisms to implement them.

3.2   Immigrants as Founders and Innovators

While the literature on immigrant entrepreneurship and innovation is not very extensive, it is nonetheless too large to be fully reviewed here. We instead outline some key research findings that provide important background for the immigration visa discussions in the next two sections.[1]

1. Immigrants account for about a quarter of US entrepreneurship and innovation. A significant body of work over the past two decades has quantified these contributions.[2] Measuring this is harder than it first appears, which results in a range of techniques and estimates. Nevertheless, research consistently finds that immigrants account for about 25 percent of new firms and patents. As a corollary, the propensity of immigrants toward entrepreneurship and innovation is higher than it is for US natives.[3] Immigrants account for about 14 percent of the US workforce and 17–18 percent of US college graduates, according to the 2016 American Community Survey. Looking specifically at science and engineering, immigrants account for 29 percent of the United States' college-educated workforce and 52 percent of its doctorates.

2. Most of the heightened impact of immigrants on US entrepreneurship and innovation comes from a greater propensity of immigrants to possess the educational backgrounds for the work. Hunt (2011, 2015) shows that immigrants' propensities toward entrepreneurship and innovation can be mostly explained through their greater educational attainment and their greater focus on the STEM fields (science, technology, engineering, and mathematics). While immigrants are more represented at the upper tail of scientific achievement[4]—accounting, for example, for a third of US-based recipients of Nobel Prizes—their most significant impact on the economy comes through the large quantity of immigrant workers trained for pursuing STEM work.

1. Kerr (2019a) provides a book-length review. Summary articles include Fairlie and Lofstrom (2014), Kerr (2017), and Kerr et al. (2016, 2017).
2. For example, Anderson and Platzer (2006); Azoulay et al. (2020); Bernstein et al. (2019); Brown et al. (2019); Kerr and Kerr (2017, 2020); Kerr and Lincoln (2010); Saxenian (1999, 2002); and Wadhwa et al. (2007).
3. The diverse literature spans Borjas (1986); Clark and Drinkwater (2000, 2006); Fairlie (2012); Fairlie and Lofstrom (2014); Fairlie, Zissimopoulos, and Krashinsky (2010); Hunt (2011, 2015); Lofstrom (2002); and Schuetze and Antecol (2007).
4. See, for example, Hart and Acs (2011); Kerr (2019a, 2019b); Peri (2007); Stephan and Levin (2001); and Wadhwa et al. (2007).

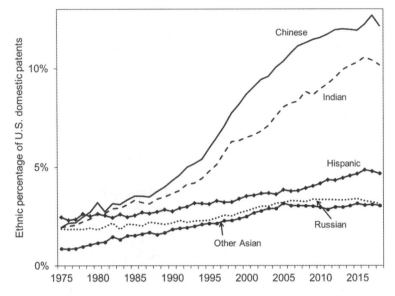

Fig. 3.1   Ethnic share of patents filed by inventors living in United States
Source: Data from US Patent and Trademark Office. Series uses ethnic naming conventions applied to inventors based in the United States.

3. Chinese and Indian immigration have been particularly strong drivers for growth in immigrant entrepreneurship and innovation. To provide an extended time horizon, figure 3.1 uses the ethnic-name-matching algorithms of Kerr (2008) to quantify the significant growth in US patents granted to individuals of Chinese and Indian ethnicity working in America. Chinese and Indian ethnic inventors accounted for less than 3 percent of US patents in 1975, but more than 22 percent in 2018. As we discuss later, this concentration is leading to long delays in obtaining US permanent residency for immigrants from China and India due to the US allocation procedures that cap the annual number of green cards that can go to petitioners who were born in any given country.

4. Immigrant entrepreneurship and innovation are quite clustered spatially and show no evidence of crowding out native activity in local areas. More than half of entrepreneurs in the San Francisco Bay Area are foreign-born, and many other leading technology clusters show high immigrant shares (Kerr and Kerr 2020). Empirical studies using geographic variation almost always find positive or no impact from high-skilled immigration on native employment and output in innovative activities in the same city.[5] This clustering

5. For example, Buchardi et al. (2019); Ghimire (2018); Hunt and Gauthier-Loiselle (2010); Kerr (2010); Kerr and Lincoln (2010); and Peri, Shih, and Sparber (2015). Lewis and Peri (2015) provide a theoretical framework and review of literature on the effects of immigration on local areas. Analyses of industries or technology areas have shown more mixed outcomes (e.g., Borjas

has substantially shifted the economic geography of innovation in America, and the lack of a crowding-out effect allows the spatial concentration of innovation to persist and grow. We note later the potential role of regional visas to counteract some of this concentration.

5. *Immigrant contributions are similarly concentrated within firms, with mixed evidence for whether native employment grows or declines.* Firms such as Microsoft and Google employ skilled immigrants to a greater degree than Procter and Gamble and Boeing. These differences can be explained in part by their physical locations and industries. Studies on whether the hiring of skilled immigrants boosts the overall employment of firms show mixed results (e.g., Dimmock, Huang, and Weisbenner 2019; Doran, Gelber, and Isen 2015; Kerr, Kerr, and Lincoln 2015b; Mayda et al. 2018), an ambiguity connected to the many ways the US visa system can be used, as described in the next section. There is evidence that high-skilled immigration is a lever used by employers to keep tech workforces younger (e.g., Kerr, Kerr, and Lincoln 2015a, 2015b; Matloff 2003).[6]

6. *Skilled immigrants receive wages at a rate comparable to similarly skilled natives.* Studies on whether immigrants receive higher or lower wages than natives yield mixed results. Legal factors, like the prevailing wage requirement for an H-1B worker, limit the extent to which pay differences could exist. Moreover, even to the degree that skilled immigrants are slightly underpaid relative to natives of similar age and background, the economics of the firm suggest a rather limited scope for this differential to influence hiring decisions. The larger wage gaps instead appear between younger skilled immigrants and older native workers, connecting to the observation above that high-skilled immigration can be a mechanism for firms to keep workforces younger.

7. *A substantial portion of skilled immigration to America begins with migration for schooling.* Immigrants who contribute to US entrepreneurship and innovation migrate at many life stages: Sergey Brin of Google migrated as a child, while Elon Musk first moved to the United States for college. The reforms below focus on entrepreneurial and employment opportunities after schooling, but Kato and Sparber (2013) demonstrate a strong link between the opportunity to remain in the United States for work and the attractiveness of US colleges to migrants. Likewise, policies that govern school-to-work transitions play an important role.

---

and Doran 2012; Bound, Khanna, and Morales 2017; Doran and Yoon 2019; Moser and San 2020; Moser, Voena, and Waldinger 2014). The clustering of entrepreneurs from a country in a narrow occupation is widespread and studied by Chung and Kalnins (2006), Fairlie, Zissimopoulos, and Krashinsky (2010), Kerr and Mandorff (2015), and Patel and Vella (2013). See also the self-employment studies of Akee, Jaeger, and Tatsiramos (2013), Fairlie and Meyer (2003), and Lofstrom (2002).

6. The transition period for native workers who are displaced appears longer in STEM-connected work than elsewhere (Kerr and Kerr 2013). Glennon (2019) considers how access to skilled immigrants influences the overseas operations of US firms.

3.3   Visas for Innovators

The research findings described in section 3.2 provide a foundation for exploring how the US immigration process can be adjusted to increase levels of entrepreneurship and innovation. This section commences by discussing the role of immigrants in invention and innovation. The bulk of these contributions come through the actions of paid employees in US businesses, and thus we focus on the frameworks that connect to the quantity and composition of these workers. Section 3.4 considers the special case of immigrant entrepreneurs who are not well aligned for employment-based visas.[7]

3.3.1   A Brief Summary of the US Immigration System

The US immigration system is vast and exceptionally complex, and we highlight here just a few important background pieces.[8] Most of the poli-

7. This chapter describes the policy environment in April 2020, when the chapter was prepared. From April 2020 until the chapter went to press in November 2020, there were a number of temporary and potentially long-term changes to US immigration policy and enforcement. Some of these actions were framed as a response to health and employment concerns related to the COVID-19 pandemic, and other countries restricted migration to some degree during the pandemic's spread. In June 2020, the Trump administration suspended new H-1B and L-1 visa issuances to most individuals outside the country through the end of the year. These restrictions followed on other restrictions emanating in April 2020, and a federal judge later issued a preliminary injunction against them. In early October, the Trump administration introduced two "interim final" regulations that would forego normal notice and commentary periods. The first, through the Department of Labor (DOL), immediately changed the calculation of the required wage for H-1B employees, effectively increasing minimum salaries. The second, through the Department of Homeland Security (DHS), required that the degrees of H-1B candidates be directly related to the proposed occupation (e.g., a candidate with a degree in mechanical engineering cannot fill a job designated for computer programming), and limited visa duration to one year for H-1B holders who work at customer or third-party sites. The DHS regulation was set to take effect in December 2020, and both DOL and DHS regulations are being legally challenged. The Trump administration also proposed a new rule to eliminate the H-1B lottery in favor of a wage-ranking system. With the November 2020 election of Joe Biden to the presidency, the future of these changes is uncertain. See White House, "Proclamation Suspending Entry of Aliens Who Present a Risk to the U.S. Labor Market Following the Coronavirus Outbreak," Executive Order, July 22, 2020, https://trumpwhitehouse.archives.gov/presidential-actions/proclamation-suspending-entry-aliens-present-risk-u-s-labor-market-following-coronavirus-outbreak/; Employment and Training Administration, "Strengthening Wage Protections for the Temporary and Permanent Employment of Certain Aliens in the United States," *Federal Register*, October 8, 2020, https://www.federalregister.gov/documents/2020/10/08/2020-22132/strengthening-wage-protections-for-the-temporary-and-permanent-employment-of-certain-aliens-in-the; Department of Homeland Security, "Strengthening the H-1B Nonimmigrant Visa Classification Program," *Federal Register*, October 8, 2020, https://www.federalregister.gov/documents/2020/10/08/2020-22347/strengthening-the-h-1b-nonimmigrant-visa-classification-program; Department of Homeland Security, "Modification of Registration Requirement for Petitioners Seeking to File Cap-Subject H-1B Petitions," October 28, 2020, https://www.dhs.gov/sites/default/files/publications/20_1028_uscis_h-1b-registration-selection-by-wage-levels-nprm-508.pdf.
8. For a primer, see Julia Gelatt, "Explainer: How the U.S. Legal Immigration System Works," Migration Policy Institute, April 2019, https://www.migrationpolicy.org/content/explainer-how-us-legal-immigration-system-works.

cies discussed below fall under the US Citizenship and Immigration Services (USCIS) within the Department of Homeland Security.

Other than citizenship, immigration to America culminates in obtaining permanent residency, also known as the "green card." Approximately 1 million green cards are granted every year, with family-based immigration being the largest category. There is no annual limit on green cards to reunite immediate family members (e.g., spouses, parents, and children) of American citizens, and up to 480,000 additional visas are provided annually for extended family. Green cards granted for employment-based purposes are subject to an annual cap of 140,000 individuals, including family members accompanying the worker. Smaller numbers of visas are issued for other purposes, such as refugee/humanitarian concerns.

In parallel, temporary visas authorize individuals to visit, study, and work in the United States. These visas are termed "nonimmigrant" as the individual does not have permanent rights to stay in the country. Temporary visas are often a predecessor to permanent residency, as more than 80 percent of employment-based green cards are issued to individuals already living and working in the United States. On the other hand, many skilled migrants work in the United States for a period of time but have no intention to stay permanently. Consequently, the levers by which policy makers might impact entrepreneurship and innovation extend beyond permanent residency admissions to cover temporary visas and, as we will return to below, how these two structures interface with each other. This section continues by describing temporary visas for employment-related purposes (versus to study or to visit).

A distinctive feature of the US temporary visa system is that it is "employer driven," meaning that a company like Microsoft or General Motors selects the worker it wants to employ and applies for a visa on behalf of the worker. This individual could be living/working abroad or be a student at a US school on a nonemployment visa. This employer-driven approach contrasts conceptually with a points-based system that scores and selects potential immigrants based on their attributes (e.g., degree, age, language skills, income). Kerr (2019a) reviews the trade-offs between the two approaches and the de facto hybrid nature of many nations. The United States has some elements of a points-like structure in that priority temporary visa categories (and permanent residency admissions) exist for persons of "extraordinary ability," but the bulk of skilled immigrant workers are admitted through temporary visas that rely on employers to select migrants.

The largest of these temporary employment-based categories is the H-1B visa for skilled foreigners working in "specialty occupations" (i.e., those requiring theoretical and practical application of specialized knowledge like engineering or accounting). Virtually all H-1B holders have a college education or higher, and the substantial majority of visas are used for computer- and STEM-related occupations. In 2017, immigrants from India accounted

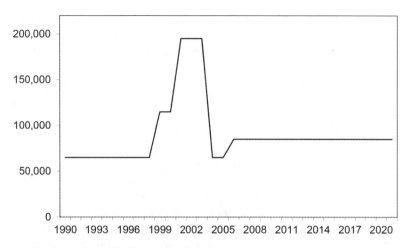

Fig. 3.2   Evolution of H-1B cap by fiscal year
Source: Data from US Citizenship and Immigration Services.

for 72 percent of H-1B visas, and immigrants from China were awarded another 13 percent. These shares have steadily risen and demonstrate the flexibility of the system to be used in ways that employers deem fit, with computer- and STEM-related occupations being attractive opportunities for firms.

H-1B holders are tied to their sponsoring firm, although visa portability is feasible with approval from the government (e.g., Depew, Norlander, and Sorensen 2017). Firms can petition for permanent residency on behalf of the worker. This "dual-intent" feature—where one can be a temporary migrant but also apply for permanent residency—is attractive to many immigrants. The H-1B visa is for three years and can be renewed once. If permanent residency is not obtained, the H-1B worker must leave the United States at the end of the second visa period for one year before applying again.

Firms must pay the visa holder the higher of (1) the prevailing wage in the firm for the position or (2) the prevailing wage for the occupation in the area of employment. Congress designed these restrictions to prevent H-1B employers from abusing their relationships with foreign workers and to protect the wages and employment of domestic workers. In 2016, the average salary for H-1B visa holders was $80,000, but there was a broad range, from midskilled employees of outsourcing firms earning $60,000 to higher-skilled workers earning greater than $150,000 (Kerr 2019b; Ruiz and Krogstad 2018).[9]

Figure 3.2 shows the annual cap on the number of new H-1B visas that

9. The minimal wage effects on R&D workers from expanding skilled immigration for innovation is different from wages being bid up from R&D stimulus described by Goolsbee (1998).

can be issued to for-profit firms. The original 65,000 cap was not binding in the early 1990s, but became so by the middle of the decade. Legislation in 1998 and 2000 sharply increased the cap over the next five years, to 195,000 visas. These short-term increases expired during the high-tech downturn, when visa demand fell short of the cap. The cap returned to the 65,000 level in 2004 and became binding again, despite being subsequently raised by 20,000 through an "advanced degree" exemption. The overall cap of 85,000 remains in place as of 2020.

Another widely used but lesser known employer-based visa is the L-1. Available for the temporary migration of foreign employees within a multinational firm, there were about 78,000 L-1 visas (including renewals) issued in 2017. Only employees who have been employed by the firm for at least one of the previous three years are eligible, and the visa has a maximum stay of seven years. Similar to the H-1B, the L-1 is a dual-intent visa, whereby it provides an opportunity to apply for a green card. Yeaple (2018) provides additional discussion of the L-1 visa.

3.3.2   Potential Reforms within the Existing System

Lawmakers have proposed several reforms that could boost entrepreneurship and innovation by, more or less, adjusting the existing system (i.e., not requiring the comprehensive immigration reform described at the end of this section). We discuss these reforms, working backward from the green card decision.

3.3.2.1   *Remove Country Caps on Employment-Based*
         Permanent Residency

The United States grants 140,000 green cards for employment-based (EB) purposes each year, a figure that includes the focal worker and his or her accompanying family members. This is not the only pathway through which an immigrant inventor or entrepreneur can obtain permanent residency as, for example, the individual may marry an American citizen and apply for permanent residency through family-based allocations. Others enter the diversity lottery that offers 50,000 green cards randomly to applicants from countries with low rates of admission to America. Nevertheless, the EB allocation is the most central and broadly accessible channel for employment-connected immigration.

In addition to these caps on the type of green card to be awarded (which we discuss in greater detail below in the context of comprehensive immigration reform), the US system has an important country-level cap. A provision within the Immigration Act of 1990, which remained in effect as of 2020, stipulated that "the total number of immigrant visas made available to natives of any single foreign state or dependent area" not exceed 7 percent. This provision was partly designed to encourage diversity in source countries of migrants.

A consequence, however, has been the development of long waiting lists for employment-based migrants from several large nations until they can obtain a green card (e.g., Kahn and MacGarvie 2018). EB immigrants from China and India face particularly long waiting times given the huge demand: recall that 85 percent of H-1B visas go to immigrants from these two countries, and figure 3.1 showed their prominent role in US innovation growth. Wait-time projections for some categories of Indian migration can stretch into the decades (priorities and wait times depend on the skill level of the EB category). Though the H-1B temporary visa can be extended beyond the typical six years (initial plus renewal) while the immigrant is waiting for a green card, the long wait times impair worker mobility across employers and their capacity to launch new ventures.

Over the last decade, attempts have been made in both the House and the Senate to amend this policy. Proposals have suggested increasing the country cap from 7 percent to 15 percent or 25 percent, and avoiding any residual, unused visas. A prominent recent example is the Fairness for High-Skilled Immigrants Act of 2020, proposed in both the House and the Senate, which sought to "eliminate the per-country numerical limitation for employment-based immigrants." Different forms of the proposal passed the House and Senate but were not reconciled before the 116th Congress ended its session.[10]

This adjustment would likely increase the attractiveness of the United States to foreign entrepreneurs and innovators. For immigrants doing innovative work in large organizations, the prospect of long waiting times can deter migration due to the uncertainty and possibly slower wage growth while on temporary status. Hunt (2017) finds that mobility is reduced by about 20 percent when waiting for green card processing. The weakened mobility of workers may also reduce the match quality between a firm and a worker, leading to lower productivity. Prospective entrepreneurs can also be discouraged if they need the permanent residency transition to start their business, due either to legal factors (visa requirements) or to the necessary confidence that the United States will be their long-term home.

3.3.2.2   Increase the Number of H-1B Visas

The most frequently proposed and debated reform to temporary migration is to raise the annual cap on the H-1B program for for-profit firms. As of

10. This section is sourced from the following (accessed December 2019): 8 U.S. Code § 1152, Numerical Limitations on Individual Foreign States, https://uscode.house.gov/view.xhtml?req=(title:8%20section:1152%20edition:prelim; Startup Act, S. 1877, 115th Congress, 2017, https://www.congress.gov/bill/115th-congress/senate-bill/1877/text#toc-H6343391472A44BF0884BAD0CFF83B119; Fairness for High-Skilled Immigrants Act of 2019, S. 386, 116th Congress, 2019, https://www.congress.gov/bill/116th-congress/senate-bill/386/text; Fairness for High-Skilled Immigrants Act of 2020, H.R. 1044, 116th Congress, 2019, https://www.congress.gov/bill/116th-congress/house-bill/1044/text; Fairness for High-Skilled Immigrants Act of 2019, S. 386, 116th Congress, 2019, https://www.congress.gov/bill/116th-congress/senate-bill/386/actions; Fairness for High-Skilled Immigrants Act of 2019: Roll Vote No. 437, *Congressional Record*, July 10, 2019, http://clerk.house.gov/evs/2019/roll437.xml.

early 2020, the H-1B visa cap was 65,000 with an additional 20,000 visas for individuals with advanced degrees from US schools. Many proposals fall in the range of 115,000 to 195,000 visas. Some prominent business leaders like Eric Schmidt, Google's former CEO, go further to advocate for an unlimited number of visas.[11] Policy makers might also consider indexing future caps to economic conditions and related factors so that Congress does not need to spend multiple years debating one-off adjustments to a nominal figure.

It is likely that such a cap increase would spur US innovation to some degree. Empirical and quantitative studies of the prior cap adjustments when binding[12] suggest this conclusion, although a study of marginal visa awards in the non-cap-binding years of 2006 and 2007 does not (Doran, Gelber, and Isen 2015).

The most frequent objection raised to a potential innovation boost is that most H-1B visa holders are not conducting innovative work (being employed in computer- and STEM-related positions more broadly). Although this is true, it remains the case that innovation would likely grow if the overall program expanded. By analogy, an expansion of the Department of Defense's budget would likely result in more tanks, even though tanks are only a small portion of the department's budget. What this objection surfaces, though, is that we do not know how the overall composition of the applicant pool would change under an expanded program. The composition could stay the same, deteriorate on average (e.g., if firms apply for more marginal visa uses), or increase (e.g., if the greater assurance of a visa led to higher-quality immigrants and to firms prioritizing more to locate in the United States).

While many advocates propose cap expansions without reference to other policies, the interaction of such an expansion with other aspects of the immigration pathway should be considered by policy makers. Most important, without potential adjustments to the 7 percent country cap regarding how EB green cards are allocated, the backlog of temporary visa holders from China and India waiting for green cards would grow substantially if only the H-1B cap were increased.

3.3.2.3   Adjust the H-1B Visa Allocation Mechanism

Additional proposals consider how the United States could adjust the allocation of H-1B visas. Prior to fiscal year 2021, the visa application period opened on April 1 of each year. In most years, the government received more

11. Schmidt said in 2017, "The single stupidest policy in the entire American political system was the limit on H-1B." S. A. O'Brien, "Alphabet's Eric Schmidt Says H-1B Visa Cap Is 'Stupid,'" CNN, May 4, 2017, https://money.cnn.com/2017/05/04/technology/eric-schmidt -h1b-visa/. Hira (2010), by contrast, provides an example of a very skeptical view on the program. In a 2019 survey of Harvard Business School alumni (Porter et al. 2019), 70 percent of respondents favored an increase in the H-1B cap of 50 percent or more. In a parallel poll of the general public, 30 percent of Democrats and 20 percent of Republicans expressed interest in such an increase.

12. For example, see Bound, Khanna, and Morales (2017); Kerr, Kerr, and Lincoln (2015a, 2015b); Kerr and Lincoln (2010); Mayda et al. (2018); Peri, Shih, and Sparber (2015).

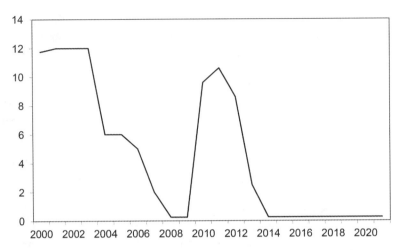

Fig. 3.3   Months until H-1B cap is reached from filing start date by fiscal year
Source: Data from US Citizenship and Immigration Services.
Notes: Cap was not reached in fiscal years 2002–2003.

applications than the available cap within the first week. The policy of the government in these oversubscribed years was to keep accepting applications for a whole week and then conduct a lottery for the applications received. Should the cap not be reached in the first week, applications were processed on a first-come, first-served basis until the cap was reached later in the year (and on that final day, USCIS conducted a mini lottery for the applications received on the day when the cap was reached). Figure 3.3 shows how rapidly the cap fills in most years. USCIS received 201,011 applications by April 5, 2019, for the 2020 fiscal year.[13] In March 2020, USCIS implemented a new two-step application process for fiscal year 2021, with a first registration from March 1, 2020, through March 20, 2020, followed by a lottery selection. Early data suggested that the government received approximately 275,000 registrations, again well in excess of the cap. At the time of writing this chapter, it was uncertain if the USCIS would further modify this new process for future years.

The lottery has important implications. A lottery randomizes applications and thus gives an equal chance to an applicant performing basic code testing for an outsourcing company as it does to one performing artificial intelligence research with a proposed salary tenfold higher. Indeed, the lottery system likely even tilts the application pool further toward more mundane uses: it is easier for a company to submit multiple applications for a routine

13. See Kumar, "H1B Visa Cap Reach Dates History FY 2000 to 2021—Graph—USCIS Data," Redbus, February 3, 2021, https://redbus2us.com/h1b-visa-cap-reach-dates-history -graphs-uscis-data/.

software developer role, knowing that the overall odds per applicant are in the range of 40 percent, than it is for a company to submit multiple applications for a scarce skill set like artificial intelligence research. (In a comparable way, it is likely that the lottery favors large companies submitting many H-1B applications over smaller companies who have more discrete needs.)

One recent change shifted in subtle ways the skill composition. USCIS has historically conducted the 20,000 visa lottery for candidates with a master's education from US schools before the 65,000 regular lottery. As candidates with master's degrees from US schools could enter both lotteries, this lottery order meant that fewer candidates with master's educations entered the regular lottery because they had already been selected. USCIS reversed the lottery order starting with the H-1B applications received in April 2020 for fiscal year 2021. By reversing the order, more of the dual lottery applicants will be chosen via the 65,000 lottery (and thus will drop out of the 20,000 exempt lottery). Estimates suggest that this change will increase by 4,000 to 5,000 individuals the number of H-1B visas awarded to holders of master's degrees. There have been some legal challenges to the proposed change, and others have argued against the switch in lottery order by noting, for example, that it would deprioritize applicants with doctorate degrees from non-US schools.[14] Pathak, Rees-Jones, and Sönmez (2020) provide an extensive analysis of this rule change and its optimality under the existing H-1B structure.

A move away from the lottery system altogether would likely increase the innovative output of the H-1B program. One mechanism frequently debated is to rank applicants by their proposed wage (which is included as part of an H-1B application). This technique would use the worker's wage as an imperfect proxy for the value of the potential immigrant to the US economy. A potential advantage of this approach is that the procedure is easy to understand and convey to the public. To the degree that wages and skills are correlated, such a prioritization would also raise the skill content of the H-1B system significantly. Sparber (2018) calculated that this change would generate a $27 billion surplus over six years, with gains even higher should better talent become more incentivized to apply.

---

14. From an applicant's perspective, one site estimated that the new lottery order would increase the likelihood that the holder of a US master's degree would obtain a visa from 51 percent to 55 percent, while reducing others from 38 percent to 34 percent. See AM22Tech Team, "What Is H1B Lottery System, Chances of Selection in Apr 2021?," AM22Tech, December 25, 2020, https://www.am22tech.com/h1b-lottery-system-changes/. Significant recent debate has also centered on the H-4 authorization that allows dependent spouses of H-1B workers with approved green card petitions to work. As of April 2020, the USCIS was considering an end to this authorization. Some H-1B holders have expressed concern that they will not be able to afford to live in the United States without a second income. It is not clear that this rule change would impact the innovation and entrepreneurship outcomes that are the focus of this chapter. Finally, several additional processing actions taken by the Trump administration appear to have aimed at reducing the number of H-1B visas awarded to IT service providers. In March 2020, a court invalidated several of these actions, and the future legal path is uncertain (Anderson, 2020a, 2020b).

There are some potential disadvantages that would need to be addressed. First, wage ranking would naturally favor some higher-priced cities and industries (e.g., New York City for finance, San Francisco for tech) over others, established companies over smaller ones, and established workers over younger ones and new college graduates. Lawmakers would need to consider what additional adjustments should complement and support wage ranking, such as regional and/or occupational caps, adjustments of school-to-work transitions, etc.[15] Second, the status implications to the temporary worker of subsequent cuts in salary compared to the initial offer use for wage ranking will need to be specified. Finally, wage ranking might also face legal challenges from groups that favor the current system, especially Indian outsourcing companies that argue the visas are compliant with the World Trade Organization's General Agreement on Trade in Services.[16]

Two other proposals are worth noting. One, which could complement wage ranking, is to establish a minimum salary level for an H-1B worker (e.g., $100,000), possibly with buffer mechanisms that would save unused visas and add them to subsequent years when demand spikes again. These thresholds would ensure that visas are allocated to purposes other than just cost minimization in IT roles.

Another proposal is to auction visas to companies (e.g., Peri 2012). Auctions would likely bring many of the same skill increases and innovation gains as wage ranking. Auctions would differ in that more of the economic surplus that immigration generates would be captured by the government, which could then use the funds as it deems fit. A challenge is that auctions would likely raise the share of H-1B visas going to companies that are already large and doing well, as they have the greatest financial capacity to bid for visas.

3.3.2.4   Adjust School-to-Work Transitions

This chapter focuses on policy reforms and how they might impact entrepreneurship and innovation in the for-profit sector. We do not provide here an in-depth treatment of potential reforms to immigration and the education system (Bound et al. 2020), which is an important early pathway for

---

15. Regional or occupation caps are also mentioned as potential H-1B reforms independent of wage ranking. Such reforms, depending upon how they were implemented, could result in a lower innovation stimulus if they shifted work out of tech clusters toward other purposes and regions. Related work on clusters includes Audretsch and Feldman (1996); Carlino and Kerr (2015); Fallick, Fleischman, and Rebitzer (2006); Feldman and Kogler (2010); Kerr and Robert-Nicoud (2020); Moretti (2019); Samila and Sorenson (2011); and Zucker, Darby, and Brewer (1998). Docquier et al. (2020), Nathan (2015), and Ottaviano and Peri (2006) are examples of work on local diversity and innovation outcomes.

16. There could also be management challenges inside companies. For example, many companies have salary bands for positions that might be stressed in a company willing to offer a higher salary in order to obtain a worker.

many who later take temporary work visas or EB green cards. However, we note several important tensions within the school-to-work transition.

US higher education is relatively unconstrained in that schools do not face caps on the number of student visas they can issue (or H-1B worker visas, as discussed later). Over the last decade, the number of foreign students in US schools has swelled to more than 1 million. Many of these students come to the United States with the hope of later obtaining a job in America (Kato and Sparber 2013). Yet the rapidly growing student population exerts pressure on the fixed supply of H-1B visas. As a consequence, many immigrant students take their first job via the Optional Practical Training (OPT) program, which lets graduates work with US companies to gain practical experience in jobs connected to their majors, lasting for up to one year in most fields and three years for STEM-degree holders.

There are an unlimited number of OPT visa extensions, with roughly 175,000 active in 2017. The OPT program accounted for about 30 percent of foreign-born students entering the US labor market during the 2000s, and today more skilled immigrants start work via OPT than through H-1B visas or permanent residency admissions (Bound et al. 2015). Many immigrants then experience the stress of repeatedly trying the H-1B lottery, with the hopes of being selected before their OPT runs out. If their OPT expires first, the student would need to leave the United States, obtain a different visa (e.g., O-1 or green card), or enter a new program (e.g., a master's degree). As the number of student and exchange visitor visas issued each year has grown to be an order of magnitude larger than the H-1B visa cap (which also covers many applicants other than graduating students), the mismatch in program sizes has become acute.

An important policy question is how the United States might smooth school-to-work transitions. Many countries provide a guaranteed right to work for a period of time for students graduating their universities (e.g., three to five years regardless of degree); even from a narrow perspective, recent graduates and younger workers tend to be fiscal contributors by paying more in taxes than receiving in benefits. Policy makers may want to consider these adjustments on their own, but they would also become important under certain reforms, contemplated above, to increase the skill content of the H-1B program. For example, with wage ranking or high H-1B minimum wages, a fresh college graduate would be disadvantaged compared to an established worker. A hybrid model would provide workers a greater defined time before they need to compete for an H-1B slot.

Another common proposal is to "staple" a green card to any advanced STEM degree granted by a qualified US school to an immigrant. The staple proposal is a conceptually simple response to the challenges of school-to-work transition, and it would likely boost entrepreneurship and innovation outcomes to some degree. A challenge to the idea is the scope of unintended consequences by attaching automatic rights to degrees. For example, comparable policies in other countries have encountered "diploma mills" that offer qualifying degrees under conditions that legislators had not anticipated.[17] Even traditional US schools have already shown an increasing reliance on foreign students to help support themselves financially (e.g., Bird and Turner 2014; Bound et al. 2020).

3.3.3   Potential Reforms to Broader Immigration Structure

Closing this section, we note briefly the larger context of US immigration reform. The proposals described above could all likely boost the entrepreneurial and innovation output of US immigration without any change to the broad structure that favors family reunification. In 2016, approximately 12 percent of US green cards went for employment-based purposes, 68 percent for family reunification, and 20 percent for other purposes (e.g., diversity, humanitarian). This allocation is quite different from those of other countries with high levels of immigration, such as Canada, where a majority of slots are for employment-based purposes.

Comprehensive immigration reform could seek to change the overall level of immigration into America (i.e., increasing or decreasing the approximately 1 million green cards issued each year) or the relative allocation of types of green cards. Proposals often connect such a move to the adoption of a point-based system, including programs seeking to reduce immigration (e.g., the 2017 proposed Reforming American Immigration for Strong Employment [RAISE] Act[18]) and those seeking to expand it (e.g., proposals from the New American Economy). It is likely that an increase in levels or a composition shift toward employment-based migrants would boost entrepreneurial and innovation outcomes. For example, Hunt (2011) shows that immigrants entering through student and work visas are more likely to conduct entrepreneurial and innovative activities than those entering via other visa types. That said, this would constitute only one element of the substantial mix of political, social, cultural, and economic factors that matter for comprehensive reform.

3.4   Visas for Entrepreneurs

While countries have for decades adopted policies to attract and admit highly skilled immigrants, there is a recent and increasing interest in attract-

17. See "UK Rolls Out New Service to Help Fight Diploma Mills and Degree Fraud," ICEF Monitor, June 15, 2015, http://monitor.icef.com/2015/06/uk-rolls-out-new-service-to-help -fight-diploma-mills-and-degree-fraud/.
18. See Julia Gelatt, "The RAISE Act: Dramatic Change to Family Immigration, Less So for the Employment-Based System," Migration Policy Institute, August 2017, https://www.migration policy.org/news/raise-act-dramatic-change-family-immigration-less-so-employment-based -system.

ing immigrant entrepreneurs. This is especially true around high-tech and high-growth start-ups.[19] As immigrants display higher rates of entrepreneurship in the United States and many other countries, policy makers often consider immigration as a way to increase the supply of would-be entrepreneurs. This has resulted in a flurry of new entrepreneur visas: for example, Australia created a visa for immigrants with entrepreneurial skills in 2012, the United Kingdom introduced a new entrepreneur visa in 2008, and Canada created a similar program in 2013.

This section considers the special case of a start-up visa for America. We first review some of the established pathways for immigrant entrepreneurs under the US system and the challenges encountered. We then examine key dimensions of start-up visas seen in other countries. This segues to a review of US legislative proposals for a start-up visa act over the last decade, which have all thus far failed to make it to law, and some of the reforms that have happened.

3.4.1   Traits of Immigrant-Founded Companies

One newly available data source to characterize the contributions of immigrant entrepreneurs is the 2014 American Survey of Entrepreneurship (ASE). The 2014 ASE asked firms about their innovation activity and R&D efforts, in addition to posing standard questions regarding firm and owner characteristics. The ASE identifies the birthplaces of firm owners, allowing us to identify companies as native owners only, immigrant owners only, or mixed ownership. We focus our analysis on new firms founded in the past five years to align with entrepreneurship activity (versus transfer of businesses across owners) and in which one of the current owners was an original business founder.

Table 3.1 presents some simple tabulations. The full and weighted sample accounts for approximately 557,000 firms, with counts rounded per Census Bureau disclosure requirements. Of these ventures, 21.3 percent are entirely immigrant owned and 4.5 percent are immigrant owned in part. The table next provides for each column the share of ventures reporting the indicated activity. Firms with immigrant owners engage modestly more in R&D and innovation than firms with only native owners. Mixed-founding teams show the greatest engagement in R&D and innovation, although this is partly because a mixed ownership team tends to be larger than a native- or immigrant-only ownership team (by definition, there must be at least two owners on a mixed team). Firms with immigrant owners are also more likely to be seeking expansion capital.

The last two rows use data on start-up financing to isolate 6,700 ventures

---

19. Anderson and Platzer (2006), Bengtsson and Hsu (2014), Fairlie (2012, 2013), Gompers, Mukharlyamov, and Xuan (2016), and Hegde and Tumlinson (2014) also consider immigrant roles among VC-backed companies and investors. Glaeser, Kerr, and Kerr (2015) and Haltiwanger, Jarmin, and Miranda (2013) describe employment growth and new firm formation.

Table 3.1   Immigrant entrepreneurship in 2014 Annual Survey of Entrepreneurs

	All firms (1)	Native only owners (2)	Immigrant only owners (3)	Mixed immigrant and native owners (4)
Ownership composition of ventures in ASE (N = 557,000)		74.2%	21.3%	4.5%
Share with granted and/or pending patents	1.5%	1.3%	1.3%	5.1%
Share reporting positive R&D expenditures	5.5%	5.1%	5.9%	10.3%
Share reporting owner(s) engaged in R&D	4.5%	4.4%	4.8%	3.7%
Share reporting workers engaged in R&D	2.4%	2.3%	2.6%	4.1%
Share seeking expansion financing	27.4%	26.7%	28.4%	33.0%
Share seeking expansion financing from venture capital firms	1.5%	1.2%	1.6%	5.1%
Ownership composition of ventures in ASE raising start-up venture and grant investment equal to or greater than $250,000 (N = 6,700)	100.0%	73.0%	13.2%	13.8%
Mean investment levels among these ventures	$1,057,000	$1,020,000	$1,265,000	$1,050,000

Notes: Sample includes firms founded in 2009–2014 where at least one of the current owners was a firm founder. Sample excludes firms where start-up funding source was unknown or not reported or owner immigrant status was unknown or not reported. Venture counts are weighted and rounded per Census Bureau disclosure requirements. Reported percentages are calculated from rounded counts.

raising $250,000 or more in private venture investment or public grants. Many start-up visa proposals suggest providing visas to immigrant founders who can raise this amount of start-up capital from either of these external financing sources. Such ventures in total account for a little over 1.2 percent of new ventures in the ASE sample. Firms with exclusively immigrant owners account for 13.2 percent of start-ups hitting these thresholds, and mixed teams account for another 13.8 percent. Ventures raising private venture investment or public grants at positive amounts less than $250,000 account for about 2 percent of the ASE sample and have comparable immigrant ownership.

These tabulations confirm several important features of immigrant entrepreneurship, including the overall role of immigrant founders and their stronger proclivity toward innovative activities (e.g., Kahn, Mattina, and MacGarvie 2017). They also provide a sense of the relative shares of existing immigrant entrepreneurship that would have qualified for visas under some proposals. Existing experiences cannot forecast latent demand for new visas that are created, but they provide a sense of what policy makers may want to target.

3.4.2   Pathways for Immigrant Entrepreneurs

Many countries encourage the immigration of wealthy individuals willing to invest in a business that provides employment in the host country. The United States has an EB-5 permanent residency track for those willing and able to invest $1.8 million into a US business. This minimum investment is an increase from the $1 million required before November 2019. If the investment is made into so-called targeted employment areas that are rural or struggle with high unemployment rates, the minimum requirement is $900,000 (up from $500,000). Going forward, USCIS plans to adjust the index every five years according to inflation. The business must generate at least 10 full-time positions for American workers. The program provides a maximum of 10,000 visas per year, and this allotment is mostly reached each year.[20]

Aspiring immigrant entrepreneurs without this personal wealth who are not US permanent residents have two primary options for building a start-up. The first option involves engaging in preliminary business planning while enrolled under F-1 status as a student, using the OPT period to launch and build the company, and then transitioning to an employment-based visa such as the O-1 or a self-petitioned green card via the EB-1A or EB-2 National Interest Waiver (NIW) category. The second option is to obtain

20. See US Department of State, "Report of the Visa Office 2018," https://travel.state.gov /content/travel/en/legal/visa-law0/visa-statistics/annual-reports/report-of-the-visa-office -2018.html; US Citizenship and Immigration Services, "About the EB-5 Visa Classification," updated March 25, 2021, https://www.uscis.gov/working-united-states/permanent-workers /about-eb-5-visa-classification.

an employment-based visa like an H-1B, engage in preliminary business planning (without engaging in unauthorized employment or violating the terms of one's employment agreement), and then pursuing a green card from one's employer or from one of the aforementioned self-petition options. Blume-Kohout (2016) provides a complete description of these and other rarer routes.

These types of immigrant pathways are not well designed for entrepreneurs. The legal fees, uncertainty, and high adjudication standard involved in obtaining an O-1, EB-1A, or EB-2 NIW and employers' general reluctance to sponsor green cards often deter aspiring entrepreneurs. Roach and Skrentny (2019) measure in STEM fields the particular underrepresentation of immigrant PhDs working in tech start-ups compared to both their native peers and also to the expressed initial desire of the immigrants to be in a start-up. In a companion piece, Roach, Sauermann, and Skrentny (2020) identify the greater risk tolerance and alignment of personality traits of foreign PhD students to start-up activity, but the authors also show a gap between the early intentions of these students to be entrepreneurs and their employment outcomes after graduation. Roach, Sauermann, and Skrentny note that the limited capabilities of the US immigration system to support immigrant entrepreneurs likely plays an important role.

Consequently, a number of local attempts have sprung up to help immigrant entrepreneurs obtain the necessary employment authorization without waiting for permanent residency. Under the American Competitiveness in the Twenty-First Century Act of 2000, Congress made institutions of higher education and nonprofit organizations exempt from the H-1B numerical cap. In 2014, the Massachusetts state legislature created an Entrepreneur in Residence (EiR) program whereby immigrant entrepreneurs with advanced STEM degrees could be sponsored on cap-exempt H-1B visas via working part-time at the University of Massachusetts Boston and part-time on their Massachusetts-headquartered start-ups. According to Global EiR Coalition, 13 such programs now exist at institutions such as the University of Colorado, Boulder, and the University of Missouri, St. Louis.[21] Some venture capital firms have also devised packages that combine employment-connected visa sponsorship (the entrepreneur works as an employee of the VC firm) with monetary investment.[22]

21. See Innovation Institute at the MassTech Collaborative, "What Is GEIR?," https://innovation.masstech.org/projects-and-initiatives/global-entrepreneur-residence-pilot-program; GlobalEIR, "Global EIR Locations," https://www.globaleir.org/global-eir-locations/.

22. See Jordan Crook, "Unshackled Is a New $3.5M Early Stage Fund That Looks a Lot Like an Accelerator," TechCrunch, November 13, 2014, https://techcrunch.com/2014/11/13/unshackled-is-a-new-3-5m-early-stage-fund-that-looks-a-lot-like-an-accelerator/. Several local policy initiatives have also sought to attract and welcome immigrant entrepreneurs more broadly (e.g., the Thrive competition in New York City and the Office of New Americans in Chicago). Some initiatives focus on specific issues that have been found to inhibit immigrant entrepreneurs from starting or growing their businesses (e.g., language barriers, difficulty navi-

3.4.3   International Examples

Even though every country promotes the unique nature of its start-up visas, the visas tend to share many common features.[23] In particular, start-up visas tend to impose minimum requirements around one or more of these criteria: (1) the degree of establishment of the company, (2) the extent of ownership of the founding team, (3) the qualifications of the entrepreneur, (4) the economic impact of the venture, and (5) the financial self-sufficiency of the entrepreneur.

- *Degree of establishment of the company*: Countries typically require that ventures be less than a certain number of years old, with Singapore setting the bar at six months versus Ireland at six years. Countries also require that entrepreneurs invest a minimum amount of money in their start-ups (at least €75,000 in the case of Ireland). On a qualitative level, countries often require that entrepreneurs submit a business plan for evaluation, as in the case of Denmark and Spain. Some countries may even require that companies be endorsed by an official body (e.g., the United Kingdom's Home Office) or that founders show evidence of professional or commercial ties within the country (e.g., Sweden).
- *Extent of ownership of the founding team*: Countries typically require that petitioners own a minimum share of their company, with Sweden and Canada both requiring that founders own a controlling stake, but with Canada permitting a founding team of up to five.
- *Qualifications of the entrepreneur*: Countries often impose requirements around language proficiency, minimum levels of related experience, and/or minimum levels of educational attainment. For example, France seeks at least a master's degree or five years of professional work experience. Australia requires petitioners be under the age of 55.
- *Economic impact of the venture*: In addition to requiring that the start-up be located in their country, countries often screen ventures based on their economic impact. Sweden, for example, requires that start-ups produce and/or sell their services or goods within Sweden. Ireland requires evidence that a given start-up plan be "capable of creating 10 jobs in Ireland and realizing €1 million in sales within three to four years of starting up." Some countries offer preferential treatment to entrepreneurs who intend to build businesses within certain high-value sectors. New Zealand, for example, waives its minimum NZ$100,000 (approxi-

gating the legal steps to start a company, or lack of capital to pilot projects), while others are generally focused on attracting more new businesses.

23. Sources for this section are given at the end of the chapter. An online appendix for the chapter describes country-level visa programs in greater detail. See S. P. Kerr and W. R. Kerr, "Immigration Policy Levers for US Innovation and Startups," NBER Appendix (Cambridge, MA: National Bureau of Economic Research), http://www.nber.org/data-appendix/c14424/201118-KK-Appendix.pdf.

mately US$70,000) investment requirement for companies related to science, information and communications technology, or "other high value export-oriented sector." Thailand's start-up visa is specifically tailored to entrepreneurs operating within 13 priority industries such as "next-generation automotive," "smart electronics," "agriculture and biotechnology," and "food for the future."

- *Financial self-sufficiency of the entrepreneur*: Countries typically require that entrepreneurs show minimum personal assets. For example, Sweden requires SEK200,000 (approximately US$23,000) available for two years.

Countries differ on the terms and pathways to permanent residency and citizenship they offer to foreign entrepreneurs. Thailand's visa is renewable every two years, though it offers no obvious path to permanent residence. Similarly, Ireland issues entrepreneur visas with an initial validity period of two years, after which the visa may be extended for three years, then for five years. However, the Irish government expressly states that it "does not provide for preferential access to citizenship for successful applicants" of its start-up visa program. By contrast, Australia offers a path to permanent residence for entrepreneurs who demonstrate "2 key success factors, or 1 key success factor and 3 supporting success factors." Examples of key success factors are employing two or more Australians, generating an annual turnover of at least AUD300,000 (approximately US$228,000), and filing a provisional patent. Supporting success factors are more qualitative, such as "adapting [one's] entrepreneurial activities into other business areas" and "receiving formal awards or recognition."

Most host countries would like to attract successful entrepreneurs, yet half of start-ups fail within the first five years. As it is hard to predict which businesses will succeed, countries often admit immigrant entrepreneurs who look promising and then observe their success over the duration of their stay. These conditional visas can be renewed (or converted to a permanent residence permit) if the business remains successful within a few years. Australia, New Zealand, Ireland, Singapore, and the United Kingdom have established versions of this approach. It is important to recognize, however, a tension in making start-up visas conditional on success. Policy makers often dream of attracting start-ups with exceptional potential for employment growth and economic impact, but these exceptional outcomes involve lots of experimentation with ideas (Kerr, Nanda, and Rhodes-Kropf 2014). Making visas conditional on success may push immigrant founders toward less risky ventures until their permanent residency is established.

A related point of tension is regional distribution. Some countries, such as Canada, provide visa set-asides or other incentives for entrepreneurs to locate outside the most prominent technological or economic clusters. (These policies mirror the reduced investment requirements for a US EB-5 visa if the investment is made into targeted employment areas. Regional policies are also frequent in employment visas.) These regional policies can serve to spread out the distribution of locations impacted by immigrant entrepreneurs, and they may be an important aspect of gaining political buy-in. It is possible, however, that constraining the spatial choices of entrepreneurs may lead to fewer start-ups pursuing high-scale growth outcomes that are often more easily pursued in prominent clusters.

3.4.4   US Start-Up Visa Proposals

Over the last decade, both Democrats and Republicans have introduced and supported approximately two dozen bills in both the House and Senate during every session of Congress in support of a start-up visa. Though the vast majority of bills have received bipartisan support, none have emerged successfully from committee, been approved by both chambers, and been enacted into law.

The spirit of most proposed bills is similar: to charge the Secretary of Homeland Security with authorizing a certain number of start-up visas— often 75,000—to entrepreneurs who satisfy minimum requirements. Requirements typically include minimum ownership (either "significant ownership" or a controlling interest), minimum funding from qualifying investors or venture capitalists, and/or the ability to generate revenue and create full-time jobs within the United States. Some bills have also stipulated that entrepreneurs possess a minimum amount in assets or have an annual income exceeding a certain threshold above the federal poverty level. Some bills have required that entrepreneurs possess either an unexpired H-1B visa or a master's degree in STEM or another relevant academic discipline from a US school.[24]

Shortly after the "Startup Act 3.0" act was introduced in the House and Senate in 2013, the Ewing Marion Kauffman Foundation published a study by Stangler and Konczal (2013) that estimated the job-creation impact of a start-up visa. When using the legislative minimum requirements and typical venture survival rates, the authors derived a lower bound, estimating that four-year-old start-ups would create nearly 500,000 new jobs after 10 years. If further assuming that half the start-up visa companies would be technology and engineering companies and their employment levels would grow beyond the minimum thresholds to reflect typical industry averages, the authors derived a larger estimate of 1.6 million new jobs. Given that their methodology did not model the potential of start-up visa companies to become high-growth, become high-scale, and positively impact innovation,

24. See Attracting and Retaining Entrepreneurs Act, S. 3510, 114th Congress, 2016, https://www.congress.gov/bill/114th-congress/senate-bill/3510/text; StartUp Visa Act of 2011, S. 565, 112th Congress, 2011, https://www.congress.gov/bill/112th-congress/senate-bill/565/text.

GDP, and productivity, the Kauffman Foundation deemed its range "conservative" and "low-end."

In 2019, the "Startup Act" was introduced on a bipartisan basis within the Senate and then referred to committee. The bill sought to authorize the Secretary of Homeland Security to issue up to 75,000 "conditional immigrant" visas to entrepreneurs who register a new business, employ at least two full-time employees, and invest or raise at least $100,000 in the business within the first year. For the following three years, entrepreneurs would be required to employ an average of at least five full-time employees in order to remove the conditional basis of their visa.[25]

3.4.5   US Modifications Related to Start-Up Founders

Although congressional proposals have failed to pass both the House and Senate, two recent reforms at the federal level influenced the potential vitality of US immigrant entrepreneurship: the "Matter of Dhanasar," and the International Entrepreneur Rule.

In December 2016, the USCIS's Administrative Appeals Office (AAO) published a decision titled the Matter of Dhanasar. The decision updated the USCIS's analytical framework for assessing eligibility for National Interest Waivers (NIWs), which permit immigrants to self-petition for a green card without an employer sponsor or related labor certification. Under a 1998 precedent, petitioners for a NIW under the EB-2 category had to demonstrate that (1) the petitioner's area of employment is of "substantial intrinsic merit," (2) any proposed benefit from the individual's endeavors will be "national in scope," and (3) the national interest would be adversely affected if a labor certification were required.[26] The 2016 revision was due in part to the belief that the "third prong was especially problematic for certain petitioners, such as entrepreneurs and self-employed individuals."

The updated criteria now require "(1) that the foreign national's proposed endeavor has both substantial merit and national importance; (2) that the foreign national is well positioned to advance the proposed endeavor; and (3) that, on balance, it would be beneficial to the United States to waive the requirements of a job offer and thus of a labor certification." In its decision, the AAO specifically noted that the first prong "may be demonstrated in a range of areas such as business, entrepreneurialism," among others. The decision also noted that the USCIS recognized "that forecasting feasibility or future success may present challenges to petitioners and USCIS officers,

25. See Startup Act, S. 328, 116th Congress, 2019, https://www.congress.gov/bill/116th-congress/senate-bill/328/text.

26. A labor certification is required to "certify to the USCIS that there are not sufficient U.S. workers able, willing, qualified and available to accept the job opportunity in the area of intended employment and that employment of the foreign worker will not adversely affect the wages and working conditions of similarly employed U.S. workers." See Employment and Training Administration, "Permanent Labor Certification," US Department of Labor, https://www.foreignlaborcert.doleta.gov/perm.cfm.

and that many innovations and entrepreneurial endeavors may ultimately fail, in whole or in part, despite an intelligent plan and competent execution" and that it did not "require petitioners to demonstrate that their endeavors are more likely than not to ultimately succeed."[27] Though not decided with the express intent of spurring US immigrant entrepreneurship, the ruling effectively reformulated the EB-2 NIW category into one that is now more favorable to aspiring immigrant entrepreneurs.

In January of 2017, the DHS, under the Obama administration, published the International Entrepreneur Rule, a rule permitting the DHS to extend a discretionary grant of parole lasting up to 30 months (2.5 years) to entrepreneurs. Entrepreneurs must (1) possess at least 10 percent ownership interest in a start-up created within the last five years, (2) have an active and central role in the operations and future growth of the entity, (3) have secured a minimum of $100,000 from government grants or at least $250,000 from a qualified US investor for the business, and (4) demonstrate evidence of substantial potential for rapid business growth or job creation. In July 2017 the DHS published a delay rule, and in May 2018 the department proposed to eliminate the rule "because the department believes that it represents an overly broad interpretation of parole authority, lacks sufficient protections for US workers and investors, and is not the appropriate vehicle for attracting and retaining international entrepreneurs."[28]

3.5   Conclusions

Immigrants have played a substantial role in US invention and entrepreneurship over the last several decades (Kerr 2019a). Further growth in these forms of immigrant contributions will be challenging under the current US immigration structure due to numerical caps at key transition points, especially the H-1B program size and the country caps on the rate at which employment-based green cards are awarded. The United States also lacks a start-up visa comparable to those developed over the last decade by many peer countries. This chapter has reviewed several policy reforms that would likely alleviate these constraints and foster greater US invention and entre-

27. See Administrative Appeals Office, "Matter of DHANASAR, Petitioner," December 27, 2016, https://www.justice.gov/eoir/page/file/920996/download; US Citizenship and Immigration Services, "Employment-Based Immigration: Second Preference EB-2," updated December 2, 2020, https://www.uscis.gov/working-united-states/permanent-workers/employment-based-immigration-second-preference-eb-2.

28. See Department of Homeland Security, "International Entrepreneur Rule," *Federal Register*, January 17, 2017, https://www.federalregister.gov/documents/2017/01/17/2017-00481/international-entrepreneur-rule; Department of Homeland Security, "International Entrepreneur Rule: Delay of Effective Date," *Federal Register*, July 11, 2017, https://www.federalregister.gov/documents/2017/07/11/2017-14619/international-entrepreneur-rule-delay-of-effective-date; US Citizenship and Immigration Services, "International Entrepreneur Parole," updated May 25, 2018, https://www.uscis.gov/humanitarian/humanitarian-parole/international-entrepreneur-parole.

preneurship going forward. Like all policy choices regarding immigration, these economic considerations are a single factor in larger political dynamics.

Start-Up Visa Information:

- Australia: https://immi.homeaffairs.gov.au/visas/getting-a-visa/visa-listing/business-innovation-and-investment-888/entrepreneur-stream#Eligibility
- Canada: https://www.canada.ca/en/immigration-refugees-citizenship/services/immigrate-canada/start-visa/eligibility.html
- Denmark: https://www.nyidanmark.dk/en-GB/Applying/Work/Start-up%20Denmark
- France: https://france-visas.gouv.fr/en_US/web/france-visas/international-talents-and-economic-attractiveness
- Ireland: http://www.inis.gov.ie/en/INIS/Guidelines%20for%20Start-up%20Entrepreneur%20Programme.pdf/Files/Guidelines%20for%20Start-up%20Entrepreneur%20Programme.pdf
- New Zealand: https://www.immigration.govt.nz/documents/forms-and-guides/inz1221.pdf
- Singapore: https://www.mom.gov.sg/passes-and-permits/entrepass/eligibility
- Spain: http://www.exteriores.gob.es/Consulados/CIUDADDEL CABO/en/InformacionParaExtranjeros/Pages/Law-on-Visas-for-Entrepreneurs.aspx
- Sweden: https://www.migrationsverket.se/English/Private-individuals/Working-in-Sweden/Self-employment.html
- Thailand: https://www.boi.go.th/index.php?page=detail_smart_visa
- United Kingdom: https://www.gov.uk/guidance/immigration-rules/immigration-rules-appendix-w-immigration-rules-for-workers#part-w5-specific-requirements–start-up

References

Akcigit, U., S. Baslandze, and S. Stantcheva. 2016. "Taxation and the International Mobility of Inventors." *American Economic Review* 106 (10): 2930–81.
Akee, R. K. Q., D. A. Jaeger, and K. Tatsiramos. 2013. "The Persistence of Self-Employment across Borders: New Evidence on Legal Immigrants to the United States." *Economics Bulletin* 33 (1): 126–37.
Anderson, S. 2020a. "H-1B Denials Remain High, Especially for IT Services Companies." *Forbes*, February 26. https://www.forbes.com/sites/stuartanderson/2020/02/26/h-1b-denials-remain-high-especially-for-it-services-companies/.
———. 2020b. "Court Invalidates Key Trump Administration H-1B Visa Policies." *Forbes*, March 11. https://www.forbes.com/sites/stuartanderson/2020/03/11/court-invalidates-key-trump-administration-h-1b-visa-policies/.

Anderson, S., and M. Platzer. 2006. *American Made: The Impact of Immigrant Entrepreneurs and Professionals on U.S. Competitiveness*. National Venture Capital Association Report.

Audretsch, D., and M. Feldman. 1996. "R&D Spillovers and the Geography of Innovation and Production." *American Economic Review* 86: 630–40.

Azoulay, P., B. F. Jones, J. D. Kim, and J. Miranda. 2020. "Immigration and Entrepreneurship in the United States." NBER Working Paper No. 27778. Cambridge, MA: National Bureau of Economic Research.

Bengtsson, O., and D. Hsu. 2014. "Ethnic Matching in the U.S. Venture Capital Market." *Journal of Business Venturing* 30 (2): 338–54.

Bernstein, S., R. Diamond, T. McQuade, and B. Pousada. 2019. "The Contribution of High-Skilled Immigrants to Innovation in the United States." Working Paper. https://web.stanford.edu/~diamondr/BDMP_2019_0709.pdf.

Bird, K., and S. Turner. 2014. "College in the States: Foreign Student Demand and Higher Education Supply in the U.S." EdPolicyWorks Working Paper Series No. 23.

Bloom, N., J. Van Reenen, and H. Williams. 2019. "A Toolkit of Policies to Promote Innovation." *Journal of Economic Perspectives* 33 (3): 163–84.

Blume-Kohout, M. 2016. *Imported Entrepreneurs: Foreign-Born Scientists and Engineers in U.S. STEM Fields Entrepreneurship*. US Small Business Administration Report.

Borjas, G. 1986. "The Self-Employment Experience of Immigrants." *Journal of Human Resources* 21: 487–506.

Borjas, G., and K. Doran. 2012. "The Collapse of the Soviet Union and the Productivity of American Mathematicians." *Quarterly Journal of Economics* 127 (3): 1143–1203.

Bound, J., B. Braga, G. Khanna, and S. Turner. 2020. "A Passage to America: University Funding and International Students." *American Economic Journal: Economic Policy* 12 (1): 97–126.

Bound, J., M. Demiric, G. Khanna, and S. Turner. 2015. "Finishing Degrees and Finding Jobs: U.S. Higher Education and the Flow of Foreign IT Workers." In *Innovation Policy and the Economy*, vol. 15, edited by William Kerr, Josh Lerner, and Scott Stern, 27–72. Chicago: University of Chicago Press.

Bound, J., G. Khanna, and N. Morales. 2017. "Understanding the Economic Impact of the H-1B Program on the U.S." NBER Working Paper No. 23153. Cambridge, MA: National Bureau of Economic Research.

Brown, J. D., J. S. Earle, M. J. Kim, and K.-M. Lee. 2019. "Immigrant Entrepreneurs and Innovation in the US High Tech Sector." Census Bureau Working Paper.

Buchardi, K., T. Chaney, T. Hassan, L. Tarquinio, and S. Terry. 2019. "Immigration, Innovation, and Growth." NBER Working Paper No. 27075. Cambridge, MA: National Bureau of Economic Research.

Carlino, G., and W. R. Kerr. 2015. "Agglomeration and Innovation." In *Handbook of Urban and Regional Economics*, vol. 5, edited by G. Duranton, V. Henderson, and W. Strange, 349–404. Amsterdam: North-Holland.

Chung, W., and A. Kalnins. 2006. "Social Capital, Geography, and the Survival: Gujarati Immigrant Entrepreneurs in the U.S. Lodging Industry." *Management Science* 52 (2): 233–47.

Clark, K., and S. Drinkwater. 2000. "Pushed Out or Pulled In? Self-Employment among Ethnic Minorities in England and Wales." *Labour Economics* 7 (5): 603–28.

———. 2006. "Changing Patterns of Ethnic Minority Self-Employment in Britain: Evidence from Census Microdata." IZA Discussion Papers 2495, Institute for the Study of Labor (IZA).

Clemens, M. A. 2011. "Economics and Emigration: Trillion-Dollar Bills on the Sidewalk?" *Journal of Economic Perspectives* 25 (3): 83–106.

Decker, R., J. Haltiwanger, R. Jarmin, and J. Miranda. 2014. "The Role of Entrepreneurship in US Job Creation and Economic Dynamism." *Journal of Economic Perspectives* 28 (3): 3–24.

Depew, B., P. Norlander, and T. Sorensen. 2017. "Inter-Firm Mobility and Return Migration Patterns of Skilled Guest Workers." *Journal of Population Economics* 30 (2): 681–721.

Dimmock, S. G., J. Huang, and S. Weisbenner. 2019. "Give Me Your Tired, Your Poor, Your High-Skilled Labor: H-1B Lottery Outcomes and Entrepreneurial Success." NBER Working Paper No. 26392. Cambridge, MA: National Bureau of Economic Research.

Docquier, F., R. Turati, J. Valette, and C. Vasilakis. 2020. "Birthplace Diversity and Economic Growth: Evidence from the US States in the Post–World War II Period." *Journal of Economic Geography* 20 (2): 321–54.

Doran, K., A. Gelber, and A. Isen. 2015. "The Effects of High-Skill Immigration on Firms: Evidence from H-1B Visa Lotteries." NBER Working Paper No. 20668. Cambridge, MA: National Bureau of Economic Research.

Doran, K., and C. Yoon. 2019. "Immigration and Invention: Evidence from the Quota Acts." Working Paper. https://www3.nd.edu/~kdoran/Doran_Quotas.pdf.

Fairlie, R. W. 2012. *Immigrant Entrepreneurs and Small Business Owners, and Their Access to Financial Capital.* US Small Business Administration Report.

———. 2013. "Minority and Immigrant Entrepreneurs: Access to Financial Capital." In *International Handbook on the Economics of Migration*, edited by A. F. Constant and K. F. Zimmermann, 153–75. Cheltenham, UK: Edward Elgar.

Fairlie, R. W., and M. Lofstrom. 2014. "Immigration and Entrepreneurship." In *Handbook on the Economics of International Migration*, edited by B. R. Chiswick and P. W. Miller, 877–911. Amsterdam: Elsevier.

Fairlie, R. W., and B. D. Meyer. 2003. "The Effect of Immigration on Native Self-Employment." *Journal of Labor Economics* 21 (3): 619–50.

Fairlie, R. W., J. Zissimopoulos, and H. A. Krashinsky. 2010. "The International Asian Business Success Story: A Comparison of Chinese, Indian, and Other Asian Businesses in the United States, Canada, and United Kingdom." In *International Differences in Entrepreneurship*, edited by J. Lerner and A. Schoar, 179–208. Chicago: University of Chicago Press.

Fallick, B., C. Fleischman, and J. Rebitzer. 2006. "Job-Hopping in Silicon Valley: Some Evidence Concerning the Microfoundations of a High-Technology Cluster." *Review of Economics and Statistics* 88 (3): 472–81.

Feldman, M., and D. Kogler. 2010. "Stylized Facts in the Geography of Innovation." In *Handbook of the Economics of Innovation*, vol. 1, edited by B. Hall and N. Rosenberg, 381–410. Oxford: Elsevier.

Ghimire, K. 2018. "Supply of Immigrant Entrepreneurs and Native Entrepreneurship." Working Paper. https://ssrn.com/abstract=3248842.

Glaeser, E., S. P. Kerr, and W. R. Kerr. 2015. "Entrepreneurship and Urban Growth: An Empirical Assessment with Historical Mines." *Review of Economics and Statistics* 97 (2): 498–520.

Glennon, B. 2019. "How Do Restrictions on High-Skilled Immigration Affect Offshoring? Evidence from the H-1B Program." NBER Working Paper No. 27538. Cambridge, MA: National Bureau of Economic Research.

Gompers, P. A., V. Mukharlyamov, and Y. Xuan. 2016. "The Cost of Friendship." *Journal of Financial Economics* 119 (3): 626–44.

Goolsbee, A. 1998. "Does Government R&D Policy Mainly Benefit Scientists and Engineers?" *American Economic Review* 88 (2): 298–302.

Haltiwanger, J., R. Jarmin, and J. Miranda. 2013. "Who Creates Jobs? Small vs. Large vs. Young." *Review of Economics and Statistics* 95 (2): 347–61.

Hart, D. M., and Z. J. Acs. 2011. "High-Tech Immigrant Entrepreneurship in the United States." *Economic Development Quarterly* 25 (2): 116–29.

Hegde, D., and J. Tumlinson. 2014. "Does Social Proximity Enhance Business Relationships? Theory and Evidence from Ethnicity's Role in US Venture Capital." *Management Science* 60 (9): 2355–80,

Hira, R. 2010. "The H-1B and L-1 Visa Programs: Out of Control." EPI Briefing Paper. Washington, DC: Economic Policy Institute.

Hunt, J. 2011. "Which Immigrants Are Most Innovative and Entrepreneurial? Distinctions by Entry Visa." *Journal of Labor Economics* 29 (3): 417–57.

———. 2015. "Are Immigrants the Most Skilled US Computer and Engineering Workers?" *Journal of Labor Economics* 33 (S1): S39–77.

———. 2017. "How Restricted Is the Job Mobility of Skilled Temporary Work Visa Holders?" NBER Working Paper No. 23529. Cambridge, MA: National Bureau of Economic Research.

Hunt, J., and M. Gauthier-Loiselle. 2010. "How Much Does Immigration Boost Innovation?" *American Economic Journal: Macroeconomics* 2 (2): 31–56.

Kahn, S., and M. MacGarvie. 2018. "The Impact of Permanent Residency Delays for STEM PhDs: Who leaves and Why." NBER Working Paper No. 25175. Cambridge, MA: National Bureau of Economic Research.

Kahn, S., G. Mattina, and M. MacGarvie. 2017. "Misfits, Stars, and Immigrant Entrepreneurship." *Small Business Economics* 49 (3): 533–57.

Kato, T., and C. Sparber. 2013. "Quotas and Quality: The Effect of H-1B Visa Restrictions on the Pool of Prospective Undergraduate Students from Abroad." *Review of Economics and Statistics* 95 (1): 109–26.

Kerr, S. P., and W. R. Kerr. 2013. "Immigration and Employer Transitions for STEM Workers." *American Economic Review Papers and Proceedings* 103 (3): 193–7.

———. 2017. "Immigrant Entrepreneurship." In *Measuring Entrepreneurial Businesses: Current Knowledge and Challenges*, edited by J. Haltiwanger, E. Hurst, J. Miranda, and A. Schoar, 187–249. Chicago: University of Chicago Press.

———. 2020. "Immigrant Entrepreneurship in America: Evidence from the Survey of Business Owners 2007 & 2012." *Research Policy* 49 (3): 103918.

Kerr, S. P., W. R. Kerr, and W. F. Lincoln. 2015a. "Firms and the Economics of Skilled Immigration." In *Innovation Policy and the Economy*, vol. 15, edited by W. R. Kerr, J. Lerner, and S. Stern, 115–52. Chicago: University of Chicago Press.

———. 2015b. "Skilled Immigration and the Employment Structures of U.S. Firms." *Journal of Labor Economics* 33 (S1): S109–45.

Kerr, S. P., W. R. Kerr, Ç. Özden, and C. Parsons. 2016. "Global Talent Flows." *Journal of Economic Perspectives* 30 (4): 83–106.

———. 2017. "High-Skilled Migration and Agglomeration." *Annual Review of Economics* 9: 201–34.

Kerr, W. R. 2008. "Ethnic Scientific Communities and International Technology Diffusion." *Review of Economics and Statistics* 90 (3): 518–37.

———. 2010. "Breakthrough Inventions and Migrating Clusters of Innovation." *Journal of Urban Economics* 67 (1): 46–60.

———. 2017. "U.S. High-Skilled Immigration, Innovation, and Entrepreneurship: Empirical Approaches and Evidence." In *The International Mobility of Talent and Innovation: New Evidence and Policy Implications*, edited by C. Fink and E. Miguelez, 193–221. Cambridge: Cambridge University Press.

———. 2019a. *The Gift of Global Talent: How Migration Shapes Business, Economy and Society.* Palo Alto, CA: Stanford University Press.

———. 2019b. "The Gift of Global Talent: Innovation Policy and the Economy." In *Innovation Policy and the Economy*, vol. 20, edited by J. Lerner and S. Stern, 1–37. Chicago: University of Chicago Press.

Kerr, W. R., and W. F. Lincoln. 2010. "The Supply Side of Innovation: H-1B Visa Reforms and U.S. Ethnic Invention." *Journal of Labor Economics* 28 (3): 473–508.

Kerr, W. R. and M. Mandorff. 2015. "Social Networks, Ethnicity, and Entrepreneurship." NBER Working Paper No. 21597. Cambridge, MA: National Bureau of Economic Research.

Kerr, W. R., R. Nanda, and M. Rhodes-Kropf. 2014. "Entrepreneurship as Experimentation." *Journal of Economic Perspectives* 28 (3): 25–48.

Kerr, W. R., and F. Robert-Nicoud. 2020. "Tech Clusters." *Journal of Economic Perspectives* 34 (3): 50–76.

Lewis, E., and G. Peri. 2015. "Immigration and the Economy of Cities and Regions." In *Handbook of Urban and Regional Economics*, vol. 5, edited by G. Duranton, V. Henderson, and W. Strange, 625–85. Amsterdam: North-Holland.

Lofstrom, M. 2002. "Labor Market Assimilation and the Self-Employment Decision of Immigrant Entrepreneurs." *Journal of Population Economics* 15 (1): 83–114.

Matloff, N. 2003. "On the Need for Reform of the H-1B Non-Immigrant Work Visa in Computer-Related Occupations." *University of Michigan Journal of Law Reform* 36 (4): 815–914.

Mayda, A. M., F. Ortega, G. Peri, K. Shih, and C. Sparber. 2018. "The Effect of the H-1B Quota on the Employment and Selection of Foreign-Born Labor." *European Economic Review* 108: 105–28.

Moretti, E. 2019. "The Effect of High-Tech Clusters on the Productivity of Top Inventors." Center for Economic Policy Research Working Paper 13992.

Moser, P., and S. San. 2020. "Immigration, Science, and Invention: Evidence from the Quota Acts." Working Paper. https://ssrn.com/abstract=3558718.

Moser, P., A. Voena, and F. Waldinger. 2014. "German Jewish Emigres and U.S. Invention." *American Economic Review* 104 (10): 3222–55.

Nathan, M. 2015. "Same Difference? Minority Ethnic Inventors, Diversity and Innovation in the UK." *Journal of Economic Geography* 15 (1): 129–68.

Ottaviano, G., and G. Peri. 2006. "The Economic Value of Cultural Diversity: Evidence from US Cities." *Journal of Economic Geography* 6 (1): 9–44.

Patel, K., and F. Vella. 2013. "Immigrant Networks and Their Implications for Occupational Choice and Wages." *Review of Economics and Statistics* 95 (4): 1249–77.

Pathak, P. A., A. Rees-Jones, and T. Sönmez. 2020. "Immigration Lottery Design: Engineered and Coincidental Consequences of H-1B Reforms." NBER Working Paper No. 26767. Cambridge, MA: National Bureau of Economic Research.

Peri, G. 2007. "Higher Education, Innovation and Growth." In *Education and Training in Europe*, edited by G. Brunello, P. Garibaldi, and E. Wasmer, 56–70. Oxford: Oxford University Press.

———. 2012. *Rationalizing U.S. Immigration Policy: Reforms for Simplicity, Fairness, and Economic Growth.* Brookings Institution Report.

Peri, G., K. Shih, and C. Sparber. 2015. "STEM Workers, H-1B Visas and Productivity in US Cities." *Journal of Labor Economics* 33 (S1): S225–55.

Porter, M. E., J. W. Rivkin, M. A. Desai, K. M. Gehl, W. R. Kerr, and M. Raman. 2019. *A Recovery Squandered: The State of U.S. Competitiveness 2019.* Harvard Business School Report. https://www.hbs.edu/competitiveness/Documents/a-recovery-squandered.pdf.

Roach, M., H. Sauermann, and J. Skrentny. 2020. "Are Foreign PhDs More Entrepreneurial? Entrepreneurial Characteristics, Preferences and Outcomes of Native and Foreign Science and Engineering PhD Students." In *The Roles of Immigrants and Foreign Students in U.S. Science, Innovation, and Entrepreneurship*, edited by I. Ganguli, S. Kahn, and M. MacGarvie, 207–28. Chicago: University of Chicago Press.

Roach, M., and J. Skrentny. 2019. "Why Foreign STEM PhDs Are Unlikely to Work for U.S. Technology Startups." *Proceedings of the National Academy of Sciences* 116 (34): 16805–10.

Ruiz, N., and J. M. Krogstad. 2018. "East Coast and Texas Metros Had the Most H-1B Visas for Skilled Workers from 2010 to 2016." Pew Research Center, March 29. https://www.pewresearch.org/fact-tank/2018/03/29/h-1b-visa-approvals-by-us-metro-area.

Samila, S., and O. Sorenson. 2011. "Venture Capital, Entrepreneurship and Economic Growth." *Review of Economics and Statistics* 93: 338–49.

Saxenian, A. 1999. *Silicon Valley's New Immigrant Entrepreneurs*. San Francisco: Public Policy Institute of California.

———. 2002. "Silicon Valley's New Immigrant High-Growth Entrepreneurs." *Economic Development Quarterly* 16: 20–31.

Schuetze, H. J., and H. Antecol. 2007. "Immigration, Entrepreneurship and the Venture Start-Up Process: The Life Cycle of Entrepreneurial Ventures." In *International Handbook Series on Entrepreneurship*, vol. 3, edited by S. Parker, 107–35. New York: Springer.

Sparber, C. 2018. "Choosing Skilled Foreign-Born Workers: Evaluating Alternative Methods for Allocating H-1B Work Permits." *Industrial Relations* 57 (1): 3–34.

Stangler, D., and J. Konczal. 2013. *Give Me Your Entrepreneurs, Your Innovators: Estimating Employment Impact of a Startup Visa*. Ewing Marion Kauffman Foundation Report.

Stephan, P., and S. Levin. 2001. "Exceptional Contributions to US Science by the Foreign-Born and Foreign-Educated." *Population Research and Policy Review* 20 (1): 59–79.

Wadhwa, V., A. Saxenian, B. Rissing, and G. Gereffi. 2007. *America's New Immigrant Entrepreneurs*. Durham, NC: Duke University Master of Engineering Management Program and UC Berkeley School of Information.

Yeaple, S. 2018. "The Innovation Activities of Multinational Enterprises and the Demand for Skilled Worker, Non-Immigrant Visas." In *High-Skilled Migration to the United States and Its Economic Consequences*, edited by G. Hanson, W. Kerr, and S. Turner, 41–70. Chicago: University of Chicago Press.

Zucker, L., M. Darby, and M. Brewer. 1998. "Intellectual Human Capital and the Birth of U.S. Biotechnology Enterprises." *American Economic Review* 88 (1): 290–306.

4

Scientific Grant Funding

Pierre Azoulay and Danielle Li

The pharmaceutical firm Novartis made use of decades of research in the development of Gleevec, a remarkably effective treatment for chronic myelogenous leukemia (CML). Between the 1960s and 1980s, numerous studies funded by the National Institutes of Health (NIH) investigated the causes of CML, documenting the role of a specific gene mutation that leads tyrosine kinase, a common cell-signaling molecule, to become overactive. This understanding pointed to an approach for treating CML—the development of compounds to inhibit tyrosine kinase—which Novartis scientists then pursued. Beyond treating CML, Gleevec also served as a proof-of-concept that ushered in a new era of targeted cancer therapeutics (Wapner 2013).

Similarly, the National Science Foundation (NSF) did not anticipate laying the foundation for secure internet commerce when it awarded grant MCS76-74294, with the general-purpose title "concrete computational complexity," to a young MIT assistant professor named Ronald Rivest. Yet Rivest, together with colleagues Adi Shamir and Leonard Adleman, used the funds to develop the first public-key cryptosystem (named the RSA

Pierre Azoulay is the International Programs Professor of Management at the MIT Sloan School of Management and a research associate of the National Bureau of Economic Research.

Danielle Li is the Class of 1922 Career Development Professor and an associate professor at the MIT Sloan School of Management, and a faculty research fellow of the National Bureau of Economic Research.

We thank Ben Jones, Bhaven Sampat, Georg von Graevenitz, and Austan Goolsbee for useful suggestions. For acknowledgments, sources of research support, and disclosure of the authors' material financial relationships, if any, please see https://www.nber.org/books-and-chapters /innovation-and-public-policy/scientific-grant-funding.

algorithm, after the initials of its developers), thus revolutionizing the field of cryptography and enabling a myriad of applications for the transmission of data using digital signatures (Rivest, Shamir, and Adleman 1978).

While they impact different sectors of the economy, Gleevec and the RSA algorithm are innovations that share three essential traits. First, although they were eventually commercialized by private firms, each owes a clear intellectual debt to research grants awarded by public-sector entities: the NIH, the Department of Defense (DoD), and the NSF. Second, the grant funds were not earmarked with these specific outcomes in mind, but rather were given for general inquiries into the fields of genetics and theoretical computer science, without any conditions with respect to the purported "usefulness" of the recipients' work. Last, while these projects eventually led to tremendous societal gains, many other projects supported by the same agencies either failed outright or generated only incremental benefits.

These features capture both the promise and the pitfalls of investing in basic science: although nascent ideas hold the potential to have widespread and substantial impacts, it is very difficult to predict whether, when, or how they might do so. Moreover, even when the value of investments is clear, as in the cases above, it is often difficult to quantify. Together, this lack of predictability and traceability has made grant funding politically vulnerable.

Emerging research, however, has begun to provide concrete evidence that grants play a critical role in enabling and sustaining innovation. In their studies of funding for biomedical research, for instance, Azoulay et al. (2019b) and Li, Azoulay, and Sampat (2017) show that NIH-funded research lays the foundation on which private-sector science builds. Over 40 percent of NIH-funded grants produce research that is cited by a private-sector patent, and a single dollar in NIH funding translates into private-sector spillovers worth twice that amount, not counting any direct value of academic research or training. Howell (2017) studies applicants to the US Department of Energy's Small Business Innovation Research (SBIR) grant program, and finds that early-stage awards approximately double the probability that a firm receives subsequent venture capital (VC) and have a large and positive impact on patenting and revenues. Her results are consistent with the view that nondilutive funding of this type allows small firms to fund technology prototyping, thereby accelerating the translation of academic results into useful products.

Economists and historians have long acknowledged the key role played by institutions in translating scientific knowledge into welfare-enhancing innovations (Dasgupta and David 1994; Mokyr 2002; Rosenberg 1979). Perhaps because grant systems are ubiquitous in the research world, they have been treated as an immutable, taken-for-granted background institution for financing basic research. Relative to prizes or patents, they have received less scholarly attention, and the ample theoretical literature on procurement (Laffont and Tirole 1993) does not appear to recognize grants as a distinct class of contractual devices, offering at best a very stylized treatment of their optimal use and design (Gallini and Scotchmer 2002; Wright 1983).[1] Yet in a growing acknowledgement of its importance, empirical studies in the past decade have begun to examine the relationship between specific modes of science funding and the rate and direction of scientific inquiry. This chapter reviews the literature on scientific grants in an effort to suggest promising avenues for reforming this important—but understudied—funding mechanism.

Throughout, we emphasize three themes.

First, grants, patents, prizes, and research contracts play overlapping and mutually supportive roles in the research-funding ecosystem, with grants most effective when research is exploratory, and when it is likely to produce ample spillovers, both across domains and over time. These two features characterize much early-stage scientific research.

Second, grant programs must be designed in ways that recognize the possibility of failure. This entails encouraging recipients to take on scientific and technological risks, exploring new research avenues rather than sticking with safer and more conventional trajectories.

Third, funding agencies could consider encouraging the systematic evaluation of grant programs by comparing outcomes among scientists, institutions, or fields that receive funding with those that accrue to "control" scientists, institution, or fields that do not.

The chapter proceeds as follows. In the next section, we identify the circumstances under which grants may be preferred over alternatives such as patents, prizes, or traditional procurement contracts. After providing a brief history of scientific grant making, we highlight key design choices faced by science policy makers when setting up a grant system: (1) delineating the scope of the grant competition and the set of potential applicants; (2) choosing a method to select meritorious applications; (3) providing incentives for the winning applicants; and (4) evaluating outcomes. We discuss the current state of knowledge regarding trade-offs entailed by alternative design choices in each of these domains, highlighting many questions still open in light of the extant evidence. We conclude with a discussion of the role of scientific grants in the wider ecosystem of R&D funding, and suggest that funders consider using randomized, controlled experimentation as a way of identifying the specific funding practices worthy of systematic adoption—or abandonment.

---

1. Notable recent exceptions include the work of Price (2019), who offers a legal analysis of grant funding, and that of Ottaviani (2020), who provides a theoretical treatment of the challenges involved in allocating funds across heterogeneous fields.

4.1   Why Fund Scientific Research through Grants?

Ever since Vannevar Bush's report *Science: The Endless Frontier*, US policy makers have generally agreed that basic scientific research "creates the fund of new knowledge from which the practical applications of knowledge must be drawn" (Bush 1945). Because scientific knowledge often exhibits the characteristics of a public good, economists have argued that it would be underprovided by the private sector (Arrow 1962; Nelson 1959), thereby providing a rationale for public expenditures devoted to the funding of scientific research.[2]

However, it is one thing to argue that there is a role for public support of scientific investments, and quite another to determine what form such support should take. In this chapter, we examine one specific type of financial support often employed in advanced economies to fund investments in research: scientific grant funding.

Grants are upfront payments for the delivery of incompletely specified and noncontractable R&D output. Unlike research prizes, the funder must pay before there is any guarantee of a successful outcome. Unlike loans, one cannot ask for grant money back if a project fails. Unlike equity investments, the success of a project does not necessarily entitle the funder to any further rights. Unlike research contracts, the funder does not tell the researcher exactly what she wants him to deliver at the end of the research period. Unlike patents, successful grant applications do not confer any right to market exclusivity.

Grant systems also face implementation challenges. Scholars have noted the inefficiency inherent in a system where much of the effort sunk into writing unfunded proposals appears to be wasted (Gross and Bergstrom 2019); they have commented on the unfairness of a system which disproportionately rewards individuals and institutions skilled at grantsmanship (Lawrence 2009), and within which female and minority applicants appear to fare less well on average than white, male, or Asian applicants (Ginther et al. 2011); they have provided evidence that peer review sometimes filters out the most novel or creative proposals (Boudreau et al. 2016), or worse,

2. To be sure, the connection between investments in research and rising living standards or improved national defense has come under increasing political scrutiny (Brooks 1996). Economists and other social scientists have also developed a more nuanced understanding of the innovation process. Over time, they have come to challenge the assumption that for-profit firms would never invest in basic research (Rosenberg 1990), they have incorporated the complex motivations that often guide scientists in their theoretical and empirical studies (e.g., Azoulay, Graff Zivin, and Manso 2011; Dasgupta and David 1994), and they have questioned the validity of the distinction between "pure" and applied research in the first place (Stokes 1997). However, this improved understanding does not overturn Arrow and Nelson's basic insight: that the free market is unlikely to provide the necessary resources for the conduct of scientific research (Balconi, Brusoni, and Orsenigo 2010).

induces scientists to skew their agenda toward projects more likely to generate results in the short term (Azoulay, Graff Zivin, and Manso 2011).

Why, then, do grants exist?

We argue that grants are likely to be the most effective—and feasible—way to fund basic research when two fundamental conditions simultaneously hold. First, when the social value of a scientific finding likely exceeds its privately appropriable value. Second, when specifying the parameters of a desired research solution ahead of time is impossible. These twin conditions would appear to characterize much exploratory and early-stage research that is often labeled "basic" or "pure." We will also discuss two subsidiary arguments in favor of grant funding over alternative mechanisms: when potential research performers face financial constraints, and when investments take the form of general-purpose research infrastructure (as opposed to specific projects).

Limited or Undesirable Appropriability. There are many cases in which the value that innovations generate for society vastly exceeds what its inventor can be paid. Consider again the case of Gleevec. In addition to being a scientific breakthrough, the drug was also a financial blockbuster for Novartis, earning the company a peak of $4.65 billion in revenue in 2015 prior to generic entry. Did the promise of such rewards under the patent system provide Novartis with sufficient incentives to develop Gleevec? While Novartis did indeed invest considerable resources in R&D once a candidate drug molecule had been identified, the vast majority of research investments that made Gleevec possible were made long before Novartis started development activities, indeed long before the idea of a treatment approach for CML even existed (Hunter 2007).

These foundational R&D investments included grants made in the 1960s for exploring the genetic basis of cancer, as well as grants made in the 1980s for the study of vascular disease. Investment in this type of knowledge is unlikely to be privately profitable: at the time the firm needs to allocate resources for a research project, there is no clear hypothesis for how it would lead to a commercializable drug, meaning that the investment would entail considerable risk for a very small chance of success. Further, even if this research did lead to a testable hypothesis in the context of drug development, the firm making this investment would be enabling other firms to build on this knowledge (for free) to develop their own (competing) drugs.[3]

---

3. A similar concern applies when considering innovations targeting the poor, such as treatments for malaria: while there is doubtless social value in addressing the problem (given the massive toll on human health exacted by this disease, particularly in sub-Saharan Africa and South Asia), neither patients nor their cash-strapped governments can afford to pay for solutions. In light of this reality, firms allocate their R&D resources toward challenges faced by wealthier consumers, who have both the ability and the willingness to pay for the fruits of innovation.

Patents, by granting firms a period of market exclusivity, arise as a natural tool to restore innovation incentives. However, they suffer from two important drawbacks. First, they do not allow for steering the direction of research beyond what the market might desire. Second, they create after-the-fact market distortions through monopoly pricing: when firms have intellectual property (IP) protections over their inventions, they will charge a higher price to would-be users relative to a competitive market. In recent years, a growing number of extraordinarily expensive drugs have heightened the salience of this tradeoff; in 2019, for instance, the FDA approved Zolgensma, a gene therapy for a rare childhood disorder priced at $2.1 million per patient. While critics argue that such prices are tantamount to extortion, drug makers counter that they are necessary to compensate for the substantial risks of the R&D process. Similarly, although less attention has been paid to more modestly priced drugs, the aggregation of smaller markups on common drugs can also limit access for poorer households and the financial health of ultimate payers such as Medicare.

Open-Ended Search and Contractability. When patents are not appropriate, why not use prizes instead? Research prizes—awarded to whoever achieves a certain outcome first—have several advantages relative to grants, the most obvious of which is the fact that prizes do not need to be paid unless research is successful. In addition, using prizes means that funders do not need to select winners before evaluating their work, making it possible to incentivize research effort from a much larger group of participants (Murray et al. 2012).

For example, in 2006, the company Netflix announced an open competition with a $1 million prize to any team that could improve its recommendation algorithm, the feature that allows the platform to guide users toward movies they are likely to appreciate, thereby boosting willingness to pay for the service. This contest drew entries from over 2,000 teams, a level of participation that would be impossible under a grant model in which winners are selected before research even begins.

However, the structure of the Netflix prize makes it impossible to replicate in many other research settings. Netflix provided entrants with a large training dataset and was able to articulate a precise, unidimensional metric for assessing both final and intermediate progress (improvement in the root mean-squared error over its current algorithm). This set of parameters was spelled out entirely at the outset, providing contestants with clarity and transparency (Lakhani et al. 2014).

Yet in many other situations, it would be impossible for a funder to spell out the conditions for winning before seeing any submissions, or to commit to a single metric or a narrow set of metrics to evaluate success. In the context of exploratory research, narrowing the question in a way that makes it easier to specify, or forcing a solution pathway on potential participants, might ultimately stifle innovation and result in suboptimal solutions.

Appropriability

Nature of Idea Search	Feasible/Desirable	Unfeasible/Undesirable
Open-ended	Patents	Grants
Known end-point	Research Contracts	Prizes

Fig. 4.1 The research-funding ecosystem

A related problem with directed search is that the value of particular research results may not appear initially obvious, as in the case of the NSF-supported discovery in Yellowstone National Park of *Thermus aquaticus*, a bacterium that retains its enzymatic properties under extremely variable temperature conditions (Brock and Freeze 1969). Indeed, this is the type of project that might easily have been singled out as an exemplar of wasteful scientific spending—that is, until Kary Mullis and the Cetus Corporation leveraged the organism's unusual properties to develop the polymerase chain reaction in the late 1980s, ushering in a new era in biotechnology with applications in far-flung domains such as forensics and paternity testing (Stern 2004).

The constraint on ex ante problem formulation suggests that the range of challenges for which innovation contests will dominate other contractual mechanisms, including grants, is perhaps narrower than their proponents have been willing to acknowledge.

Together, appropriability conditions and the nature of idea search are dimensions that can guide policy makers as they navigate the landscape of institutions supporting the production of scientific knowledge.

As depicted in figure 4.1, grants are most suitable in the upper-right quadrant, when appropriating the market returns associated with knowledge production is either infeasible or undesirable, and when the formulation of problems worth solving cannot be scripted in advance. Patents share with grants the ability to harness scientific or technological creativity in a decentralized way, but differ from them in relying on market incentives to stimulate and direct investments. Like grants, prizes promise to direct innovation efforts toward aims that the market might neglect if left to its own devices. Unlike grants, this mechanism requires advanced specification of the problems worth addressing in order to be effective. Finally, research contracts might operate best in environments where the "deliverable" can be well specified and appropriability concerns do not loom large (such as in the defense context, with one large paying customer able to specify objectives, with associated penalties for nonperformance).

We end this section with two additional arguments that might sometimes push patrons of science to favor grant funding over alternative mechanisms.

Financial Constraints. Grants may be particularly effective in cases where researchers are financially constrained. Patents and prizes reward innovators after they have invested in R&D when R&D efforts turn out to be successful. By design, then, this requires innovators to put up capital and bear substantial risk up front. This is likely to limit both the set of people and organizations who can afford to engage in R&D, and the nature of the R&D they do engage in. Although debt and equity markets exist, a large literature in finance suggests that financial frictions nonetheless lead firms, large and small, to underinvest in innovation generally, and in high-risk projects in particular (Froot, Scharfstein, and Stein 1993; Howell 2017; Krieger, Li, and Papanikolaou 2018; Nanda and Rhodes-Kropf 2016). Venture capital investors routinely refer to "financing risk" to describe how otherwise sound projects may fail to obtain additional capital for continued exploration. The high cost of designing and running experiments that sufficiently reduce uncertainty likely explains why VC activity has been circumscribed to a narrow range of sectors (Kerr and Nanda 2015).

Although limiting for firms, financial constraints become prohibitive for individual scientists seeking to finance their investigations, especially in fields that necessitate specialized capital equipment (as in condensed matter physics) or expensive materials (such as mice with a particular genetic profile). Without grants, it would be impossible for junior scientists to establish their laboratories and independent research identities. While some universities can afford to provide generous "start-up packages" to their new employees, most institutions are limited in their ability to support researchers absent external grants (Stephan 2012). Relying on localized funding of this type may widen disparities in science, hampering the opportunities available to those at less wealthy institutions.

Supporting Human Capital and Other Research "Infrastructure." Because the potential of a given research trajectory is difficult to predict and can shift over time, investments in specific research projects may afford less durable payoffs than investments in research "infrastructure," whether in the form of physical or human capital.

Patents, contracts, and research prizes are not useful tools in this regard because they are necessarily directed to specific ends. Grants, however, are more flexible. While they are frequently used to fund projects (as in the case of the R01, the traditional project grant awarded by the NIH), they can also be used to fund institutions (such as when the Department of Energy, or DOE, funds the construction of a new light source at the synchrotron located at Brookhaven National Laboratory) or public goods (e.g., the Sloan Foundation underwriting the Digital Sky Survey, which has created detailed, open-access, three-dimensional maps of the universe).

Investments in scientific training and apprenticeship are also typically financed through grants. For instance, Stanford graduate student Sergey Brin was supported by a dissertation fellowship from the NSF when he teamed up with fellow graduate student Larry Page to design BackRub, a prototype World Wide Web search engine that leveraged hyperlinks between pages to develop an "importance" ranking for a set of 24 million web pages (Page et al. 1998). By 1998, Page and Brin had obtained funding that allowed them to move their growing operation away from campus and to incorporate Google, Inc. (Hart 2004). In the United States at least, nearly all scientific apprenticeships are funded through grants, whether in the form of individual fellowships as above, in the form of training grants awarded to specific institutions, or indirectly as budget items in traditional project grants.

To summarize, we view scientific grants—such as those used in government-sponsored research—as a particularly effective way of supporting research when outcomes are open ended and when ensuring the broadest range of spillovers is viewed as a feature rather than a bug. These traits describe a great deal of "basic" or exploratory research—the bedrock of the innovation ecosystem.

4.2   A Short History of the Scientific Grant

Given the importance of grants, how should science funders organize the grant-making process? In this section, we consider how scientific endeavors have historically been supported, focusing on the origins of the peer review–based systems that have come to dominate modern grant making.

The earliest precursors of the modern scientific grant were patronage systems widely practiced in Europe, Asia, and the Middle East in both the ancient and early modern periods. For scientists like Galileo, for instance, pursuing knowledge in "experimental philosophy" meant securing the support of a wealthy patron, whose generosity was grounded in a mix of utilitarian and status-seeking motivations. Sustaining the interest of a benefactor often came at the price of skewing one's investigations toward topics the patron found tasteful or prestigious (Westfall 1985).

As capital requirements increased over time, scientists began to seek public support. In Europe, financial backing took different forms, from the founding of science departments within long-established universities to the establishment of freestanding "intramural" research institutes—such as the Physikalisch-Technische Reichsanstalt in Germany (Cahan 1982) or the Pasteur Institute in France (Hage and Mote 2010)—where teaching activities did not take place.

"Encouragements" from the French Académie des Sciences, 1831–1850.

The earliest recorded grant system was administered by the Paris-based Académie des Sciences following a large estate gift from Baron de Montyon. Finding itself constrained in its ability to finance the research of promising but not-well-established savants, the academy seized on the flexibility afforded by the Montyon gift to transform traditional grands prix into "encouragements": smaller amounts that could broaden the set of active researchers. Even though the process was highly informal (the names of the early recipients were not published in the academy's *Compte rendus*), it apparently avoided suspected or actual cases of corruption (Crosland and Gálvez 1989). Throughout the 19th century, however, the academy struggled to convince wealthy donors to abandon their preference for indivisible, large monetary prizes in favor of these divisible encouragements.

The Royal Society's Experience, 1849–1914. The "government grants" administered by the British Royal Society were another early precursor of modern grant systems. Over the 64 years of the program's existence, 2,316 grants assisted the investigations of 938 scientists. In 1851, it accounted for about 50 percent of all the funds appropriated by the British Parliament in the aid of science, declining to 9 percent on the eve of the World War I, when it was terminated (MacLeod 1971). Although its grants were primarily awarded to members of the society located in and around London, the selection process eventually came to function like an early form of peer review. After facing initial accusations of bias, the society reformed its process, leading to the creation of discipline-specific committees with members elected to four-year terms.

Ultimately, the Victorian-era government grant appears to have withered both because of its trustees' ambivalence about expanding its scope (for fear that a more ample budget would invite the government to meddle in the Royal Society's affairs) and because of the growing influence of universities. It would take 40 years and another world war to create a window of opportunity for reinventing the scientific grant, this time on the other side of the Atlantic.

Rise of Philanthropic Foundations. Before World War II, science funding in the United States was dominated by philanthropic foundations such as the Carnegie, Guggenheim, and Rockefeller foundations. The magnitude of the scientific-research outlays of the federal government and large industrial firms, such as DuPont, General Electric, and AT&T, may have been more significant, but these entities were not patrons of science. Rather, they designed and performed the research they paid for.[4]

The scientific foundations were staffed by professional "managers of science" who cultivated a personal network so they could remain informed

4. For instance, the intramural campus of the National Institutes of Health traces its roots back to a one-room "Laboratory of Hygiene" founded in 1887 as part of the Marine Hospital Service.

about the scientists and fields worthy of support, but their financial backing targeted institutions (in particular science departments within universities) rather than individual scientists (Kohler 1976). In the early 1930s, the Great Depression and its associated financial pressures forced the Rockefeller Foundation to suspend its institutional grant program and rely instead on "project grants" that amounted to about $6,700 per year (about $125,000 adjusted for inflation) for a typical three-year period (Schneider 2015).[5] However, the similarities between this scheme and modern government grants are superficial. Grant officers did not rely on peer review, nor did they call for applications in open competitions. Rather they appeared to have exercised considerable discretion in selecting winning projects. Unsurprisingly, these informal practices tended to reinforce the power of scientific elites (Barany 2018, 2019).

Post–World War II Transition. The investigator-initiated, renewable, peer-reviewed scientific grant emerged in its modern incarnation shortly after World War II, as officials in the US Public Health Service (PHS) maneuvered to transform a wartime strategy to procure specific research products into a broader grant program.

The window of opportunity was the impending expiration of biomedical research contracts awarded by the Office of Scientific Research and Development (OSRD), the federal agency created to coordinate scientific research for military purposes during World War II. After much bureaucratic infighting (Fox 1987), PHS staff secured the transfer of these contracts to NIH and their transmutation into "contract grants," a term probably chosen to create ambiguity. Using the authority vested in NIH by the Cancer Act of 1944, PHS staff laid the foundation of scientific grant making by the middle of 1946. This included the creation of sixteen study sections to review the scientific merits of individual applications, overseen by an academic council nominally in charge of: deciding on the final list of recipients (Van Slyke 1946); rules governing grantees' salaries and pensions, as well as the purchase of equipment; an explicit commitment to protect the freedom of investigators as they performed their investigations; and the choice of an 8 percent overhead rate over the direct costs of grants so as to minimize "unfairness to less wealthy institutions where establishment of research projects would cause an actual burden to administrative operations" (Fox 1987). Over time, additional policies were implemented to complement solicitations on broad topics with more targeted calls for research in specific areas (Myers 2020).

---

5. Focusing on individual investigators rather than academic departments was met by resistance on the part of the staff in charge of selecting recipients. Alan Gregg, one of the Rockefeller Foundation's key officers, explicitly argued against the practice in a 1937 memorandum, stating that a grant operation was tantamount to setting up a "a huge dispensary of chicken feed" (Schneider 2015, 280). In what may be a prescient cautionary note, the memo stated that "the hesitant uncertainty of short-term grants all but insults the intelligence if not the sincerity of the recipient and certainly makes a mockery of long-term planning" (Schneider 2015, 309).

By the late 1940s, the NIH had become preeminent in medical research as a result of its extramural grant program, expending more than half of all federal funds for medical research. It had strong and growing support in Congress and a powerful constituency in the research community, since a majority of recipients appeared to consistently hail from lower-status institutions not represented in study sections (Munger 1960; Strickland 1989).[6] This apparent success explains in large part why, when it finally emerged in 1950, the NSF also chose investigator-initiated grants awarded to university researchers as its primary contractual mechanism, though peer review appears to have initially played a less significant role in its practices, compared with the NIH (Baldwin 2018).

Modern Developments. Since the 1950s, scientific grants have spread to many other parts of the US federal government (Departments of Energy, Defense, and Agriculture), to some state governments (such as the California Institute for Regenerative Medicine), and to the nonprofit sector (e.g., the March of Dimes, the American Cancer Society, the Bill and Melinda Gates Foundation, the Howard Hughes Medical Institute, the Chan-Zuckerberg Initiative, etc.). Diffusion outside the United States has been slower. In 2007, the European Union established the European Research Council (ERC), an organization that shares many of the practices pioneered by NIH and NSF in the United States, with an initial annual budget of €7.5 billion (König 2017). Interestingly, grants had not figured prominently in the funding of science in the countries of continental Europe until the ERC's founding. This suggests that a certain scale is required to justify the costs of administering a peer-review system capable of processing tens of thousands of applications on a yearly basis.

In advanced economies, "extramural" grant systems (such as those operated by NSF or ERC) coexist with "intramural" institutes (such as the National Laboratories in the United States, the Centre National de la Recherche Scientifique in France, the Max Planck Institutes in Germany, or Riken in Japan), where the allocation of funds is the outcome of layered administrative processes. In a first step, the overall budget for each institute or laboratory is the result of a political process reflecting national priorities, historical allocations, and the clout of laboratory leaders with senior civil servants. In a second step, a bureaucratic process disburses funds to particular laboratories within each institute, typically headed by a director overseeing medium-sized teams of scientists, technicians, and postdoctoral fellows. Finally, each director has the decision-making power to allocate her budget across specific projects.

To our knowledge, there is no empirical evidence to date that can speak

---

6. Study sections are standing committees charged with evaluating the scientific merits of grant proposals.

to the relative merits of extramural funding, through a decentralized, investigator-initiated process, versus intramural funding, filtered through a decision-making hierarchy. It is possible that hierarchs have better information about the relative quality of projects and initiatives pitched to them by the scientists within their institutions, relative to arm's-length peer reviewers without access to "soft information." The other side of the coin, of course, is that poor accountability at the top of the hierarchy makes these same leaders susceptible to influence activities, since the struggle for resources within each institution is necessarily zero-sum. In the rest of this chapter, we restrict our attention to the design of extramural grant systems.

4.3   A Guide to Designing Grant Programs

As illustrated in the introduction, grant-funding programs have been instrumental in supporting the development of many important innovations. In this section, we explore issues policy makers face when setting up a new—or reforming an already existing—scientific grant system. In particular, we describe the current state of knowledge and highlight open questions pertaining to the following elements of such systems: developing goals and expectations, choosing the scope of what is to be supported, selecting among applications, monitoring recipients' activities, supporting translation and commercialization efforts, and, finally, evaluating the grant program's overall impact. These choices can be consequential because, as persuasively documented in Stephan (2012), the availability and nature of grant funding plays an important role in shaping scientists' careers and research incentives.

4.3.1   Developing Goals and Expectations

Investing in scientific research requires patience and a tolerance for failure. Imagine a $1 million project with a 0.00001 percent chance of leading to a cure for cancer. In practice, relatively few individual organizations have the risk tolerance to spend $1 million on a single investment that will fail 99.99999 percent of the time.

Yet imagine there are 200,000 such potential projects, all with a 0.00001 percent chance of success. If their probabilities of success are independent, then these projects collectively represent a $200 billion investment with an 87 percent chance of success. Because of the enormous social value of finding a cure for cancer, almost everyone would agree that this would be a worthwhile portfolio of investments. Yet risk-averse performers are unlikely to invest in any of the component $1 million dollar investments as stand-alone projects.

As this simple example illustrates, it is important for funders to think of their investments as part of a broader social portfolio of projects, whether they are supported by government agencies, private-sector firms, or non-profit entities (Goodin, Hatfull, and Malik 2016). Even when the failure rate of individual projects is high, the risk inherent to a diverse portfolio of the same projects may be low enough to make the entire effort worthwhile from a social point of view.

This same portfolio logic can be extended to the design of grant-making organizations and processes: it is important to create grant mechanisms that are diverse in the scientific research areas they support, in their time horizons and risk preferences, and in the expertise and experiences of those who decide how funds are ultimately allocated.

4.3.2   Defining Program Scope

Funders must first choose what type of research to support. This decision has both a "horizontal" and a "vertical" dimension. Horizontally, funders must choose a research domain or set of domains to support (e.g., a set of disease areas). Vertically, funders must decide where in the research "value chain" to focus (e.g., on early-stage as opposed to "scaling-up" efforts). From a portfolio perspective, it is important that the ecosystem of grant programs cover as much of this space as possible (e.g., with some funders focusing on established research domains and others launching new areas of inquiry).

One obvious way to reinforce the portfolio mindset is for funders to seek out intellectual "white spaces"—areas of the scientific landscape that have not, to date, received much public or private attention. However, a key concern with white spaces is that it is often difficult to determine whether there has been little research in an area because scientific opportunities are scarce or because resources are. Indeed, these tend to be self-reinforcing: areas may not receive funding because there has been little progress to date, but that lack of progress may itself result from a persistent lack of support.[7]

Because of these factors, establishing a new research area may require a dedicated and sustained effort. In 1958, the division of research grants at NIH created a study section dedicated to genetics. In addition to recruiting distinguished scientists to serve as members, the new genetics study section took it upon itself to define research standards in this emerging domain, through the organization of symposia that resulted in volumes codifying key methodological aspects of genetics research. In the space of 20 years, the number of applications related to this field increased by an order of magnitude (Crow and Owen 2000).

Today, a similar white-space effort might be needed to explore alternative treatments for Alzheimer's disease. A long-standing hypothesis in the Alzheimer's field holds that a protein fragment called beta-amyloid accumulates in the brain, creating neuron-killing clumps that cause the disorder. For

---

7. White space can also exhibit a geographical dimension. Ganguli (2017) studies a grant program funded by George Soros that provided grants to over 28,000 Soviet scientists shortly after the end of the USSR, in an environment where public support of science had all but evaporated. Not only did these grants more than double publications on the margin; they also induced scientists to remain in the science sector.

many years, NIH funding for Alzheimer's focused primarily on this amyloid hypothesis, to the detriment of other research streams centered on oxidative stress, neuroinflammation, and another protein called tau (Begley 2019). As drug candidates based on amyloids have repeatedly failed, the Alzheimer's research community is increasingly seeing the importance of cultivating a diverse set of treatment hypotheses.

Funders who are unwilling or who lack the resources to commit to a sustained effort to address research white spaces can have a stronger impact by funding research in already established research areas. Doing so allows them to take advantage of knowledge spillovers. Indeed, one of the hallmarks of knowledge production is that ideas, once produced, can be freely used by others as inputs in their own research efforts. When a funder supports research in an already active research area, the scientists they fund can have a larger impact by learning from and contributing to the work of other researchers in the same area.

This approach, however, can also lead to excessive duplication of effort—for example, "priority races" in which different teams of scientists compete to be the first to publish a discovery, often keeping their work secret in the meantime (Hill and Stein 2020). One way to balance a desire to generate spillovers with the need to avoid duplication is to conceive of white spaces not just in terms of research topics but rather in terms of vertical research type. For example, the NIH is clearly the dominant funder of biomedical research, especially "mature basic research" (i.e., projects that have generated enough preliminary evidence to prove their conceptual soundness but that are not necessarily directed toward an immediate application). Given this, new funders may wish to locate their activities "upstream" of the NIH by providing seed funding to de-risk very early-stage ideas, allowing scientists to generate the preliminary findings necessary to obtain follow-on NIH funding. Alternatively, they may consider locating "downstream" to support translational infrastructure that helps science transition out of the laboratory.

4.3.3   Developing Research Priorities

Having defined the general scope of a grant program, funders must next choose how to set specific research priorities within their domain. Broadly, funders can elect to be "top down" or "mission oriented" (i.e., generating priorities internally and then seeking applications related to those priorities) or "bottom up" or "investigator initiated" (i.e., allowing applicants to propose their own projects, so that research priorities are determined after the fact).

Both models are used in practice. The family of federal agencies modeled after the Defense Advanced Research Projects Agency (DARPA) typically operate top down. Advanced Research Projects Agency–Energy (ARPA-E), for example, identified a gap in energy research on materials for semiconductors and responded by designing a funding program called SWITCHES, which focuses on the development of high-voltage (approximately 200–2,000 V), high-current-power semiconductor devices and circuits that, upon ultimately reaching scale, could offer affordable breakthrough performance in power electronics, in terms of higher efficiencies, higher switching frequencies (and therefore smaller packages), and higher temperature operation (ARPA-E 2013). In such a program, the funder determines the priority area and then solicits applications on that topic.

In contrast, an agency like NIH largely operates from the bottom up, relying on investigator-initiated grants. Applicants can submit proposals on any of a broad range of topics and methods, which will then be peer reviewed in one of the agency's 178 chartered study sections (e.g., "Synapses, Cytoskeleton and Trafficking," "Behavioral Genetics and Epidemiology," or "Child Psychopathology and Developmental Disabilities"). In this model, the agency's research priorities emerge organically through the application and evaluation process, rather than being specified ahead of time.

The relative merits of a mission-oriented versus investigator-initiated approach are a long-standing object of debate in the science policy community (Mazzucato 2018), one not always informed by compelling empirical evidence. In our view, the appropriate approach depends on the nature of the research that funders intend to support. Returning to our two-by-two classification system from section 4.1, top-down programs can be better justified when the funder is confident that it knows and can specify the output that it would like. Meanwhile, bottom-up approaches make sense when funders want to support the most promising areas of research but lack the information to identify those areas on their own.

For example, it is unsurprising that top-down models are common at DARPA, which focuses on R&D for technologies that are relevant for defense. Because DARPA is a branch of the Department of Defense—which is the ultimate buyer for many of these research products—its officials are likely to have a good sense of what the DoD's needs are, making it easier for them to specify research priorities ahead of time.

In contrast, the NIH is charged with funding research that may eventually lead to improvements in health. The time lags between initial R&D can be long, running into the decades (Li, Azoulay, and Sampat 2017). In such a case, it is unlikely that NIH administrators will be informed enough to accurately identify and solicit applications in the most promising research areas. Asking them to pick priority areas may therefore lead to an inefficient allocation of funds (Aghion, Dewatripont, and Stein 2008). A bottom-up, investigator-initiated grant process may do a better job of aggregating the collective wisdom of scientists in the relevant communities.

In practice, of course, there are many hybrid models that attempt to capture the advantages of both approaches. The NIH resorts to Requests for Applications (RFAs) to focus the energy of the scientific community on areas that are thought to have been neglected or to have fallen between the interstices at the boundaries of its peer-review committees (Sampat 2012). This has also proved a flexible way to respond to congressional pressures to fund research on specific diseases (Godefroy 2011).[8]

Meanwhile, reflecting an awareness that a top-down setting of priorities may lead to inefficient allocations, agencies like DARPA and ARPA-E have a rigorous process of "program peer review" in establishing research priorities (Azoulay et al. 2019a). At ARPA-E, for instance, proposed programs need to survive a gauntlet of critiques, some coming from existing program directors, others coming from leaders in the relevant technical community. Using this feedback, the program manager will refine the problem domain, and only then might the agency director approve the program. This type of iterative review with community feedback is therefore a method through which administrators can attempt to overcome their informational disadvantage in identifying high-potential research priorities.

In summary, and echoing our earlier point about research portfolios, society might be best served by an ecosystem of funders, some of which set specific agendas in cases where research priorities are clear, and others that embrace the wide interests of their relevant scientific communities when research goals are more exploratory.

4.3.4   Grant Evaluation: Peer Review and the Determination of "Scientific Merit"

Once a pool of applications has been collected, grant agencies must select winners and losers. In the modern era, this process has become synonymous with peer review, although the term covers a wide spectrum of practices, and one can imagine grant systems operating without peer review—as many such systems historically did (Baldwin 2018).[9] Under the traditional model of peer review, applications are read and scored by multiple evaluators, who then discuss and vote on which applications to fund. This raises three important design questions: who should evaluate the proposals, what types of evaluative input should funders seek from evaluators, and how should these potentially divergent signals be aggregated? We discuss each in turn.

Choosing Evaluators. First, what kinds of people should grant funders seek advice from when evaluating applications? Whereas subject matter experts may have better information about the quality of an application,

8. One note of caution concerns the potential difficulty of convincing scientists to shift their work into new areas via specific RFPs. Recent research by Myers (2020) suggests that established scientists are relatively "inelastic" in the sense that they are unlikely to switch their research interests in response to small amounts of funding or a small likelihood of funding. Myers's research suggests instead that it would be cheaper to target funds for research in new areas to younger scientists who are more flexible in their research interests.

9. For example, the Office of Naval Research (ONR), established in 1946, could only award contracts by statute. These contracts, however, functioned much like grants, with minimal emphasis on deliverables. Only in 2011 did ONR began initiating peer review of ongoing basic research programs across its science and technology departments (Klunder 2013).

they may also have preferences—supporting their field, handicapping a competitor—that impede their objectivity. Similarly, reviewers with technical expertise may have a better sense of a project's feasibility, but those with industry or policy expertise may have a better sense of its potential. In a study of NIH peer review, Li (2017) shows that although scientists are biased in favor of applicants in their own fields, they are also substantially better informed. Rather than striving to eliminate conflicts of interest entirely, funders should balance potential for bias against the value of an expert's information.

Determination and Use of Scientific Merit Scores. In addition to seeking advice from human subject experts, how much should funders rely on quantitative metrics like publications and citations? Recent empirical studies have shown that following algorithmic advice or other quantitative "rules" may yield better outcomes. Kleinberg et al. (2018) demonstrate that algorithms may be better at predicting recidivism among arrestees; Hoffman, Kahn, and Li (2018) show that following algorithmic job test recommendations yields better outcomes than relying on the opinions of human recruiters. This evidence concords with an older stream of research in psychology that compares "clinical" and "actuarial" approaches to decision-making and typically finds the latter to be associated with superior outcomes (Dawes, Faust, and Meehl 1989).

These studies, however, focus on predicting traits—a worker's job tenure, for instance—that involve less creativity and variability than assessing scientific potential. Li and Agha (2015) show that human review scores predict eventual research output above and beyond what would be suggested by quantitative metrics alone. In this case, funders should focus on understanding the comparative advantage of human and metrics-based assessments. In the case of the NIH, Li and Agha (2015) show that the relative contribution of humans relative to quantitative metrics is higher among top-scoring applications.[10] This suggests a policy in which quantitative metrics can be used to make initial screens, allowing peer reviewers to focus their expertise on distinguishing among top performers with a higher chance of being funded.

Finally, funders must also decide how rigidly to adhere to the funding recommendations of external reviewers. Most peer-review systems allow for projects to be funded "out of order"—that is, they allow program administrators to promote or demote specific projects when doing so would enable the agency to pursue a specific priority.[11] Ginther and Heggeness (2020)

10. Cole, Cole, and Simon (1981) and Pier et al. (2018) cast doubt on the fidelity of peer evaluators after finding low rates of agreement between reviewers assessing the merits of the same NSF or NIH grant applications.

11. In fact, administrative discretion has been an important feature of peer-review systems implemented within scientific journals and funding bodies alike, ever since the Royal Society of London instated the practice in 1831 (Moxham and Fyfe 2018). Baldwin (2018) documents

studied the careers of applicants to a postdoctoral fellowship program at NIH and found that "promoted" applicants (those who scored below a cutoff but were nonetheless funded) secured less research funding in the long run, relative to applicants who were "passed over" (i.e., those who scored above the cutoff but were not appointed). It is of course possible that these applicants fared better on other metrics, but at the very least this evidence should convince agencies to carefully record instances when they choose to deviate from typical funding rules, and track the outcomes that result over time.

Aggregating Opinions. Given a chosen set of evaluators (human or otherwise), how should organizations aggregate potentially disparate opinions? The most common approach is to simply take an average; this does a good job of capturing reviewers' overall assessments, but such averaging could plausibly lead to the selection of more conventional and less risky projects. NIH grant applicants often complain that one bad review is enough to torpedo a proposal, even though the most original projects may be more likely to garner negative reviews because they do not fit neatly within established scientific paradigms. Rather, it is possible that diversity of opinion might itself be a marker of creative potential, in which case funders should look closely at grants with a high *variance* in evaluator scores.

A related approach, similar to that used by the Gates Foundation, is to issue reviewers a limited supply of "gold stars." This forces reviewers to think carefully about how to allocate their stars across projects (Kolev et al. 2019). One could also issue reviewers a limited number of "rotten tomatoes," which have the capacity to sink a proposal. Both these approaches are used in the private sector by venture capitalists considering which start-up firms to invest in. Malenko, Nanda, and Rhodes-Kropf (2019) surveyed VC firms on their aggregation practices and show that, for early-stage investments, venture capitalists often work on an advocacy model in which a start-up can be funded as long as one partner is willing to serve as its champion. This advocacy approach prioritizes a project's upside potential, which can make sense for investments in early-stage firms, when capital commitments are relatively low and there is still a great deal of uncertainty about a firm's potential. For investments in more mature firms, the authors show that majority voting and consensus models are more common. This practice makes it easier for a single partner to block an investment and thereby focuses on minimizing downside risk. This approach might apply to the scientific-funding environment in the case of "big science" projects involving large outlays in specialized physical capital.

Viewing the question from a portfolio perspective, it is important for funders to select some projects that represent "safer" bets, and others that

how the NSF came to place more emphasis on external referee opinions as a strategy to insulate some of its funding decisions from congressional criticism.

are higher-impact but potentially riskier. In doing so, funders should strive to match their selection processes to the goals of the program. For example, the NIH may want to consider adopting an advocacy model (ranking based on maximum scores) in their transformative research program, but may want to continue using average scores in evaluating renewals of existing project grants.

4.3.5 Postaward Program Management

A funder's task need not conclude after it has selected award recipients. Rather, funders must decide the extent to which they want ongoing involvement with funded researchers. The pure prize approach, in which funders reward scientists for past successes, requires little to no postaward management. At the other end of the continuum, grant officers can be involved in the choice of collaborators and the determination of intermediate milestones, with ongoing monitoring and possible early termination of the project. Goldstein and Kearney (2020) use internal data from ARPA-E to document that program staff modify projects frequently, especially timelines, and that these changes are more sensitive to poor performance than to strong performance. They conjecture that such "active project management," when combined with high upfront risk tolerance, can be used to enhance the productivity of mission-oriented public research funding.

In addition to explicit directives, funders implicitly shape scientists' research trajectories through their choice of whether and how to conduct reviews for grant renewal. While some programs are explicitly one shot, grants that hold the promise of renewed funding give funders a lever to continue influencing scientists' research efforts. The majority of life-science labs in the United States, for instance, rely on continual renewals of NIH grants (which last three to five years per cycle) in order to operate. This type of staged funding enables funders to deepen their financial commitment only after ideas have shown some promise. Indeed, staged funding is also standard practice in venture finance: by investing smaller initial amounts, firms can afford to take risks on early-stage projects while preserving the option to abandon projects that show no initial promise (see Kerr, Nanda, and Rhodes-Kropf [2014] for an overview of private sector VC financing).

Under such models, scientists have a strong incentive to demonstrate productivity and success in order to renew their funding. These incentives work best when the funder has a clear sense of what behaviors it would like scientists to adopt, has a way to measure these outcomes, and is cognizant of the potential for unintended consequences. A renewal policy that emphasizes publication counts, for instance, may lead scientists to waste time on weak projects (or engage in data mining) in order to seek a publication, rather than accepting initial failures and moving on. Fearing failure, scientists may also take fewer risks initially, steering their work toward safer but potentially less impactful projects.

To address these concerns, organizations that seek to encourage scientific risk taking must match their rhetoric with deeds. For example, medical investigators at the Howard Hughes Medical Institute (HHMI) receive funding for an initial period of five years, but the first renewal decision appears rather lax, focusing mostly on whether the funded scientists have made use of the freedom an HHMI investigatorship allows to branch out in new directions. Azoulay, Graff Zivin, and Manso (2011) show that these failure-tolerant policies influence how scientists lead their laboratories, the types of personnel they employ, and the methods and questions they choose to investigate. Compared to a matched class of NIH funding recipients (who face a more traditional output-based renewal process), HHMI investigators produce very highly cited publications at a higher rate, as well as more "duds" with few or no citations, which is what one would expect if they chose to privilege "exploration" at the expense of "exploitation" of traditional scientific approaches.

4.3.6   Translation and Impact

Though grants are mechanisms that enable funders to support basic research, one of their fundamental rationale is that investment in basic science underwrites technological progress through commercialization and other translation efforts (Bush 1945). Yet the majority of academic research supported by agencies like the NSF and NIH does not yield follow-on economic activity in a direct way, whether in the form of patenting, licensing, or entrepreneurship. And for the subset of ideas that are commercialized, few make it past the so-called valley of death to reach a wider audience (Beard et al. 2009; Contopoulos-Ioannidis, Ntzani, and Ioannidis 2003).

One potential barrier to greater translation is the fact that scientists, left to their own devices, do not necessarily consider engagement with industry as an integral part of their job description (Barham, Foltz, and Melo 2020; Cohen, Sauermann, and Stephan 2019). For this reason, policy makers need to consider the desirability and feasibility of incorporating "translation incentives" into the design of grant systems. As an approximation, it is useful to distinguish a passive approach, whereby obstacles to commercialization (such as unclear or limited IP rights) are removed, from an active approach, whereby funders are directly involved in helping their awardees commercialize their research.

Passive Translation: IP Rights and Grant Policy. In the United States, the Bayh-Dole Act (passed in 1980) allows researchers and universities to retain IP rights to inventions supported by federal funding, whereas previously such rights would have in most cases resided with the government. This change contributed to an already growing trend in university patenting and licensing, as documented by Mowery et al. (2001). Part of this increase reflects organizational investments that universities made in establishing technology transfer offices to facilitate the licensing of inventions that emerged from academic labs. Implicit in this logic is that academic scientists may lack the knowledge, time, or interest to manage the commercialization of their inventions; they may not know which companies to approach or how to negotiate licensing agreements. Technology transfer offices therefore provide a set of services that complement the scientists' technical expertise. Reflecting this reality, universities and scientists typically split revenues associated with an invention, although the extent to which academics respond to the level of the negotiated royalty rate is in dispute (Hvide and Jones 2018; Ouelette and Tutt 2020).

Hausman (2019) studies the impact of Bayh-Dole on measures of real economic activity, in order to better understand the role that university science plays in shaping invention and entrepreneurship in the local economy. She finds that employment, wages, and corporate innovation appear to increase as a result of Bayh-Dole: these measures of economic output rose more rapidly after Bayh-Dole in counties near universities and in industries more closely related to the local university's areas of innovative expertise.

However, a key critique of Bayh-Dole (and other IP rights–focused policies) is that an increased emphasis on patenting may weaken universities' commitments to "open science." Williams (2013) and Murray et al. (2016) both consider the value of open access in scientific research. Williams focuses on IP rights related to human genes and finds that genes sequenced by the private firm Celera, and therefore subject to its IP, were less likely to be the subject of follow-on research and product development, relative to comparable open-access genes sequenced by the Human Genome Project. Murray et al. (2016) further examine how IP rights shape the nature of the follow-on research that investigators pursue. The authors show that open access to scientific inputs—in this case, genetically engineered mice—encouraged entry by new researchers and led to a greater diversity of research paths. Together, these and other studies document an IP policy trade-off when policy makers decide whether to allow scientists (and their employers) to patent findings that emerge out of public or even nonprofit funding. While strong IP rights provide incentives for the development and commercialization of technologies that would otherwise remain in an embryonic state, they may also reduce access for innovators building on the initial work, thereby limiting the scope of nondirected spillovers (Scotchmer 1991; Walsh, Cho, and Cohen 2005).

One hybrid approach is to allow universities to patent and license their inventions to private-sector firms, but to maintain free access for academic or other nonprofit users. Such "research exemptions"—a hotly debated (and litigated) area of IP law—potentially retain the incentive benefits of IP rights while maintaining some commitment to open science (Dent et al. 2006).

Active Translation and the "ARPA Model." In addition to removing IP barriers, grant funders can take a more active approach to midwifing the translation of scientific results into prototypes or technologies, as one particular aspect of postaward management mentioned above. This orientation toward commercial impact has been a hallmark of DARPA-style funding, but these efforts have probably been made easier insofar as the Department of Defense is both the funder and ultimate buyer of the inventions that arise from its support. A fairer test of active translation efforts might therefore involve a funder in a domain where technological inputs must be purchased on the open market (Azoulay et al. 2019a).

The ARPA-E "tech-to-market" (hereafter T2M) program and personnel provide a proof-of-concept for active funder involvement, although one that must still be regarded as an ongoing experiment rather than accepted best practice. Before receiving award funds, ARPA-E performers are required to develop a T2M plan in close coordination with ARPA-E's T2M advisors. Commercialization strategies developed to meet this requirement include training and the development of the business information necessary to understand market needs, and tailoring technology development to address those needs. ARPA-E also helps awardees develop relationships with relevant government agencies, technology transfer offices, companies, investors, and other organizations to facilitate transition to the commercial phase (National Academies of Sciences, Engineering, and Medicine 2017).

Regardless of the approach espoused by grant system designers, one uncontroversial theme emerges from scholarship on this topic: funders should attempt to lower the cost faced by their awardees while sharing the output of their work with a diverse audience, including other researchers who may produce follow-on work, as well as researchers in industry who may have the expertise and financial wherewithal to develop early-stage ideas and take them closer to market. One way to do so is for funding agencies to assist in building institutions that make it easier to access materials and knowledge. For instance, in the life sciences, the ability to build on prior research often depends on access to biological specimens—cell lines, tissue cultures, etc. Furman and Stern (2011) demonstrate that biological resource centers, which certify the fidelity of biological materials and facilitate their distribution, substantially amplify the impact of published research, sometimes doubling the number of citations it receives. From the grant funder's perspective, these types of investments can vastly increase the overall returns to its R&D investments.

4.4   Toward a Science of Science Funding

Finally, as with any other investment, funders of scientific research should understand the impact that their resources have. This provides an opportunity to build on strengths in their existing funding model and to improve on weaknesses.

Yet evaluation is difficult without some initial planning. Imagine that a foundation awards a grant to a scientist, and two years later she has trained three graduate students and published 10 additional articles, several of them in prominent journals. In order to assess the impact of this grant, it is not enough to tabulate these outputs, however impressive they appear. Rather, one needs to understand what her research achievements would have been had she not received any support. This is analogous to the challenge that scientists face when assessing the impact of a medical treatment: how does one know whether the patient got better because of the treatment or because of something else?

In medicine, scientists address this challenge by comparing outcomes for treated patients with outcomes for a control group of similar patients who were not treated. Funders of scientific research can do the same by collecting data on similar scientists who were not funded. To begin assessing the value of a grant, one should compare research outcomes between funded and unfunded groups. This comparison is valid if funded and unfunded applicants are similar. If applicants are rejected because they are substantially less qualified, then they would likely have worse research outcomes than funded applicants, even in the absence of funding. Such a comparison would tend to overstate the role of the grant.

The most effective way to address this problem is to randomize who gets funding. This is akin to randomization in medical trials, or A/B testing in business settings. When applied in the science-funding setting, randomized evaluations seek to determine the impact of grant funding or grant programs by comparing the outcomes of a group that receives funding or is subject to a particular set of grant policies (the treatment group) with the outcomes of a group that is not (the control group). Because the two groups are randomly assigned, their respective members do not differ systematically at the start of the evaluation, allowing researchers to attribute any differences in outcomes that may emerge to the causal impact of the grant or grant policy.

Randomized controlled trials (RCTs) have become the gold standard for policy evaluation and evidence-based decision-making. Many governments and foundations use RCTs to assess the efficacy of their programs, and a variety of organizations have emerged, inspired by organizations such as the Poverty Action Lab, to facilitate these experiments. To design an effective and fair RCT evaluation, it is important to appreciate the institutional context and goals at hand. For example, HHMI grants are aimed at encouraging scientists to pursue risky avenues of research, even if doing so means that in many cases experiments will fail and scientists may have little to publish. In this case, an RCT that focuses on counting publications would be inappropriate because publication counts do not reflect the underlying goal of the organization. For reasons such as these, we believe that the most effective evaluations arise from collaborations between agency staff and external program evaluators.

In many cases, there is reluctance to implement RCTs because of their perceived costs or inefficiencies. Funders, for instance, may understandably not want to randomly allocate their scarce funds to unqualified scientists. Yet even when a full-scale RCT is infeasible, it is still possible to perform some kind of randomization. For example, funders could devise a two-step approach in which applicants are first screened to eliminate those that are below a baseline level of acceptable quality; funding could then be randomized within the set of remaining applicants.[12] This would ensure a level of quality control while still enabling funders to better understand the impact of their programs.

In addition, there are often other naturally occurring "experiments" that allow researchers to assess the impact of funding. For example, funding cutoffs—so-called pay lines—create opportunities to use a regression discontinuity design where one compares outcomes for those just above and just below the cutoff. The idea is that because their scores are actually quite close, these applicants are likely to be more similar to each other than the average funded applicant is to the average unfunded applicant. Therefore, differences in their outcomes can be attributed more readily to the grant. Azoulay et al. (2019b), Howell (2017), and Jacob and Lefgren (2011) are all examples of this type of analysis applied to grant funding.

When a fully randomized or "natural" experiment is not possible, an alternative approach is to collect basic data on the characteristics of applicants— for instance, highest education, year of graduation, undergraduate and graduate institution, prior funding history, and keywords describing primary fields of research—and use the variables to make sure that one is comparing funded and unfunded scientists who look similar in terms of education, past research productivity, and other observable traits.

It is also important to consider the unit of analysis. An individual-level analysis typically yields an estimate of the average effect of being "treated" by funding, that is, the impact of funding for a typical scientist. Funders, however, may be interested in understanding their impact on a field of research as a whole. In this view, it is not enough to compare treatment and control outcomes at the level of the individual scientist because two applicants may have similar ideas. If funding enables one scientist to publish her results ahead of another, that yields a big impact from the perspective of her individual output, but it may not yield as large an impact on her field because that research idea would have been performed regardless. In order to assess the impact of funding on an entire area, one can still apply the same techniques as those described above, but focusing on fields rather than individuals as the unit of "treatment." For example, if one decides to focus funding on translational research in diabetes, one may compare the number of new clinical trials in diabetes to those in other, similar disease areas.

Finally, an informative program evaluation requires that funders collect information on research outcomes. While the overall desired impact of a

12. Fang and Casadevall (2016) propose a modified lottery scheme in this exact spirit.

program may be to improve life expectancy for patients with a particular health condition, the long lags involved, as well as the traceability challenges mentioned in the introduction, may make it infeasible to deploy metrics that are directly welfare relevant. In contrast, it may be easier to measure narrower, or intermediate, outputs in the innovation process. Before discussing the merits of such "surrogate markers" for impact, it is worth remembering that the outcomes funders track invariably morph into the incentives scientists face. Programs that only track publications (perhaps in "high-impact" journals) will provide recipients with an incentive to publish, but may not necessarily stir their interest in seeing their work translated or commercialized. Conversely, funders who carefully tabulate their awardees' patents may unwittingly lead them to patent unimportant work, as seems to have been the case with patent-promotion policies in China (Long and Wang 2019).

The most common metrics used in funding-program evaluations include:

- *Bibliometric Measures.* These include publications, publications in top journals, or "blockbuster publications"—that is, those that receive citations above some absolute threshold (e.g., in the top 1 percent, given their vintage). While not a panacea, such metrics are correlated with subsequent breakthrough discoveries (Lawani and Bayer 1983). They should be considered a basic part of any impact evaluation, even if they can appear far removed from the effect that funders wish to produce in their respective domains.[13]

- *Commercial or Applied Impact.* A weakness of publication-based measures is that they may fail to capture the impact of a scientist or research program outside academia. For mission-oriented organizations in particular, one may want to consider other metrics, such as patents generated (Goldstein and Kearney 2017), clinical trials initiated (Kolev et al. 2019), or the incorporation of start-up firms with growth ambitions (Kearney 2020).

- *Career Outcomes.* Funders may be interested in supporting scientific training rather than specific projects, in which case impact assessments should include measures of career traction or influence—for example, job appointments and promotions, as well as the number and placement of students the researcher trains (Azoulay, Greenblatt, and Heggeness 2020).

Jaffe (1998) provides a seven-point "wish list" for innovation metrics that science policy makers should have in mind when evaluating the impact of funding programs. First, metrics should have a high signal/noise ratio; sec-

---

13. A related point is that work on the development and validation of a citation-based metric has been a vibrant area of inquiry in the emerging "science of science" field. Recent efforts include attempts to distinguish "consolidating" from "disruptive" publications in science, using a combination of backward references and forward acknowledgments (Funk and Owen-Smith 2017; Wu, Wang, and Evans 2019).

ond, error in measurements should be uncorrelated with other phenomena of interest; third, the relationship between the proxy and the underlying phenomenon of interest should be linear, or at least of known functional form; fourth, the relationship between the proxy and the underlying concept should be stable over time; fifth, there should be stability across settings (institutional, geographic) in the relationship between the proxy and the underlying concept; sixth, the metric should not be susceptible to easy manipulation or inflation; seventh, it should be possible to consistently track the metric at different levels of aggregation (geographic or institutional).

This list makes for sobering reading since it can be argued that most, if not all, of the metrics used in program evaluations to date fall short in at least one respect. This suggests that funders should consider collecting information for a battery of outcomes rather than a single proxy. We also note that the scientific enterprise tends to generate digital breadcrumbs that, when systematically collected and parsed, can help alleviate traceability challenges and narrow the gap between bibliometric data and welfare-relevant outcomes. For instance, the wide availability of genetic sequence information as metadata attached to publications has made it possible for researchers to trace the impact of basic genetics research from the laboratory all the way to clinical trials, and the market availability of diagnostic tests (Kao 2020; Williams 2013).

In addition to impact evaluation, there could be significant returns to examining design elements of the funding system. Is scientific funding more effective when it holds scientists accountable for the precise content of the investigations they proposed (as is the case for NIH and NSF), or when it gives them the flexibility to alter the content of their research in the middle of a funding cycle (as is the case in the HHMI investigator program)? Should evaluator sentiment be averaged to generate priority scores, or can quadratic voting approaches be used to incorporate the intensity and variance in evaluator sentiment when scoring proposals? Should young and established investigators' proposals be evaluated in the same pool, or on separate tracks? These are empirical questions whose answers can only be provided through the careful design of tailored experiments.

Given the high potential returns to evaluation and experimentation, we end this section by pondering why the scientific community, funding agencies, and nonprofit foundations have been so reluctant to "turn the scientific method on themselves" (Azoulay 2012). Conservatism on the part of those benefiting from the status quo certainly plays a role, but resistance to experimentation does not only reflect self-serving motives. First, there are objective obstacles to experimentation in this setting, namely, the long lags involved for welfare-relevant outcomes to be realized, and the scale required to power experiments in order to detect meaningful differences in a world where "tail" outcomes are inherently more informative than "average" outcomes.

Second, science policy makers might fear that the nuanced implications from careful analysis could open the door to budgetary restrictions, whereas the emphasis on carefully cherry-picked anecdotes does not entail a similar degree of political risk. Paradoxically, the routinization of experimentation in scientific funding might require the imposition of a mandate from political institutions.

4.5 Conclusion

The investigator-initiated scientific grant is an important metainstitution with distinctly American origins, and one of the touchstones of the US "National Innovation System" (Nelson 1993). Yet it would be surprising if the initial design choices made by institutional entrepreneurs such as Vannevar Bush and C. James van Slyke in 1945 continued to provide a comprehensive blueprint for policy makers seeking to meet the challenges of scientific discovery in the 21st century.

While this chapter has attempted to grapple with some of the delicate trade-offs present in the design of science-funding institutions, we end the chapter by emphasizing a small number of core principles for policy makers.

First, though much of our discussion emphasizes the dangers of skewing the scientific agenda toward the short term, doing so may often be viewed by policy makers as a feature rather than a bug, especially in periods of crisis such as wartime or global pandemics.[14] As a consequence, a large share of grants often stipulate fairly specific aims that go well beyond curiosity-driven scientific exploration (as in the case of SBIR grants). Our assessment of the costs and benefits of grants relative to other instruments may not apply with the same force when the dividing line between "grants" and "contracts" becomes blurred in this way.

Second, there is great worth in maintaining a diversity of approaches to grant making. The analysis of grant systems should therefore be regarded as a portfolio evaluation problem. A crucial activity for science policy makers is therefore the identification of gaps in the ecosystem of funding. Traditionally, topic white space has been most salient, but we believe that it could be at least as productive to identify gaps with respect to risk orientation. As an example, at present neither the NIH nor the NSF has in its arsenal a mechanism providing grantees with a truly long-term horizon to plan their investigations (e.g., seven to ten years).[15]

---

14. Even outside these clear emergencies, the seeming inability of grant mechanisms to "deliver goods quickly" is often deplored, for example by patient advocates and lobbying groups in the context of the NIH and the "war on cancer" (Rettig 1977).

15. Recently, the National Institute of General Medical Science, the NIH's component institute focused on "basic" biological research, initiated the R35 Maximizing Investigators' Research Award, which is a step in this direction, though the time horizon of the award is only five years.

Third, in the nonprofit and public sector alike, funders have proved surprisingly reluctant to submit changes in the administration of their grants to rigorous evaluation. Nor do funders typically routinize the collection of outcome information regarding the applicants they did not choose to support. The lack of an experimental mindset partly explains why so many important questions regarding the design of grant systems remain without clear answers, and also why specific advice provided to policy makers must be tempered. Rather than chase the latest funding fad (e.g., "people not projects," a modified funding lottery, a "translational" institute, replacing grants with prizes, etc.), turning the scientific method on the funding process could yield novel insights with the potential to accelerate scientific discoveries (Azoulay 2012). Within this framework, federal funding agencies and philanthropic funders could encourage randomized experimentation of grant-making practices—whether they pertain to peer review, time horizon, or intellectual property policies—and carefully evaluate the results before adopting them at scale.

In sum, scientific grant funding is an important part of the policy toolkit for encouraging innovation, particularly in basic research. In this chapter, we have covered a range of examples—from the NIH to the NSF to the DoD to the DOE—of agencies that have used varying types of grant mechanisms to support both incremental and high-risk R&D. By adopting a more scientific approach to studying the grant-funding processes, policy makers can refine these tools to support new research challenges and needs.

References

Aghion, Philippe, Mathias Dewatripont, and Jeremy C. Stein. 2008. "Academic Freedom, Private Sector Focus, and the Process of Innovation." *RAND Journal of Economics* 39 (3): 617–35.

ARPA-E. 2013. *Final Assistance Funding Opportunity Announcement, Strategies for Wide-Bandgap, Inexpensive Transistors for Controlling High Efficiency Systems (SWITCHES): DE-FOA-0000942.* Washington, DC: Department of Energy.

Arrow, Kenneth. 1962. "Economic Welfare and the Allocation of Resources for Invention." In *The Rate and Direction of Inventive Activity: Economic and Social Factors,* 609–25. Princeton, NJ: Princeton University Press.

Azoulay, Pierre. 2012. "Turn the Scientific Method on Ourselves." *Nature* 484 (7392): 31–32.

Azoulay, Pierre, Erica Fuchs, Anna P. Goldstein, and Michael Kearney. 2019a. "Funding Breakthrough Research: Promises and Challenges of the 'ARPA Model.'" In *Innovation Policy and the Economy,* vol. 19, edited by Josh Lerner and Scott Stern, 69–96. Chicago: University of Chicago Press.

Azoulay, Pierre, Joshua Graff Zivin, and Gustavo Manso. 2011. "Incentives and Creativity: Evidence from the Academic Life Sciences." *RAND Journal of Economics* 42 (3): 527–54.

Azoulay, Pierre, Joshua S. Graff Zivin, Danielle Li, and Bhaven N. Sampat. 2019b. "Public R&D Investments and Private-Sector Patenting: Evidence from NIH Funding Rules." *Review of Economic Studies* 86 (1): 117–52.

Azoulay, Pierre, Wesley H. Greenblatt, and Misty L. Heggeness. 2020. "Long-Term Effects from Early Exposure to Research: Evidence from the NIH 'Yellow Berets.'" NBER Working Paper No. 26069. Cambridge, MA: National Bureau of Economic Research.

Balconi, Margherita, Stefano Brusoni, and Luigi Orsenigo. 2010. "In Defence of the Linear Model: An Essay." *Research Policy* 39 (1): 1–13.

Baldwin, Melinda. 2018. "Scientific Autonomy, Public Accountability, and the Rise of 'Peer Review' in the Cold War United States." *Isis* 109 (3): 538–58.

Barany, Michael J. 2018. "A Postwar Guide to Winning a Science Grant." *Physics Today*, March 20.

———. 2019. "Rockefeller Bureaucracy and Circumknowing Science in the Mid-twentieth Century." *International Journal for History, Culture and Modernity* 7: 779–96.

Barham, Bradford L., Jeremy D. Foltz, and Ana Paula Melo. 2020. "Academic Engagement, Commercialization, and Scholarship: Empirical Evidence from Agricultural and Life Scientists at U.S. Land-Grant Universities." NBER Working Paper No. 26688. Cambridge, MA: National Bureau of Economic Research.

Beard, T. Randolph, George S. Ford, Thomas M. Koutsky, and Lawrence J. Spiwak. 2009. "A Valley of Death in the Innovation Sequence: An Economic Investigation." *Research Evaluation* 18 (5): 343–56.

Begley, Sharon. 2019. "The Maddening Saga of How an Alzheimer's 'Cabal' Thwarted Progress toward a Cure for Decades." *STAT*, June 25.

Boudreau, Kevin J., Eva C. Guinan, Karim R. Lakhani, and Christoph Riedl. 2016. "Looking Across and Looking Beyond the Knowledge Frontier: Intellectual Distance, Novelty, and Resource Allocation in Science." *Management Science* 62 (10): 2765–83.

Brock, Thomas D., and Hudson Freeze. 1969. "Thermus aquaticus gen. n. and sp. n., a Nonsporulating Extreme Thermophile." *Journal of Bacteriology* 98 (1): 289–97.

Brooks, Harvey. 1996. "The Evolution of U.S. Science Policy." In *Technology, R&D, and the Economy*, edited by Bruce L. R. Smith and Claude E. Barfield, 15–48. Washington, DC: Brookings Institution.

Bush, Vannevar. 1945. *Science: The Endless Frontier*. Washington, DC: US General Printing Office.

Cahan, David. 1982. "Werner Siemens and the Origin of the Physikalisch-Technische Reichsanstalt, 1872–1887." *Historical Studies in the Physical Sciences* 12 (2): 253–83.

Cohen, Wesley M., Henry Sauermann, and Paula Stephan. 2019. "Not in the Job Description: The Commercial Activities of Academic Scientists and Engineers." NBER Working Paper No. 24769. Cambridge, MA: National Bureau of Economic Research.

Cole, Stephen, Jonathan R. Cole, and Gary A. Simon. 1981. "Chance and Consensus in Peer Review." *Science* 214 (4523): 559–67.

Contopoulos-Ioannidis, Despina G., Evangelia E. Ntzani, and John P.A. Ioannidis. 2003. "Translation of Highly Promising Basic Science Research into Clinical Applications." *American Journal of Medicine* 114 (6): 477–84.

Crosland, Maurice, and Antonio Gálvez. 1989. "The Emergence of Research Grants within the Prize System of the French Academy of Sciences, 1795–1914." *Social Studies of Science* 19 (1): 71–100.

Crow, James F., and Ray D. Owen. 2000. "Kay Wilson and the NIH Genetics Study Section." *Genetics* 155 (1): 1–5.

Dasgupta, Partha, and Paul David. 1994. "Towards a New Economics of Science." *Research Policy* 23 (5): 487–521.

Dawes, Robyn, David Faust, and Paul E. Meehl. 1989. "Clinical versus Actuarial Judgment." *Science* 243 (4899): 1668–74.

Dent, Chris, Paul Jensen, Sophie Waller, and Beth Webster. 2006. "Research Use of Patented Knowledge: A Review." OECD Directorate for Science, Technology and Industry Working Paper #2006/2. https://www.oecd.org/science/inno/36311146.pdf.

Fang, Ferric C., and Arturo Casadevall. 2016. "Research Funding: The Case for a Modified Lottery." *mBio* 7 (2): e00422–16.

Fox, Daniel M. 1987. "The Politics of the NIH Extramural Program, 1937–1950." *Journal of the History of Medicine and Allied Sciences* 42 (4): 447–66.

Froot, Kenneth A., David S. Scharfstein, and Jeremy C. Stein. 1993. "Risk Management: Coordinating Corporate Investment and Financing Policies." *Journal of Finance* 48 (5): 1629–58.

Funk, Russell J., and Jason Owen-Smith. 2017. "A Dynamic Network Measure of Technological Change." *Management Science* 63 (3): 791–817.

Furman, Jeffrey, and Scott Stern. 2011. "Climbing Atop the Shoulders of Giants: The Impact of Institutions on Cumulative Knowledge Production." *American Economic Review* 101 (5): 1933–63.

Gallini, Nancy, and Suzanne Scotchmer. 2002. "Intellectual Property: What is the Best Incentive System?" In *Innovation Policy and the Economy*, vol. 2, edited by Adam Jaffe, Josh Lerner, and Scott Stern, 51–77. Cambridge, MA: MIT Press.

Ganguli, Ina. 2017. "Saving Soviet Science: The Impact of Grants When Government R&D Funding Disappears." *American Economic Journal: Applied Economics* 9 (2): 165–201.

Ginther, Donna K., and Misty L. Heggeness. 2020. "Administrative Discretion in Scientific Funding: Evidence from a Prestigious Postdoctoral Training Program." *Research Policy* 49 (4): 103953.

Ginther, Donna K., Walter T. Schaffer, Joshua Schnell, Beth Masimore, Faye Liu, Laurel L. Haak, and Raynard Kington. 2011. "Race, Ethnicity, and NIH Research Awards." *Science* 333 (6045): 1015–19.

Godefroy, Raphael. 2011. "The Birth of the Congressional Clinic." Working Paper, Paris School of Economics.

Goldstein, Anna P., and Michael Kearney. 2017. "Uncertainty and Individual Discretion in Allocating Research Funds." August 7. https://ssrn.com/abstract=3012169.

———. 2020. "Know When to Fold 'Em: An Empirical Description of Risk Management in Public Research Funding." *Research Policy* 49 (1): 103873.

Goodin, Michael M., Graham F. Hatfull, and Harmit S. Malik. 2016. "A Diversified Portfolio." *Annual Review of Virology* 3: vi–viii.

Gross, Kevin, and Carl T. Bergstrom. 2019. "Contest Models Highlight Inherent Inefficiencies of Scientific Funding Competitions." *PLoS Biology* 17 (1): e3000065.

Hage, Jerald, and Jonathon Mote. 2010. "Transformational Organizations and a Burst of Scientific Breakthroughs: The Institut Pasteur and Biomedicine, 1889–1919." *Social Science History* 34 (1): 13–46.

Hart, David. 2004. "On the Origins of Google." National Science Foundation, August 17. https://www.nsf.gov/discoveries/disc_summ.jsp?cntn_id=100660.

Hausman, Naomi. 2019. "University Innovation and Local Economic Growth." Working Paper, Hebrew University of Jerusalem.

Hill, Ryan, and Carolyn Stein. 2020. "Race to the Bottom: Competition and Quality in Science." Working Paper, Massachusetts Institute of Technology.

Hoffman, Mitchell, Lisa B. Kahn, and Danielle Li. 2018. "Discretion in Hiring." *Quarterly Journal of Economics* 133 (2): 765–800.

Howell, Sabrina T. 2017. "Financing Innovation: Evidence from R&D Grants." *American Economic Review* 107 (4): 1136–64.

Hunter, Tony. 2007. "Treatment for Chronic Myelogenous Leukemia: The Long Road to Imatinib." *Journal of Clinical Investigation* 117 (8): 2036–43.

Hvide, Hans K., and Benjamin F. Jones. 2018. "University Innovation and the Professor's Privilege." *American Economic Review* 108 (7): 1860–98.

Jacob, Brian A., and Lars Lefgren. 2011. "The Impact of Research Grant Funding on Research Productivity." *Journal of Public Economics* 95 (9–10): 1168–77.

Jaffe, Adam. 1998. "Measurement Issues." In *Investing in Innovation: Creating a Research and Innovation Policy That Works*, edited by Lewis Branscomb and James Keller, 64–84. Cambridge, MA: MIT Press.

Kao, Jennifer. 2020. "Charted Territory: Evidence from Mapping the Cancer Genome and R&D Decisions in the Pharmaceutical Industry." Working Paper, UCLA.

Kearney, Michael. 2020. "Translating Science through Startups: Evidence from the National Science Foundation's I-Corps Program." Working Paper, Massachusetts Institute of Technology.

Kerr, William R., and Ramana Nanda. 2015. "Financing Innovation." *Annual Review of Financial Economics* 7: 445–62.

Kerr, William R., Ramana Nanda, and Matthew Rhodes-Kropf. 2014. "Entrepreneurship as Experimentation." *Journal of Economic Perspectives* 28 (3): 25–48.

Kleinberg, Jon, Himabindu Lakkaraju, Jure Leskovec, Jens Ludwig, and Sendhil Mullainathan. 2018. "Human Decisions and Machine Predictions." *Quarterly Journal of Economics* 133 (1): 237–93.

Klunder, Matthew L. 2013. "Establishment and Implementation of a Peer Review Program within ONR." Office of Naval Research Instruction 3966.1A, November 14. https://www.onr.navy.mil/-/media/Files/Research/ONR-Instruction-39661 A.ashx?la=en.

Kohler, Robert E. 1976. "The Management of Science: The Experience of Warren Weaver and the Rockefeller Foundation Programme in Molecular Biology." *Minerva* 14 (3): 279–306.

Kolev, Julian, Pierre Azoulay, Yuly Fuentes-Medel, and Fiona Murray. 2019. "Expert Evaluation in Innovation: The Role of Distance and Consensus in Project Selection." Working Paper, Southern Methodist University.

König, Thomas. 2017. *The European Research Council*. Cambridge, UK: Polity Press.

Krieger, Joshua, Danielle Li, and Dimitris Papanikolaou. 2018. "Missing Novelty in Drug Development." NBER Working Paper No. 24595. Cambridge, MA: National Bureau of Economic Research.

Laffont, Jean-Jacques, and Jean Tirole. 1993. *A Theory of Incentives in Procurement and Regulation*. Cambridge, MA: MIT Press.

Lakhani, Karim R., Wesley M. Cohen, Kynon Ingram, Tushar Kothalkar, Maxim Kuzemchenko, Santosh Malik, Cynthia Meyn, Greta Friar, and Stephanie Healy Pokrywa. 2014. "Netflix: Designing the Netflix Prize (A)." Harvard Business School Case 615–015.

Lawani, Stephen M., and Alan E. Bayer. 1983. "Validity of Citation Criteria for Assessing the Influence of Scientific Publications: New Evidence with Peer Assessment." *Journal of the American Society for Information Science* 34 (1): 59–66.

Lawrence, Peter A. 2009. "Real Lives and White Lies in the Funding of Scientific Research." *PLoS Biology* 7 (9): e1000197.

Li, Danielle. 2017. "Expertise vs. Bias in Evaluation: Evidence from the NIH." *American Economic Journal: Applied Economics* 9 (2): 60–92.

Li, Danielle, and Leila Agha. 2015. "Big Names or Big Ideas: Do Peer-Review Panels Select the Best Science Proposals?" *Science* 348 (6233): 434–38.

Li, Danielle, Pierre Azoulay, and Bhaven N. Sampat. 2017. "The Applied Value of Public Investments in Biomedical Research." *Science* 356 (6333): 78–81.

Long, Cheryl Xiaoning, and Jun Wang. 2019. "China's Patent Promotion Policies and Its Quality Implications." *Science and Public Policy* 46 (1): 91–104.

MacLeod, R. M. 1971. "The Royal Society and the Government Grant: Notes on the Administration of Scientific Research, 1849–1914." *The Historical Journal* 14 (2): 323–58.

Malenko, Andrey, Ramana Nanda, and Matthew Rhodes-Kropf. 2019. "Investment Committee Voting and the Financing of Innovation." Working Paper, Boston College.

Mazzucato, Mariana. 2018. "Mission-Oriented Innovation Policies: Challenges and Opportunities." *Industrial and Corporate Change* 27 (5): 803–15.

Mokyr, Joel. 2002. *The Gifts of Athena: Historical Origins of the Knowledge Economy*. Princeton, NJ: Princeton University Press.

Mowery, David C., Richard R. Nelson, Bhaven N. Sampat, and Arvids Ziedonis. 2001. "The Growth of Patenting and Licensing by U.S. Universities: An Assessment of the Effects of the Bayh-Dole Act of 1980." *Research Policy* 30 (1): 99–119.

Moxham, Noah, and Aileen Fyfe. 2018. "The Royal Society and the Prehistory of Peer Review." *The Historical Journal* 61 (4): 863–89.

Munger, Mary G. 1960. *Growth of the External Programs of the National Institutes of Health*. Statistics and Analysis Branch, Division of Research Grants, National Institutes of Health.

Murray, Fiona, Philippe Aghion, Mathias Dewatripont, Julian Kolev, and Scott Stern. 2016. "Of Mice and Academics: Examining the Effect of Openness on Innovation." *American Economic Journal: Economic Policy* 8 (1): 212–52.

Murray, Fiona, Scott Stern, Georgina Campbell, and Alan MacCormack. 2012. "Grand Innovation Prizes: A Theoretical, Normative, and Empirical Evaluation." *Research Policy* 41 (10): 1779–92.

Myers, Kyle. 2020. "The Elasticity of Science." *American Economic Journal: Applied Economics* 12 (4): 103–34.

Nanda, Ramana, and Matthew Rhodes-Kropf. 2016. "Financing Entrepreneurial Experimentation." *Innovation Policy and the Economy*, vol. 16, edited by Josh Lerner and Scott Stern, 1–23. Chicago: University of Chicago Press.

National Academies of Science, Engineering, and Medicine. 2017. *An Assessment of ARPA-E*. Washington, DC: National Academies Press.

Nelson, Richard R. 1959. "The Simple Economics of Basic Scientific Research." *Journal of Political Economy* 67 (2): 297–306.

Nelson, Richard R. 1993. *National Innovation Systems*. New York: Oxford University Press.

Ottaviani, Marco. 2020. "Grantmaking." Working Paper, Bocconi University.

Ouellette, Lisa Larrimore, and Andrew Tutt. 2020. "How Do Patent Incentives Affect University Researchers?" *International Review of Law and Economics* 61 (March), article 105883. https://doi.org/10.1016/j.irle.2019105883.

Page, Lawrence, Sergey Brin, Rajeev Motwani, and Terry Winograd. 1998. "The PageRank Citation Ranking: Bringing Order to the Web." Working paper, Stanford University.

Pier, Elizabeth L., Markus Brauer, Amarette Filut, Anna Kaatz, Joshua Raclaw,

Mitchell J. Nathan, Cecilia E. Ford, and Molly Carnes. 2018. "Low Agreement among Reviewers Evaluating the Same NIH Grant Applications." *Proceedings of the National Academy of Sciences* 115 (12): 2952–57.

Price, W. Nicholson, II. 2019. "Grants." *Berkeley Technology Law Journal* 34 (1): 1–66.

Rettig, Richard. 1977. *Cancer Crusade: The Story of the National Cancer Act of 1971.* Princeton, NJ: Princeton University Press.

Rivest, Ronald L., Adi Shamir, and Leonard Adleman. 1978. "A Method for Obtaining Digital Signatures and Public-Key Cryptosystems." *Communications of the ACM* 21 (2): 120–26.

Rosenberg, Nathan. 1979. "Technological Interdependence in the American Economy." *Technology and Culture* 20 (1): 25–50.

———. 1990. "Why Do Firms Do Basic Research (with Their Own Money)?" *Research Policy* 19 (2): 165–74.

Sampat, Bhaven N. 2012. "Mission-Oriented Biomedical Research at the NIH." *Research Policy* 41 (10): 1729–41.

Schneider, William H. 2015. "The Origin of the Medical Research Grant in the United States: The Rockefeller Foundation and the NIH Extramural Funding Program." *Journal of the History of Medicine and Allied Sciences* 70 (2): 279–311.

Scotchmer, Suzanne. 1991. "Standing on the Shoulders of Giants: Cumulative Research and the Patent Law." *Journal of Economic Perspectives* 5 (1): 29–41.

Stephan, Paula E. 2012. *How Economics Shapes Science.* Cambridge, MA: Harvard University Press.

Stern, Scott. 2004. *Biological Resource Centers: Knowledge Hubs for the Life Sciences.* Washington, DC: Brookings Institution Press.

Stokes, Donald. 1997. *Pasteur's Quadrant: Basic Science and Technological Innovation.* Washington, DC: Brookings Institution Press.

Strickland, Stephen P. 1989. *The Story of the NIH Grants Program.* Lanham, MD: University Press of America.

Van Slyke, C. J. 1946. "New Horizons in Medical Research." *Science* 104 (2711): 559–67.

Walsh, John P., Charlene Cho, and Wesley M. Cohen. 2005. "View from the Bench: Patents and Material Transfers." *Science* 309 (5743): 2002–3.

Wapner, Jessica. 2013. *The Philadelphia Chromosome: A Genetic Mystery, a Lethal Cancer, and the Improbable Invention of a Life-Saving Treatment.* New York: The Experiment.

Westfall, Richard S. 1985. "Science and Patronage: Galileo and the Telescope." *Isis* 76 (1): 11–30.

Williams, Heidi L. 2013. "Intellectual Property Rights and Innovation: Evidence from the Human Genome." *Journal of Political Economy* 121 (1): 1–27.

Wright, Brian D. 1983. "The Economics of Invention Incentives: Patents, Prizes, and Research Contracts." *American Economic Review* 73 (4): 691–707.

Wu, Lingfei, Dashun Wang, and James A. Evans. 2019. "Large Teams Develop and Small Teams Disrupt Science and Technology." *Nature* 566 (7744): 378–82.

5

Tax Policy for Innovation

Bronwyn H. Hall

5.1 Introduction: Some Questions

Innovative activity on the part of firms and individuals is viewed by most economists as a key driver of productivity and economic growth. However, there are good arguments that from a social welfare perspective innovation will be undersupplied by such market agents. One of the ways in which policy makers hope to encourage innovative activity is via the treatment of such activity in the corporate tax system. The two key tax policies that bear directly on innovative activity are various tax credits and superdeductions for R&D expenses (cost reductions for an innovative input) and reduced taxes on profits from intellectual property (IP) income, commonly known as IP boxes.

This article reviews what we know about these two types of tax policy, one addressed to innovation input choice, and one based on innovation output. In the process I attempt to provide at least partial answers to the following questions:

1. How does taxation affect innovation?
2. Why are there special tax incentives for innovative activity?
3. What are the consequences of different R&D design choices?

Bronwyn H. Hall is professor of economics emerita at the University of California, Berkeley, an international research associate of IFS London, a visiting professor at MPI Munich, and a research associate of the National Bureau of Economic Research.

I thank Laurie Ciaramella, Fabian Gaessler, Ben Jones, Jacques Mairesse, James Poterba, and anonymous reviewers for helpful comments on earlier drafts. Prepared for the NBER Conference on Innovation and Public Policy, Washington, DC, March 13, 2020 (postponed due to COVID-19). For acknowledgments, sources of research support, and disclosure of the author's material financial relationships, if any, please see https://www.nber.org/books-and-chapters/innovation-and-public-policy/tax-policy-innovation.

4. Do patent boxes spur innovation?

5. How does the introduction of a tax measure in one jurisdiction affect other jurisdictions?

Before doing so, however, I highlight the broader topic of which the discussion here is only a part. The impact of taxation on innovative activity goes beyond these targeted measures to encompass personal and corporate taxes imposed for other purposes. For an example, see Akcigit et al. (2018), who examine the relationship between patents and citation-weighted patents and the level of personal and corporate taxation at the US state level. They find that higher taxes reduce the quantity, quality, and location of innovation as proxied by patent measures, both for individuals and even more strongly for firms.

This chapter focuses only on those tax instruments that directly target innovative activity, but it should be kept in mind that the broader tax environment may also matter and may influence the efficacy of innovation-related tax policies. The chapter is structured as follows: Section 5.2 defines innovative activities and discusses the rationale for their support. Sections 5.3 and 5.4 provide a detailed examination of the policy design issues and practices associated with innovation tax incentives, including the current use of these policies around the world. I then summarize the evidence for their effectiveness in section 5.5. Section 5.6 focuses on the use of the R&D tax credit in the United States and how it might be designed in the future. Section 5.7 concludes and discusses some of the broader questions that arise from the review in the earlier sections.

5.2 Innovation Activity and the Rationale for Its Support

At least since the work of Arrow (1962) and Nelson (1959), economists have understood that innovative activity in the form of R&D is likely to generate unpriced spillovers to other firms and to the overall economy, implying that these resources may be undersupplied due to the (relative) ease of their imitation. Arrow also noted two additional factors that influence the supply of innovation: the associated risk and uncertainty that cannot be diversified away or insured against, and asymmetric information/moral hazard problems when the innovator and his financier are not the same. These features of R&D investment lead to a high cost of financing, especially for new firms and small and medium-sized enterprises (SMEs).

However, R&D is only one component of innovative activity. When we look at the other components, it is less clear a priori that the spillovers will be as large, although this is an area about which we know relatively little empirically. The components of innovation spending by firms include the following:

- Research (basic and applied)
- Development (including experimental research and design)
- Purchase of external IP. including patents, copyrights, trademarks, and technical know-how
- Purchase, installation, and use of technologically more advanced equipment
- Software and database activities
- Training of employees in new processes or in supporting new products
- Marketing associated with the introduction of new or improved goods and services
- Costs of organizational innovation

The extent of potential spillovers obviously varies across the type of spending, as does appropriability via IP protection or other means. A distinction that was highlighted long ago by Nelson (1959) and recently modeled more explicitly by Akcigit, Hanley, and Serrano-Velarde (2013) is that between basic and applied R&D. The former is expected to have greater and less predictable spillovers than the latter, which would argue that it be targeted by R&D policy. It might also be argued that the returns from the purchase of new equipment as well as software and database development are largely internalized by the firm and therefore require less subsidy. However, the returns to training expense depend very much on both its specific (to the firm) nature and also on the degree to which employees are able to capture these returns in their wages in the future. The extent to which training employees raises the cost of wages because it increases the value of the employees' outside options makes the allocation of the returns from such training between private and social more complex.

Beyond the usual market-failure arguments of government policy toward private innovation expenditure, it is important to note that there is another argument in favor of government policy toward research and innovation. This argument is the fact that the production of public goods (in the realms of health, environment, defense, etc.) may be greatly enhanced by research targeted toward them. This kind of research will be undersupplied for the usual reasons of lack of appropriability and risk, but is also directed toward goods which themselves can be undersupplied because of their nonrival and/or nonexcludable nature. Economists sometimes refer to this as the double externality problem, especially in the context of environmental innovation.

5.3   Tax Policies for Innovation

If we accept the rationale for the government role in encouraging innovation, what policies are commonly used to this end? There are several, some of which take the form of increasing firm incentives, and some of which involve direct spending by the government. The main difference between the two is that modifying the incentives for innovation generally leaves the direction of innovation in the hands of firms, while direct spending allows the government a larger role in choosing the projects that will be funded.

The potential incentive measures include reduced taxes, depending on the level of innovation inputs or outputs of the firm, as well as the granting of intellectual property rights (IPRs), such as patents on new inventions. Drawbacks to these instruments are that the firm may choose privately profitable avenues of innovation that do not add much to social welfare. A leading example is the development of "me too" drugs, slightly improved versions of existing remedies that take a large market share and therefore profits from the drugs they displace, but provide only a small benefit in terms of increases in consumer welfare. In the case of IPRs, there is an additional cost due to the creation of some ex post market power that may restrict output or raise the cost of follow-on innovation.

Direct spending by government consists of subsidies for R&D or innovation, often targeted to a particular type of firm or project, as well as government-performed R&D directed toward the public good (e.g., health research, defense, etc.). Targeted subsidies, especially those that choose specific projects to support, tend to have high administrative costs for evaluation and auditing. Nevertheless, they are widely used around the world (EYGM 2017; Hall and Maffioli 2008). As Cohen and Noll (1991) point out, one drawback of these kinds of government projects is that political support arising from the beneficiaries may make them difficult to terminate when they are unsuccessful, especially if they are large, create local employment, and require considerable investment before a path to success is seen. Nevertheless, one can also point to successful projects of this type, especially in the area of space exploration.

In this chapter I focus on tax-related incentive measures to encourage innovation. The next few sections discuss issues in the design of tax measures and the two commonly used tax incentives that directly target innovative activity: R&D tax credits and superdeductions, and IP boxes (reduced taxes on the profits from innovation).

5.3.1 Some Issues in Design

Before describing the most commonly used tax instruments, it is useful to review the features of these instruments that are more likely to make them effective at achieving their goals. First, is the policy instrument visible to the firm's decision-makers? That is, given limited attention and bounded rationality, does it affect the company's bottom line enough so that it becomes salient in decision-making? Related to this, are there significant accounting and reporting costs required to make use of the instrument?

Second, does the time horizon of benefits match that of the subsidized investment? That is, does the instrument reduce cost or increase income in the near term, when the firm may have losses due to investment spending? Third and related, is the system stable enough to allow forward planning by the firm regarding its investment strategy?

Fourth, does the instrument target activities with greater potential spill-overs, such as basic research, standard setting, or spending at universities and nonprofit research organizations, rather than incremental innovation of existing products in which a firm already has a strong market position? Also, given the evidence that SMEs face larger financial constraints, does it target their activities?

Fifth, what is the appropriate level of the tax subsidy? In principle, it should be designed to lower the cost of private R&D capital to a level that induces the socially optimal level of private R&D. What we usually observe is a different quantity: the gap between the social and private rate of return to R&D. This is generally found to be quite large, but imprecisely determined (Hall, Mairesse, and Mohnen 2010; Lucking, Bloom, and Van Reenen 2019). One reason for the indeterminacy is that the social return to R&D is an unintended consequence of the individual firm's decisions. That is, the firm attempts to set its expected return to some estimate of the cost of capital, whereas no such mechanism determines the social rate of return. At the macroeconomic level, Jones and Williams (1998) use an endogenous growth model to suggest that the optimal R&D investment level for the United States may be as high as four times the current level.

The problem of determining the optimal subsidy using the estimated private and social returns to R&D is illustrated in figure 5.1, which presents a stylized version of the impact of a tax subsidy on R&D spending by the firm. The horizontal axis gives the level of R&D spending and the vertical axis its price in terms of cost of capital or rate of return. The firm's return

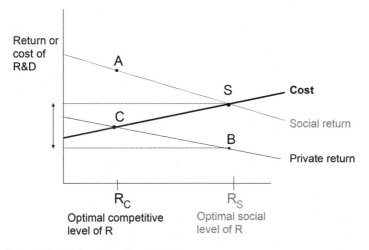

Fig. 5.1   Determining the optimal subsidy

to R&D is assumed to slope downward, as does the return to society as a whole, but society's return is higher because of spillovers. The cost of capital is assumed to increase with an increase in R&D, although this is not essential for the argument and it could be constant. What we usually observe in the various econometric studies of R&D returns is the gap between point A (the social returns to the firm's choice of R&D) and point C (the private returns to R&D at the firm, chosen to be equal to the expected cost of capital). In order to move the firm's R&D from the competitive level R_C to the socially optimal level R_S, the subsidy required is a reduction in cost from point S to point B, which is not necessarily of the same magnitude as A–C, unless the return lines are parallel.

Obviously, even this picture is oversimplified. First, there is no reason to think that the ordering of R&D projects by rate of return is the same for private and social rates. That is, the social return curve may not be a simple downward-sloping curve when plotted against R&D spending ordered by the firm's preferences. In addition, the magnitude of the spillover gap will vary by country, industry, and technology type. Attempts to take account of these factors in policy design will necessarily be fairly crude and are usually confined to attempts to distinguish basic from applied research and development.

A final design question is whether the instrument is comparatively easy to audit. That is, do the tax authorities find it straightforward to identify expenditure or income that is qualified for the tax measure? This has proved to be difficult for many governments (Cowx 2020; Guenther 2013, 2015) and also can discourage firms from using the measures (Appelt et al. 2016, 2019; Guenther 2015).

5.3.2   The Practice of Corporate Tax in the Innovation Area

A number of features in the corporate tax system can be seen to subsidize innovation. As mentioned, the most obvious are the widely used R&D tax credit or superdeduction, and the various IP boxes (reduced tax rates on income generated by intellectual property such as patents, design rights, copyright, and trademarks). Tax credits are a reduction in taxes that are based on a measure of R&D spending, whereas an R&D superdeduction allows for expensing of R&D at a rate higher than the 100 percent commonly used.[1] In some cases these measures are targeted toward basic research, university cooperation, and the use of public nonprofit research organizations.

But there are other instruments that favor innovative activity. The first

1. The main difference between the two is that the superdeduction portion is reduced by one minus the corporate tax rate, whereas the credit does not depend on the level of the tax rate on corporate profits. If the credit is recaptured, as has sometimes been the case, it will behave like a superdeduction, assuming the firm is profitable. In the case of a loss-making firm, the comparison between a credit and superdeduction will depend on the precise carryforward rules and the discount rate faced by the firm.

and most important is the investment tax credit or accelerated depreciation, which reduces the cost of acquiring new equipment and IT. Surveys of innovation spending based on the Oslo Manual (OECD/Eurostat 2018), such as those reported by Eurostat, show that in many countries the most important share of innovation spending is the acquisition of new equipment—that is, IT hardware and software related to innovation—rather than R&D spending (Eurostat 2020).

Another tax feature that may favor or disfavor innovative activity is the relative treatment of debt versus equity finance. If debt is favored due to the tax deductibility of interest expense, the cost of intangible, nonsecurable finance is relatively more expensive than investment in tangible assets (Hall 1992).

However, the most commonly used corporate tax instrument specifically targeted toward innovation is the R&D tax credit. Given that this instrument has been used at least since the 1980s in some countries, there is considerable experience with its design. The first design problem is that basing a credit on the total R&D spending by a firm can be expensive, given the relative smoothness of R&D spending within the firm. That is, most R&D will be done anyway, and it would be desirable only to subsidize an incremental amount. The difficulty is to measure that increment—that is, what would the firm have done in the absence of the tax credit? Using the firm's own past history of spending has the negative effect of greatly reducing the nominal incentive offered by the credit due to the impact an increase today has on the increment available in the future (figure 5.A.1 and Hall 1993). So although incremental schemes can be cheaper, they have been abandoned or greatly modified over time by several countries (e.g., the United States and France).

A tax credit or superdeduction may not be useful unless there are taxes to be paid, so the better-designed instruments allow for loss carryforwards of the tax benefits, to reduce future taxes. This can be especially helpful for start-ups, although it still leaves them facing higher costs for their initial investments. Administratively, one way to handle this problem is that introduced by the Netherlands: reduced social charges on science and engineering employment for R&D.[2] This is an attractive design, as the audit cost is relatively low, and it is immediately effective in reducing the firm's costs, avoiding the carryforward problem. The downside is that it may be more complex to administer in the case of purchased external R&D. The effectiveness in this case will depend to some extent on whether the supplying firm passes the reduced cost of their R&D through to the buyer.

A second drawback to using a social charge reduction as an R&D incentive is that in some countries the accounts for social security and retirement pensions are administered quite separately from the general government

---

2. As discussed later in the chapter, the United States introduced a limited version of this instrument for small businesses in 2016.

budget. It is not always easy to make up for reducing the social charges from the general government budget for administrative reasons and would require additional legislation.

Recently a number of countries have introduced so-called IP boxes, which permit considerably reduced corporate tax rates on income that is generated by a firm's intellectual property such as patents, copyrights, designs, and trademarks. Such a tax instrument is often justified as subsidy to or reward for innovative activity. However, the rationale is a bit more complex than that, as I describe in what follows.

In most developed economies, the share of company assets that is intangible has grown in recent years to the point where it is larger than tangible assets in some firms (Corrado, Hulten, and Sichel 2009; R. E. Hall 2001; Lev 2018). Many of these intangibles are in fact intellectual property, covered by some form of exclusivity right. Because intangibles do not necessarily have a physical location, it is fairly easy to move them to a low tax jurisdiction, enabling lower tax obligations (Dischinger and Riedel 2011; Mutti and Grubert 2009). A common strategy is to pay royalties for the use of the IP to the low-tax country, creating income there, and cost in the source (high-tax) country, reducing the total taxes to be paid (Bartelsman and Beetsma 2003). This strategy has not escaped the attention of tax authorities and governments, and in an effort to persuade the IP assets to stay home, it is appealing to offer lower tax rates on their income. Such a tax strategy on the part of governments also reflects a view that encouraging IP asset creation and location in the country is likely to persuade firms to retain skilled jobs and R&D there.

The above argument implies that although the encouragement of innovative activity and IP creation may be a motive for lowering taxes on IP income, countries are effectively forced to do this by the presence of many low-tax jurisdictions around the world into which such income could migrate.[3] It is also worth noting that three of the countries that have introduced IP boxes recently are Cyprus, Liechtenstein, and Malta, who presumably did so mainly to attract tax revenue rather than to discourage IP income from leaving.[4]

The design of IP boxes has proved even more challenging than the design of R&D tax credits. First, what IP should be covered? All the extant boxes include patent rights, but the other choices include trademarks, designs and models, copyrights (sometimes restricted to software), domain names, and trade secrets/know-how (Alstadsæter et al. 2018). From a spillover perspective, the rationale for subsidizing some of these alternative IPRs appears

3. The well-known use of Ireland as an IP-related tax haven by Apple is only the tip of a very large iceberg (Ting 2014), although see Hines (2014) for a fact-based review of the evidence that suggests the problem may be less serious than is sometimes believed.

4. These three countries combined account for fewer than 0.2 percent of European patent applications. Author's computations from European Patent Office (2019).

questionable. For example, trademarks are traditionally used for consumer protection purposes, but also to secure and maintain some degree of pricing power by preventing imitation. A similar argument applies to domain names. In the case of trade secrets or know-how, it is unclear how one could even measure the associated income.

Second, how is IP income to be measured and expenses to be allocated between IP and non-IP activities? Third, is acquired or existing IP to be covered, or only IP newly developed in the country in question? This latter feature has now been to some extent standardized in the Organisation for Economic Co-operation and Development (OECD) and EU economies by the nexus principle of the base erosion and profit-shifting (BEPS) rules (OECD 2015).[5] Fourth, should any tax benefits for the R&D associated with the patent be recaptured, to avoid too generous an incentive? In practice, different countries have reached different answers to these questions, so there is a wide variation around the world in implementation of patent boxes (Alstadsæder et al. 2018; Gaessler, Hall, and Harhoff 2021).

5.3.3   Comparing R&D Tax Incentives and Patent Boxes

What is the difference between these two tax incentives, and should we prefer one over the other? There are two obvious differences. First, R&D tax credits do not cover innovation that is not generated via R&D, and patent boxes do not cover nonpatentable innovation. Second, R&D tax incentives directly target an input to innovation that is under control of the firm, whereas patent boxes target an output, which may be affected by and indeed largely due to external causes and "luck." Obviously, in an expectational sense, the availability of lower taxes on patent income feeds back into the firm's decision-making process, but it seems rather indirect compared to a subsidy of an innovation input. In addition, tax benefits ex post (in some cases many years ex post) do not really help with the immediate problem of financing the investment.

Besides the fact that R&D tax credits are directly related to the firm's decisions on the cost and location of innovative activity, there are a number of other reasons that they differ from patent boxes. Patent boxes target the most appropriable part of innovation, which are the innovative activities that already receive a reward via the exclusivity of the patent. They also effectively subsidize patent assertion, some of which is "patent trolling" because all the income of firms that specialize in patent litigation and enforcement is patent income.[6] Relatedly, they provide an additional incentive to renew patents that might otherwise be abandoned, thus extending potential mar-

5. The nexus approach requires a link between the income benefiting from the IP regime and the extent to which the taxpayer has undertaken the underlying R&D that generated the IP asset (OECD 2015).
6. The definition of a patent troll is controversial, but it generally means an entity that specializes in asserting patents against producers in situations where the legal costs are so high

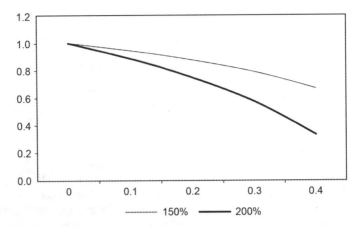

Fig. 5.2   **B-index for R&D deduction versus corporate tax rate**

ket power and raising search costs for inventors. Depending on the precise design of the patent box (gross income versus net income), they may provide an incentive to choose projects with high expenditure unrelated to R&D, since the size of the non-R&D budget will affect the amount claimed as a tax reduction.

IP boxes are more likely to face much higher audit cost than the R&D tax credit, which is already one of the most contentious areas of tax compliance (Sullivan 2015; US Congress Joint Economic Committee 2016). The tax reduction claimed depends on the allocation of a company's income and expense between its IP and non-IP assets, something that is rife with difficulty given complementarity. This fact is probably one of the reasons that some countries have chosen to use a gross income definition for patent income.

Before leaving this review of R&D tax credits versus patent boxes, it is useful to consider the recent EU proposal for a common corporate tax base in Europe, which includes a superdeduction of 150 percent, to replace patent boxes and existing R&D tax credit schemes (d'Andria, Dimitrios, and Agnieszka 2018). It is worth pointing out that the effectiveness of this instrument depends on the corporate tax rate. Warda (2001) defined the B-index as the marginal pretax profit a company needs to generate to break even when spending one unit on R&D. This index is equal to one when there is no special tax treatment for R&D. Figure 5.2 shows the B-index as a function of the corporate tax rate (from 0 to 0.4) for two different proposed superdeductions (150 percent and 200 percent).[7] The reduction in R&D cost is clearly much

---

that the firm will reach a financial settlement with the troll rather than defend itself, even if it believes that the patent is invalid or is not infringed.

7. See the appendix and Warda (2001) or OECD (2019b) for the derivation and detailed definition of the B-index.

higher for higher corporate tax rates than for lower—something to keep in mind when setting the level of the superdeduction.

5.4 The Facts

In this section of the chapter, I briefly summarize the current use (as of 2019) around the world of the two main innovation-related tax policies: R&D tax credits and superdeductions, and the patent box. For more detailed information on these instruments, see EYGM (2017), Lester and Warda (2018), and OECD (2019b).

5.4.1   R&D Tax Credits

From its beginnings in the 1970s and 1980s in the United States and Canada, this policy instrument is now very widely used. In 2000, 19 countries currently in the OECD provided some form of tax relief, as compared to 2018, when 32 out of 36 OECD countries, along with Brazil, China, and Russia, did. The latest figures given in EYGM (2017) suggest that 42 countries worldwide have some kind of tax scheme that reduces the cost of doing R&D. Implementation of these schemes varies widely across countries in a number of dimensions:

- Whether the scheme is a credit against taxes or a superdeduction (>100 percent) of R&D expense, or even a reduction in social charges for R&D employees
- The size of the credit or deduction
- Whether it is an incremental versus a level credit
- Whether or not SMEs are treated more favorably
- Details of the expense allowed
- Whether unused credits can be carried forward to be used when the firm is profitable

Comparing the tax credit policies across countries is usually done by computing the user cost of R&D capital, taking into account its tax treatment (R. E. Hall and Jorgenson 1967), or by computing the B-index, defined above. In general, these measures are computed for a profitable firm that increases its R&D in a single year. However, the OECD has recently developed a database of the effective subsidy rate from R&D tax incentives that is available on its website (OECD 2019b), covering the years 2000 through 2018. This database provides separate estimates for profitable and loss-making firms, as well as for SMEs if they face different tax treatment. In general, loss-making firms receive a slightly smaller subsidy and SMEs a slightly larger subsidy (see also Lester and Warda 2018).

Figure 5.3 shows the countries that offer some form of R&D tax relief in 2017, distinguishing between those administered via the corporate profits tax and those that also include a reduction in social charges on R&D

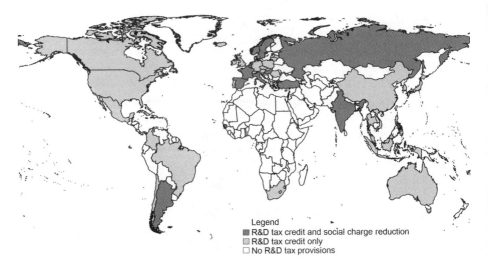

Fig. 5.3   Countries with R&D tax relief

employees. In the appendix I present figures that show the pattern of the R&D tax subsidies over time, based on the OECD (2019b) data.

5.4.2   IP Boxes

At the time of writing, 22 countries have introduced some kind of IP box, most of them in Europe. Tables comparting the various IP boxes can be found in Alstadsæder et al. (2018) and Evers, Miller, and Spengel (2015).

As in the case of R&D tax schemes, there is a wide variation in the rules surrounding IP boxes across countries:

- Variations in IP covered (sometimes even informal IP)
- Variations in the treatment of income and expense; reduced tax rate on gross IP income in some countries, rather than net IP income
- Recapture of past R&D expense deductions in some cases
- Rules on whether purchased or preexisting IP is eligible, or whether further development of the income-generating product in the relevant country is necessary (modified by BEPS, as described in section 5.3.2)
- Whether use is affected by controlled foreign corporation (CFC) rules[8]

Figure 5.4 shows the countries that have introduced a patent box as of 2019, many of them quite recently. Almost all are in Europe, mostly in West-

8. CFC rules specify that if a company in a tax haven is controlled from the home country, taxes are imposed on income received in the low-tax country at the domestic rate. However, the European Court of Justice has limited the application of CFC rules within the European Economic Area, so they do not affect patent transfers to patent box countries within the EU (Bräutigam, Spengel, and Steiff 2017). See also Deloitte Consulting (2014).

Fig. 5.4   Countries with a patent box in 2019

ern Europe. The only exceptions to this are Israel, India, Japan, and Turkey (not shown on the graph). Note also that several very small European countries with relatively little innovative activity have introduced a patent box but are not visible on the graph: Andorra, Liechtenstein, Malta, and San Marino.

5.5   Recent Research on Innovation Tax Policy Evaluation

5.5.1   R&D Tax Credit Evaluation

Evaluating the R&D tax credit involves at least three questions: (1) Does the credit increase business R&D as intended? (2) Do private rates of return to R&D decline, as they should, since the effect of the tax credit is to lower the cost of capital? (3) Do other firms receive increased R&D spillovers as a result of higher spending from the credit? The first has been very well studied and I summarize the results here. The second is often misinterpreted, with policy makers looking for high private returns from subsidized R&D, rather than the relatively low returns that would be expected if the effect of the tax credit is to lower the cost and therefore the required rate of return to R&D. The third question is the most important but also the most difficult, and there are few if any studies that look specifically at this question, although there are many studies of R&D spillovers more broadly (Hall, Mairesse, and Mohnen 2010).

Since the early and somewhat skeptical work of Mansfield (1984, 1986), evidence on the effectiveness of R&D tax credits has accumulated to show that they are generally effective at increasing business R&D, with a price elasticity of minus one or higher (Hall and Van Reenen, 2000). Such a result generally passes the simple cost-benefit test when compared with direct funding of R&D projects. Simulation evidence such as that reported in Hall (1993) and Mulkay and Mairesse (2013) has shown that the increase in R&D spending approximately balances or even exceeds the lost tax revenue.

Recent research generally confirms the evidence surveyed in Hall and Van Reenen (2000). For example, Chang (2018) uses US state-level data instrumented by federal tax changes to find elasticities of R&D to its tax-adjusted price of –2.8 to –3.8. Mulkay and Mairesse (2013) use the 2008 tax changes in France to find a price elasticity of –0.4 or higher, and Dechezleprêtre et al. (2016) use a regression discontinuity approach to find an elasticity of –2.6 for SMEs in the UK. Similarly, Agrawal, Rosell, and Simcoe (2020) use a difference-in-difference analysis of a change in the eligibility of Canadian small firms for the credit to find estimated elasticities well within the range of previous work. They also show a larger effect for firms that received the tax credit as refunds due to a lack of tax liability. Guceri and Liu (2019) use similar data with an exogenous shift in eligibility thresholds to find an elasticity of –1.6. See also Acconcia and Cantabene (2017) for a study of the impact of Italian R&D tax credits on financially constrained and unconstrained firms. Blandinieres, Steinbrenner, and Weiss (2020) provide a metaregression analysis of the various estimates of the tax-adjusted price elasticity of R&D, and generally center on –1 as the consensus estimate.

One problem that is particularly important for the analyses of US data is that of obtaining the appropriate measure of research and experimentation (R&E) expenses incurred by the firm. The legislation defines the expense eligible for the credit as research and experimentation excluding routine development. However, the only publicly available data on research at the firm level is that reported in the 10-K filings at the US Securities and Exchange Commission and available to researchers via Standard and Poor's Compustat. This definition of R&D is broader than the definition eligible for the credit. Because almost all the few studies that use the actual US IRS data on R&E expense claimed do not match these data to the 10-K data at the firm level, we have only an approximate idea of the difference between the two numbers (Altshuler 1989; Cowx 2020).

Rao (2016) compares the actual R&E expense claimed and reported to the tax authorities to the R&D reported on the 10-K for a sample of about 60 firms between 1981 and 1991, finding substantial discrepancies.[9] Using

---

9. The qualified research expenditures (QREs) for the tax credit average 37 percent of 10-K-reported R&D for these firms (Rao, private communication, April 2020). However, these numbers are also confounded by another source of discrepancy: the tax credit R&D is domestic only, whereas the R&D on the 10-K is worldwide. The firms in question are largely

the actual R&E expense and controlling for endogeneity in the relation-ship between the tax price and R&E, she finds a tax price elasticity of –1.6, which is very similar to those found using the public R&D data. This result does raise a further question about the R&D production function, because it suggests that the disallowed portion of the R&D is complementary to the eligible R&E expense. This in turn justifies the restricted definition as lowering the cost of the tax instrument (except for the increased audit cost) while not reducing its impact.

Cowx (2020) studies the impact of R&D tax credit uncertainty on the level of R&D. She finds that a higher IRS audit risk is associated with lower levels of R&D, especially for more financially constrained firms and those with lower-quality information environments for tracking QRE expense. These effects presumably dampen the effectiveness of the credit and make the strong findings of an impact in the literature more surprising.

Two recent studies have examined spillovers from tax credit–induced R&D. The first is the previously mentioned Dechezleprêtre et al. (2016). Following on Bloom, Schankerman, and Van Reenen (2013), they measure the technological closeness between firms using patent data, and show that increases in R&D (due to changes in eligibility for the tax credit) in one firm increases the patenting in firms that are technologically close to that firm. Aggregating over all such firms, they find that patenting overall increases 1.7 times the direct impact on the targeted firm. Interestingly, they find no such impact (positive or negative) for firms that are close in product market space. The implication of their work is that tax-induced increases in R&D do indeed generate technological spillovers that are fairly large in magnitude.

Balsmeier et al. (2020) base their study on the California R&D tax credit that was introduced in 1987. They find the usual increase in R&D and pat-enting in response to the credit. However, in contrast to Dechezleprêtre et al. (2016), in their data when firms are close in technology space, competitors' market value reacts negatively to the increase. They also find that there is a general tendency for firms to pursue existing lines of research with the increased R&D rather than striking out in new directions. One major dif-ference from the Dechezleprêtre et al. study is the sample: here firms of all sizes are examined, rather than only SMEs, which may help to explain some of the differences in the findings.

There is one further impact of changes in the tax treatment of R&D that should be considered: the possibility that rapid changes in the tax price of R&D may have the effect of increasing its cost rather than its quantity. This is because the supply of scientists and engineers is fairly inelastic in the short run, since it takes time to produce them. In that setting one might expect the

---

multinational enterprises (MNEs), so there will be a fair amount of R&D done outside the United States in their numbers. Thus the true fraction of domestic R&D that is QRE will be somewhat higher.

wages of existing R&D workers to increase in response to greater demand. This is what Goolsbee (1998) found for the United States, measuring a wage elasticity of about 0.3 with respect to R&D. Using data on 15 OECD economies, Wolff and Reinthaler (2008) find an upper bound to the long-run wage elasticity of 0.2, while Lokshin and Mohnen (2013) found a similar positive elasticity of about 0.2 for the Netherlands. Note that if the overall impact of the tax credit is unity, these findings suggest that the majority of the impact does go to the quantity of R&D, rather than the price.

5.5.2   R&D Tax Price as an Instrument for R&D

As argued in the introduction, the primary goal of tax policy toward innovation is increases in productivity and economic growth, via subsidies to innovative activity. Evaluating the success of these policies involves first asking whether they increase innovative activity, as discussed above, and second whether the increase leads to higher productivity at the firm level, greater spillovers to other firms, and ultimately higher economic growth. In the case of R&D or other investment policies, it is tempting to use the tax price of the investment as an instrument for the investment in a productivity or growth equation. Here I consider whether this procedure is justified.

My focus is on R&D investment, but much of the discussion applies to other forms of investment policy. There are two considerations that make instrumenting R&D by its tax price problematic: (1) the usual question of whether the instrument is a valid instrument and (2) the fact that R&D is an investment. That is, the problem is inherently dynamic. If the tax price is lowered in the current year, it is expected to increase current R&D investment, and possibly future R&D investment, assuming the tax change is quasi-permanent. However, it will do nothing for the past knowledge or R&D stock, which is the relevant driver of productivity and performance. This does not invalidate the instrument, but it weakens its power. Attempting to unpack the contribution of different lags of R&D (in order to use varying tax prices as instruments) in this kind of equation has long been shown to be extremely difficult due to the high serial correlation of R&D over time within firm, sector, or country.

The validity of the tax price as an instrument using the two requirements of correlation with the R&D choice and lack of correlation with the disturbance in the productivity or growth equation depends to some extent on the level of aggregation. For firms, if the future tax price depends on the current level of R&D investment, as it has done in some countries at some times, the tax price is presumably endogenous to the current output, given the current output influence on the future R&D-output profile of the firm. This is less of a worry if the tax price is the same regardless of the firm's current and future tax positions, although in this case there will be limited variability across firms for identification. Quasi-natural experiments involving eligibility changes such as those in Dechezleprêtre et al. (2016) and Agrawal, Rosell, and Simcoe (2020) are the solution in this case.

For investigation of the relation between R&D tax policy and growth at the country level, things are much more problematic. Low productivity growth or low R&D spending is arguably a driver of the introduction and strengthening of R&D tax incentives. For the 20 countries shown in the appendix, in recent years the raw correlation between the tax price of R&D and the country's R&D intensity is not negative, as expected, but positive and equal to 0.38, lending support to this view. Controlling for the country's mean of R&D intensity over time weakens the positive correlation somewhat, but it is still significantly positive. In any case, fixed effect estimation of that kind is inappropriate if our interest is in the impact of R&D tax credits on R&D and performance. Therefore, use of tax price as an instrument for R&D in this context requires a more careful dynamic model to control for the past history of R&D and its cost.

5.5.3   Patent Boxes

The evaluation of the effectiveness of patent boxes depends somewhat on what they are trying to achieve. Does their implementation aim to prevent taxable income from migrating to low-tax countries, or to encourage the production of knowledge and intangible assets within a country? In addition, some have questioned whether the presence of a patent box induces the transfer of patent ownership to a country without any positive benefits for the economy other than the taxation (at a low rate) of some additional corporate income.

A number of studies have been conducted on the patent box, looking at different aspects of these questions. In practice, the variation in patent box features across countries and the limited number of countries in which they had been introduced until recently mean that the use of the patent box as a "natural experiment" produces somewhat imprecise and sometimes conflicting results. Accounting for all the features leaves little variation for identification of their effect. In addition, it has always been possible to transfer patent income to a low-tax jurisdiction even without a patent box, so one might expect that the additional patent transfer induced by the patent box would be small (Bartelsman and Beetsma 2003).

Gaessler, Hall, and Harhoff (2021) survey the research that looks at the effect of introducing a patent box on patent transfer to and from a country. We then investigate the question using our own data and several features of the patent box, examining both the incentive to transfer patents to a patent box country and the impact on patentable invention and R&D in the country. We are able to extend the analysis to 2016, by which time 17 countries had a patent box in place for at least two years.

Our review of the literature finds a large number of studies that have looked at the relationship between taxation and patenting, a subset of which have examined patent boxes and the location of patents. Almost none have examined other impacts of the patent box. In general, the level of corporate taxes appears to reduce the incentive to locate patents in a country, consistent with what Akcigit et al. (2018) found for US state data (Boehm et al. 2015; Griffith, Miller, and O'Connell 2014; Karkinsky and Riedel 2012).

The evidence on patent location and ownership transfer in response to the introduction of a patent box has been studied by a number of other researchers (Alstadsæter et al. 2018; Bösenberg and Egger 2017; Bradley, Dauchy, and Robinson 2015; Ciaramella 2017). In general, both location and transfer respond to lower tax rates on patent income, although the studies vary considerably in their approach: observation at patent, country, or firm level; the set of patents observed (pre-grant only or including postgrant); whether initial location or transfer is examined. Because of this variability, it is difficult to extract the precise magnitude of the impact from the various estimates. Gaessler, Hall, and Harhoff (2021) find that the transfer impact is modest: if the difference between the corporate tax rate and the patent income tax rate in the potential recipient country falls by 10 percent, that leads to an 18 percent increase in patent transfers over the next three years, with most of the impact coming in the final year. However, like Alstadsæter et al. (2018) and Bradley, Dauchy, and Robinson (2015), we find that if there is a further development requirement for existing patents and those acquired from abroad, the impact disappears. As the nexus requirement of BEPS has eliminated the ability to simply benefit from transferring patents, we would expect the patent box impact on transfer to disappear in the future.

An interesting finding in Gaessler, Hall, and Harhoff is that patent ownership transfer is significantly discouraged by the size of the patent income tax rate in the sending company; there is an 18 percent reduction in transfer if the tax rate on patent income changes by 10 percent. This result is entirely consistent with the view that patent boxes are introduced in order to keep patent ownership and related activities in the country, rather than primarily to attract new patents.

Does the presence of a patent box increase patentable invention in a country? This is difficult to see in the aggregate data because all countries have an upward trend in patenting during the period. To examine this question, Gaessler, Hall, and Harhoff estimated regressions for the log of European patent (EP) filings in a country-year on the patent box rate, corporate tax rate, log population, log GDP per capita, log R&D per GDP, and country and year dummies, and found an insignificant impact of the patent box on patented invention. We also found similar insignificant results for the level of business R&D spending in the country. If there is no requirement for further development of the transferred patents, both patented invention and business R&D in the country actually decline significantly. That is, with a further development requirement on the use of the patent to reduce taxes, there is no impact on domestic patented invention or R&D. Once that requirement is in place (as required by the nexus principle), there seems to be a disincentive for domestic innovation. We caution, however, that sample sizes are small given the limited number of countries under investigation.

The only other paper to look at the impact of the patent box on R&D is that by Mohnen, Vankan, and Verspagen (2017), who find an increase in R&D person-hours in response to the patent box in the Netherlands. This may reflect the difference in the way the patent box (which is actually an innovation box) is administered in that country, as it has covered nonpatentable R&D since 2010.

Summarizing the results from these studies, I conclude first that patent boxes reduce patent ownership transfers from the country introducing them. They also induce some transfers to the country, but only if income from existing and/or acquired patents without development condition is covered. In addition, others have found that CFC rules do reduce patent ownership transfer by multinationals. More valuable patents by the usual metrics are the ones transferred, confirming the relationship of patent value metrics to the income generated by the related invention/innovation (Alstadsæter et al. 2018; Dudar, Spengel, and Voget 2015; Gaessler, Hall, and Harhoff 2021). However, there is little evidence that the introduction of a patent box increases either patentable invention or R&D investment in a country, controlling for country characteristics and overall time trends.

5.6 The R&D Tax Credit in the United States

5.6.1 History and Current Status

In the United States, the R&D tax credit (properly called the Research and Experimentation Tax Credit) has a long and varied history. It was first introduced in 1981 as an incremental credit, and it did not take long for economists to point out that the design was flawed, in that forward-looking firms would perceive an effective rate of the credit that was substantially lower than the statutory rate (table 5.A.1; Altshuler 1989; Eisner, Albert, and Sullivan 1986). In response, in 1990, the rolling base amount for the incremental credit was switched to a fixed base, determined by the 1984–1988 R&D-to-sales ratio times the current sales. This base is still in use, although it is obviously becoming more and more irrelevant as time passes.

Since its inception, R&D spending eligible for the credit has been restricted to QREs, which are typically about 65–75 percent of total R&D, although Rao (2016) uses a small sample of firms from the Statistics of Income data to report that QREs are only 37 percent of total R&D.[10] This is for two reasons:

10. In Rao's case the denominator of this percentage also accounts for R&D performed outside the United States, which is ineligible for the credit. This explains why her number is lower.

the desire to target expenditures that are more likely to generate spillovers, and to reduce the cost to the government of the tax credit. The definition of "qualified research" is research relying on a hard science that is intended to resolve technological uncertainty related to development of a new or improved business component, product, process, internal-use computer software, technique, formula, or invention to be sold or used in the taxpayer's trade or business. The emphasis in the definition is on the need for testing to resolve uncertainty and the use of engineering, computing, biological, or physical science. If the research passes this test, QREs are defined as follows:

- Wages paid to employees for qualified services (in practice, 69 percent of spending; US Congress, Office of Technology Assessment 1995)
- Supplies, excluding land or depreciable tangible property used in the R&D process (about 15 percent)
- 65 percent of contract research expenses paid to a third party performing qualified research, regardless of success (about 16 percent)

The main exclusions here are therefore capital spending for R&D (which is typically about 10 percent of its cost) as well as some end-stage development and social science research for marketing or other purposes. The extent to which development involves the resolution of uncertainty is the main area of auditing contention.

The US R&E tax credit has been continuously renewed, extended, and expanded at least 16 times since its introduction, with the exception of a one-year lapse between July 1995 and June 1996. As of July 1996, the credit has generally been computed based on the following formula:

$$20\% \times (\textit{Qualified Research Expenses less Base Amount}) + 20\%$$
$$\times (\textit{Basic Research Payments})$$

The base amount equals the fixed-base percentage multiplied by the taxpayer's average annual gross receipts for the preceding four tax years. The base amount cannot be less than 50 percent of the taxpayer's QREs for the current tax year. The fixed-base percentage represents the ratio of the taxpayer's QREs for the base period of 1984 through 1988 to gross receipts for the same period. When introduced in 1996, the fixed-base percentage could not exceed 16 percent; currently the limit on the base amount is 50 percent of total R&D. For start-up companies (as specially defined for the credit), the fixed-base percentage is generally 3 percent, but gradually shifting to a base determined by the fifth to tenth year of the startup. All of these figures must be adjusted in the case of acquisition or disposition, and are subject to recapture by the corporate tax rate, reducing their level. They are also subject to the alternative minimum tax (AMT). Finally, basic research payments are those made to a university or nonprofit organization on a contract basis.

Effective with the PATH (Protecting Americans from Tax Hikes) Act of 2015, the R&D tax credit was made permanent rather than temporary. In addition, two exceptions to the exclusion of the R&E credit from offsetting AMT liability were made: (1) small businesses with gross receipts less than $50 million averaged over the past three years are excepted and (2) small businesses may claim up to $250,000 of R&E tax credit as a payroll tax credit against the employer share of Old-Age, Survivors, and Disability Insurance taxes. The current system contains two options for computing the credit, which differ in the definition of the base amount: (1) regular, defined as a fixed base equal to the average gross receipts over the preceding four years times the ratio of research expenses to gross receipts for the 1984–1988 period; and (2) alternative simplified credit (ASC), a fixed base defined as 50 percent of the average QRE for the three preceding tax years. The statutory credit rate for the regular credit is 20 percent, while that for the ASC is 14 percent. There is also a two-year carryback and a 20 year carryforward of the credit available for firms without taxes in the current year.

It is helpful to illustrate the complexity of the R&E tax credit computation via a few hypothetical scenarios. I present three here: (1) the regular credit, (2) the ASC, and (3) the special provisions for start-ups. All three examples avoid the complications induced by carryforwards in the case of losses and the ceilings on the amount that can be claimed. The regular credit presumes that the firm existed in a similar form during the 1984–1988 period. An example of a firm that can benefit from the regular credit is the following: Assume the total QRE-to-sales ratio in 1984–1988 is 8 percent, and the firm spends $0.9 billion out of sales of $10 billion (9 percent QRE intensity) during a subsequent year. The fixed base for the regular credit will be $0.8 billion $= .08 * 10$ billion, and the available credit will be $0.20 * (0.9–0.8) = \$20$ million. If we assume that QRE and sales are roughly constant for three years prior to the year of interest, the ASC for the firm will be zero, because the fixed base will be the same as the current R&D. So firms that are relatively stable but show some growth in QRE between the 1980s and the present will prefer the regular credit. Obviously, this will be a shrinking percentage of the firms as time passes, both because of firm exit and because the firm's profile in the late 1980s will become less relevant to its present spending.

The ASC computation is more likely to benefit firms whose sales are growing, but whose QRE intensity has remained the same or declined over time. It is also available to a larger number of firms, because it does not require data from the 1980s. For example, consider a firm whose sales over five years are 50, 55, 60, 65, and 70, and whose QRE intensity is 0.05 over the same period. The fixed bases in the final two years will be 2.75 and 3, implying credits of $0.14 * (3.25–2.75) = 0.07$ and $0.14 * (3.5–3.0) = 0.07$ respectively. Assuming either that the firm did not exist in 1984–1988 or that its QRE intensity was

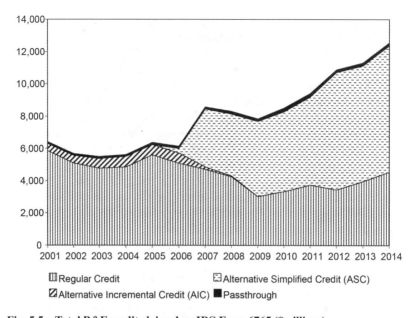

Fig. 5.5   Total R&E credit claimed on IRS Form 6765 ($millions)
Source: US Department of Treasury Statistics of Income (SOI), https://www.irs.gov/statistics
/soi-tax-stats-corporation-research-credit.

higher than 0.05 during that period, in this example the firm will choose the ASC, because the regular credit would yield zero.[11]

Some start-up firm scenarios are shown in figure 5.A.3. For its first 10 years, a start-up firm will follow a relatively complex set of computations that are designed to transit the firm from a fixed-base percentage of 3 percent to one that is more reflective of the particular firm's circumstances. The result is some fairly extreme heterogeneity, depending on the particular pattern of QRE and sales growth in the firm. For a stylized R&D-intensive startup (Scenario 4) with high QRE intensity in the first three years and steady sales growth, the average credit is about 12 percent of QRE in the first six years, declining to 2 percent by year 11. The marginal credit shows a similar pattern (see the appendix for details).

Figure 5.5 shows the actual evolution of the use of the different methods of computing the R&D credit between 2001 and 2014; unfortunately the Statistics of Income (SOI) detail is not available on the website prior to 2001 or post 2014. The figure shows that the amount devoted to the credit doubled between 2006 and 2012, and that the ASC accounts for an increas-

11. This analysis ignores the impact of the increased QRE in the current period on the amount of credit available in the future. That impact will reduce the total value of the credit, but not to zero, so the ASC will still be preferred to the regular credit.

| Table 5.1 | Statutory, effective, and average R&E credit rates by computation method for corporate taxpayers, 2013 (in percent) |

Rate	Regular method: Unconstrained by minimum base	Regular method: Constrained by 50% minimum base	Alternative Simplified Credit (ASC)
Statutory credit rate	20	20	14
Reduced credit rate (due to recapture)	13	13	9.1
Effective credit rate with no carryforward[a]	13	6.5	5
Effective credit rate with average carryforward[b]	10.7	5.3	4.1
Average credit rate[c]	5.6	6.5	5.2
Share of returns[c]	5	44	51
Share of qualified research expenses (QREs)[c]	3	28	69

Source: US Department of Treasury (2016).
[a]This assumes that firms have sufficient tax liability to use the full credit in the current year.
[b]According to OTA calculations, on average 82 percent of the current-year credit will eventually be used.
[c]According to OTA calculations using the 2013 SOI corporate sample. Returns not reporting information in appropriate fields for the calculations were dropped. This eliminated 9 percent of returns, which only accounted for 1 percent of the reported credit.

ing share of the credits claimed, as expected. The small amount claimed under the alternative incremental credit (AIC, described in the appendix) before its elimination in 2009 perhaps accounts for its discontinuation in favor of the ASC. The figure also shows the so-called pass-through amounts of the credit, which are those claimed by S corporations, partnerships, and Schedule C sole proprietorships; they are a very small percentage of the total throughout the period.

Several factors make the R&E credit rate actually experienced by the firm considerably less than the statutory rate of 20 or 14 percent. Table 5.1 presents some computations that illustrate this point; they were done by the US Office of Tax Analysis (OTA) using a sample of corporate tax returns during the 2013 year along with an assumed discount rate of 5 percent. Note first that the majority of returns and of returns weighted by QRE choose to use the ASC computation, which depends on QRE from the past three years, and therefore has a similar impact on the future credit available as the former AIC. The table analyzes three scenarios: a firm using the regular credit and unconstrained by the requirement that the base amount of QRE be 50 percent or higher;[12] a firm using the regular credit, but constrained by the 50 percent requirement; and a firm using the alternative simplified credit.

The first two lines show the relevant statutory credit rate and its value

12. In 2013, this requirement essentially means that the firm's R&D growth rate must be about 2.5 percentage points annually above the sales growth rate over the approximately 25-year period since the late 1980s. It is therefore no surprise that only a small share of firms are unconstrained under the regular method.

when reduced by the recapture under a corporate income tax rate of 35 percent. The next line shows the effective rate with no carryforward. This computation incorporates the impact of increasing the QRE this year on the future base; note that in the rare unconstrained case, there is no impact on the future base. This result was the original intent of the 1989 legislation. Obviously this intent has been lost as time has passed and more firms use the ASC. Line 4 corrects the effective rate for the fact that in many cases the credit will be carried forward due to insufficient tax in a given year, and in some cases will be lost due to firm exit, etc. This reduces the effective marginal credit rate even further. Finally, line 5 shows the average credit rate—that is, the credit claimed divided by the total QRE of the claimants who elected each of the three scenarios in 2013.

Note three observations about this table: First, the average credit rates (credit/QRE) are remarkably similar under the three methods. Second, the average credit rate is not that different from the marginal effective rate, except in the little-used unconstrained regular method. Third, the marginal effective credit rate is rather low, which is consistent with the OECD (2019b) figure, which shows that the US provides a lower tax subsidy to R&D than the other 30-plus OECD countries that offer a tax credit.

5.6.2   Some Thoughts on Design of the Tax Credit

Earlier it was suggested that the relevant considerations for design of tax policy toward innovation are saliency to the firm, appropriate time horizons, targeting those areas where the private-social return gap is large, and reducing auditing cost. To these might be added some consideration of the cost of the policy in relation to its benefits. In this section I consider whether there are potential improvements in the R&E tax credit toward these ends.

The current take-up of the R&E tax credit suggests that it is visible to many firms. Holtzman (2017) reports the result of a short survey of CEOs, CFOs, and tax directors at 40 companies across size and industry about the 2015 PATH Act changes. The responses were uniformly positive about its impact both on take-up and on increasing R&D, especially the impact of permanence. However, the fact that a majority of firms have switched to the ASC, which uses QRE spending in the recent past to construct a base, does suggest that the effective current credit rate (marginal or average) may be considerably lower than the 14 or 20 percent intended by the legislation. It is also true that the United States has one of the lowest effective rates among OECD economies with a research tax credit. If the goal is to encourage a substantial increase in R&D spending on the grounds that the social return is much higher than the private, it would be desirable to use a much higher credit rate along with an incremental form of the credit, to avoid the loss of inframarginal tax revenue.

With respect to targeting, in the appendix I show some detailed computations of the operation of the credit for start-up firms. These show that the start-up version of the R&E tax credit is more generous than that available to established firms, at least for firms with high R&D intensities, but that after about five years, the incentive declines considerably for the same reasons as the above. It is an open question whether the current design is anything close to optimal.

There are some remaining open questions about the design of the credit. First, does recapturing the credit for profit-making firms make sense? The effect is to provide a larger credit rate to firms with losses than to firms with profits. Second, would it be simpler for auditing purposes to define eligible R&D the same way the accounting standards define it, in order to simplify both recordkeeping and auditing? This would increase QRE by about 40 percent so that it has consequences for the cost of the credit.

5.7 Conclusion and Discussion

In this article I have reviewed the main tax policies designed to encourage innovative activity and the evidence about their effectiveness. The strongest conclusion is not new: R&D tax credits do increase R&D and roughly pay for themselves, in the sense that the increased spending meets or exceeds the lost tax revenue. Conflicting evidence exists for the proposition that the R&D thus induced spills over to other firms that are close in technological space. More research is needed on this question. There also has been little study of the specific impact of R&D induced by the credit on the return to R&D, which theory predicts should decline if the cost of R&D capital has declined. The literature on the R&D tax credit also suggests that the increased audit and compliance cost associated with more complex tax credit schemes may not be justified.

Finally, one could argue that the introduction of the IP box is in part an attempt to reward a broader concept of innovative activity than that which is simply R&D-related. Although this may be true, it also has the effect of rewarding successful R&D in addition to subsidizing its cost with tax credits in many cases, and for a number of reasons discussed above it may not be the ideal solution to the question of incentivizing innovative activity more broadly. One hopes that policy makers will develop better methods in the future. Further research might also be directed to study of the nonpatent use of IP boxes and their effectiveness.

Based on this review, a number of broader policy questions suggest themselves. First, are the current tax subsidies enough? That is, do countries provide enough support for R&D and innovative activity? It is well known that although imprecisely measured, the social returns to R&D itself are much higher than the private returns (for the micro evidence, see Hall, Mairesse, and Mohnen 2010; for the macro evidence, see Coe and Helpman 1995; Kao, Chiang, and Chen 1999; Keller 1998).

Looking in more detail at the international spillover evidence, Branstetter (2001) and Peri (2004) find that domestic spillovers are larger than those from other countries, while Park (1995) and van Pottelsberghe (1997) find that spillovers from foreign R&D are more important for smaller open economies than for the United States, Japan, and Germany. The absorptive capacity of the recipient country is also important for making use of R&D spillovers (Guellec and van Pottelsberghe 2001). All of this suggests that the optimal policy may vary depending on country size, openness, and level of development. One fairly extreme view is offered by Jones and Williams (1998) using an endogenous growth model to argue that the socially optimal R&D investment in the United States is at least four times the actual investment.

Although most of this literature is focused on R&D rather than innovative activity more broadly, the conclusions are that tax incentives for innovation should be even larger than they are already, and also that those for larger economies are more important for global welfare. The evidence also highlights a second question: Would these policies achieve higher welfare if they were better coordinated between countries? If so, how could that be done? There are two reasons why coordination might be a good idea: the presence of cross-border spillovers and the avoidance of wasteful tax competition.

The latter has been found both for US states and across the OECD and the EU. Using eight large OECD economies 1981–1999, Bloom, Griffith, and Van Reenen (2002) find that domestic R&D responds to the foreign cost of R&D with an elasticity of about unity, roughly equal and opposite to the domestic cost response. Corrado et al. (2015) find similar results for 10 EU countries, 1995–2007. Wilson (2009) finds similar, but even larger, results for US states, where the mobility of R&D is arguably even higher. Note, however, that equal and opposite elasticities do not imply zero-sum effects, although they do imply that total worldwide R&D will respond more strongly to R&D tax credits in the larger economies, as suggested by Park and van Pottelsberghe. A related finding by Schwab and Todtenhaupt (2018) is that European multinationals increase their patenting and R&D activity overall when a patent box is introduced in one of the countries in which they operate. This result suggests that the global impact of an innovation incentive could be positive precisely because MNEs tend to house their innovation activity in larger countries already.

Appendix

The B-Index

"The B-index is a measure of the level of pre-tax profit a 'representative' company needs to generate to break even on a marginal, unitary outlay on R&D (Warda, 2001), taking into account provisions in the tax system that allow for special treatment of R&D expenditures."[13] It is defined as follows:

13. From OECD (2019a).

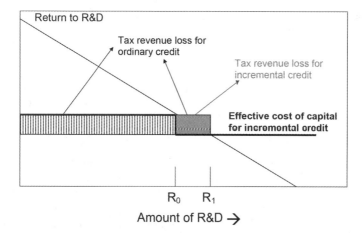

Fig. 5.A.1   Firm increasing R&D from R_0 to R_1

$$B - index \equiv \frac{1 - A}{1 - \tau}$$

where τ is the corporate tax rate and A represents the combined reduction in taxes due to R&D spending: credit, superdeduction, and any increased depreciation allowances for investment in R&D equipment. If R&D is simply expensed, as it is in most countries, $A = \tau$ and the B-index is unity. See the reference in the footnote for further details and the more complex formulas used when losses can be carried forward or backward.

Incremental Tax Credits

Unlike ordinary investment, R&D spending, once established, tends to be fairly smooth from year to year within a firm (Hall 1992; Hall, Griliches, and Hausman 1986). The appeal of incremental R&D tax credits is that they target the marginal decision to increase R&D rather than subsidizing inframarginal R&D that would have been done anyway. The drawback is that every firm is different, and the best way to figure out a firm's presubsidy R&D level is to look at its past history. Thus, incremental credits tend to be based on the firm's own R&D history, which implies that a firm can directly affect its future credit availability.

Figure 5.A.1 illustrates the tax cost savings from using an incremental credit to subsidize a firm with an established ongoing R&D budget. The figure assumes that the tax authority is able to identify precisely the point R_0 at which the cost of capital needs to be lowered in order to induce the firm to increase its R&D to R_1. The tax revenue loss in the case of an incremental credit is shown in the gray rectangle (the difference in the cost of R&D capital times the amount of increased R&D). To achieve the same increase

Table 5.A.1 Effective credit rate as a function of the discount rate

Discount rate	Effective marginal credit rate	
Nominal credit rate	US in 1981 at 30%	ASC at 14%
1.0	0.0	0.0
0.95	$0.030 = 0.3 * 0.10$	$0.077 = 0.14 * 0.55$
0.9	$0.057 = 0.3 * 0.19$	$0.083 = 0.14 * 0.59$

in R&D using a level or volume credit would cost both the gray rectangle and the rectangle with vertical lines, a much higher cost for the same impact.

As was first pointed out by Eisner, Albert, and Sullivan (1986) and Altshuler (1989), the downside of the incremental credit is that it is weakened by the fact that an increase in R&D today causes a decrease in credit availability in the future.

The following argument explains why incremental tax credits are so difficult to design when they are based on past R&D spending by the firm. Define the following variables:

θ = tax credit rate
R = R&D
π = current profit
Π = Present discounted value of profits
β = discount rate

Assume that the spending eligible for the credit is the amount above the average of the last three years of spending on R&D.[14] If in year t the firm increases R_t by ΔR_t, the tax credit benefit to the firm is $\Delta \pi_t = \theta \Delta R_t$. However, for the next three years, this increase is in the base R&D, so there is a cost each year given by $(\theta/3) \Delta R_t$. Therefore, the marginal tax benefit of a one-unit increase in R&D at year t is not θ, but the following:

$$\frac{\partial \Delta \Pi_t}{\partial \Delta R_t} = \theta \left[1 - \frac{(\beta + \beta^2 + \beta^3)}{3} \right].$$

Table 5.A.1 shows the effective tax credit as a function of the discount rate faced by the firm, based on the above formula, for two different statutory credit rates, 20 and 14 percent. The first two columns show the effective credit rate according to the rules as they existed in 1981–1986 for constrained and unconstrained firms, while the third second column shows the effective marginal rate under the current ASC.

The only reason there is an effective credit at all from these versions of the incremental tax credit is because the future cost to the base R&D of increasing R&D today is discounted.

14. This was the situation in the United States when the credit was first introduced in 1981. The current ASC uses 50 percent of the average of the last three years of spending.

Tax Treatment of Start-Ups in the United States

The PATH legislation of 2015 contains the following provisions for computing the fixed-base QRE against which the increment eligible for the tax credit can be computed. This computation applies to companies that incorporated after December 31, 1983, or had fewer than three years with QREs and revenue between January 1, 1984, and December 31, 1988. The fixed-base percentage is calculated according to the code as follows:

- §41(c)(3)(B)(ii)(I) 3 percent for each of the taxpayer's first five taxable years beginning after December 31, 1993, for which the taxpayer has qualified research expenses
- §41(c)(3)(B)(ii)(II) in the case of the taxpayer's sixth such taxable year, 1/6 of the percentage which the aggregate qualified research expenses of the taxpayer for the fourth and fifth such taxable years is of the aggregate gross receipts of the taxpayer for such years
- §41(c)(3)(B)(ii)(III) in the case of the taxpayer's seventh such taxable year, 1/3 of the percentage which the aggregate qualified research expenses of the taxpayer for the fifth and sixth such taxable years is of the aggregate gross receipts of the taxpayer for such years
- §41(c)(3)(B)(ii)(IV) in the case of the taxpayer's eighth such taxable year, 1/2 of the percentage which the aggregate qualified research expenses of the taxpayer for the fifth, sixth, and seventh such taxable years is of the aggregate gross receipts of the taxpayer for such years
- §41(c)(3)(B)(ii)(V) in the case of the taxpayer's ninth such taxable year, 2/3 of the percentage which the aggregate qualified research expenses of the taxpayer for the fifth, sixth, seventh, and eighth such taxable years is of the aggregate gross receipts of the taxpayer for such years
- §41(c)(3)(B)(ii)(VI) in the case of the taxpayer's tenth such taxable year, 5/6 of the percentage which the aggregate qualified research expenses of the taxpayer for the fifth, sixth, seventh, eighth, and ninth such taxable years is of the aggregate gross receipts of the taxpayer for such years
- §41(c)(3)(B)(ii)(VII) for taxable years thereafter, the percentage which the aggregate qualified research expenses for any five taxable years selected by the taxpayer from among the fifth through the tenth such taxable years is of the aggregate gross receipts of the taxpayer for such selected years

For purposes of the calculation, the resulting fixed-base percentage is multiplied by the average of the taxpayer's gross revenue for the four years prior to the calculation year.[15] The fixed-base percentage should only change for purposes of meeting the consistency rule or adjusting for an acquisition or disposition.

---

15. It seems clear, although not specifically mentioned, that if fewer than four years are available prior to the calculation year, the average over the years available should be used.

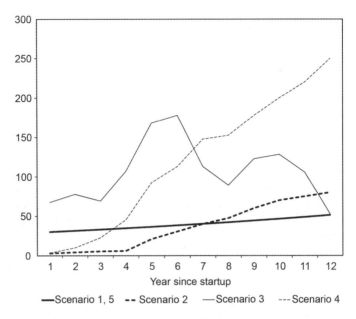

Fig. 5.A.2   Sales trend scenarios for start-up firms

Figures 5.A.2–5.A.4 show the implication of this form of computation for startups with varying patterns of R&E spending and sales growth. There are five scenarios:

1. Steady, slow sales growth with R&E to sales of 3 percent every year
2. Very low sales for four years, followed by fairly rapid increase, with the R&E intensity falling over the same period as sales are established
3. A pattern taken from a random high-tech startup on Compustat with uneven but growing sales and rapidly growing R&E intensity
4. High initial R&E spending accompanied by rapid sales growth that eventually stabilizes the R&E intensity at the relatively high level of 15 percent
5. Same as 1, but with the R&E-to-sales ratio at a constant 5 percent

If I have interpreted the computation rules correctly, the results are a bit strange. Prior to year six, the average credit share seems more or less directly related to whether the firm has an R&E intensity above 3 percent. However the differences between firms that begin with 15 percent, or 30 percent R&E intensity, do not seem that great. At year six, however, the impact of the 1/6 rule is to give all the synthetic firms an average credit that is close to the statutory 14 percent rate, since their past histories are downweighted greatly. Following year six, the average credit share declines similarly for all the scenarios, whether growing or not, with the exception of the scenario with fluctuating sales, as one would expect. Average is of course not marginal,

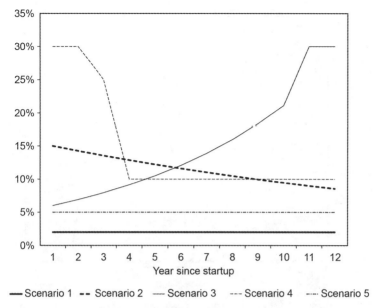

Fig. 5.A.3   QRE to sales for start-up firms

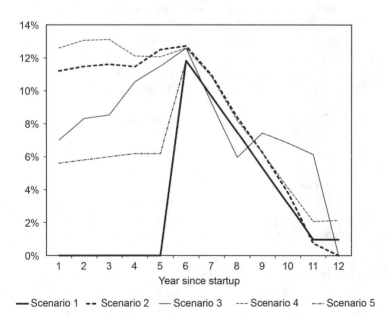

Fig. 5.A.4   Amount of tax credit as share of QRE for start-up firms

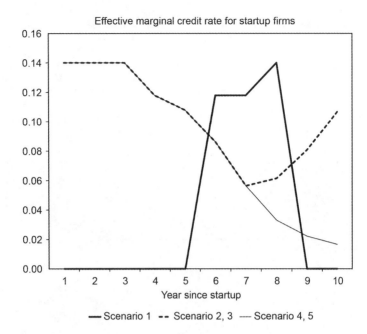

Fig. 5.A.5   **Effective marginal credit rate for start-up firms**

but it may be what is salient for the firm, as it is visible on their tax return. It is also what will be computed when a firm does pro forma forecasting to assess the appropriate R&D profile for which to plan.

Marginal rates that take into account the impact of current increases on the future fixed base are also rather heterogeneous, as shown in figure 5.A.5.[16] For Scenario 1, there is no eligibility in the first four years because the QRE intensity is quite low. Scenarios 4 and 5 are eligible throughout, and so their effective marginal credit declines to nearly zero at the end of the period when current increases affect future eligibility for four years. Scenarios 2 and 3 are not eligible at the end of the period because their QRE intensity has stopped growing, and this is reflected in marginal rates that increase again (because assuming that they remain below the base in future periods means it is not costly to increase QRE now).

Additional Figures: R&D Tax Subsidy Rates 2000–2018 around the World

Figures 5.A.6 and 5.A.7 show the R&D tax subsidy rates (1-B index) for large profit-making firms that offer some kind of R&D tax credit or superdeduction.

16. In computing these marginal rates I have used a discount rate of 0.95, which has been used in much of the earlier work by OTA and others. I have also used perfect foresight to forecast future QRE.

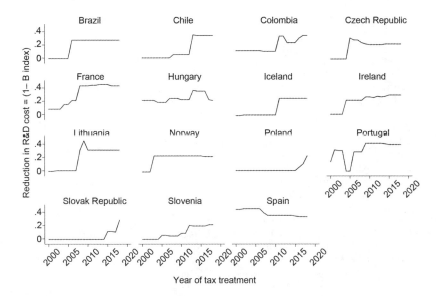

Fig. 5.A.6   Tax subsidy rate trend for the more generous countries
Source: OECD (2019c).

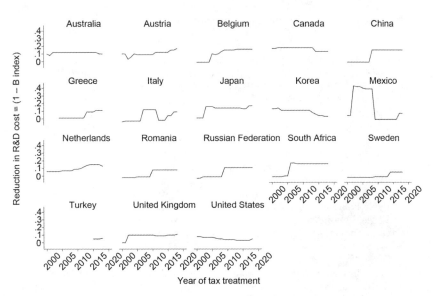

Fig. 5.A.7   Tax subsidy rate trend for the less generous countries
Source: OECD (2019c).

References

Acconcia, Antonio, and Claudia Cantabene. 2018. "Liquidity and Firms' Response to Fiscal Stimulus." *The Economic Journal* 128 (613): 1759–85.

Agrawal, Ajay, Carlos Rosell, and Timothy Simcoe. 2020. "Tax Credits and Small Firm R&D Spending." *American Economic Journal: Economic Policy* 12 (2): 1–21.

Akcigit, Ufuk, John Grigsby, Tom Nicholas, and Stefanie Stantcheva. 2018. "Taxation and Innovation in the 20th Century." NBER Working Paper No. 24982. Cambridge, MA: National Bureau of Economic Research.

Akcigit, Ufuk, Douglas Hanley, and Nicolas Serrano-Velarde. 2013. "Back to Basics: Basic Research Spillovers, Innovation Policy and Growth." NBER Working Paper No. 19473. Cambridge, MA: National Bureau of Economic Research.

Alstadsæter, Annette, Salvador Barrios, Gaetan Nicodeme, Agnieszka Maria Skonieczna, and Antonio Vezzani. 2018. "Patent Boxes Design, Patents Location, and Local R&D." *Economic Policy* 33 (93): 131–77.

Altshuler, Rosanne. 1989. "A Dynamic Analysis of the Research and Experimentation Credit." *National Tax Journal* 41: 453–66.

Appelt, Sylvia, Matej Bajgar, Chiara Criscuolo, and Fernando Galindo-Rueda. 2016. "R&D Tax Incentives: Evidence on Design, Incidence and Impacts." OECD Science, Technology and Industry Policy Paper No. 32. Paris: OECD Publishing. http://dx.doi.org/10.1787/5jlr8fldqk7j-en.

Appelt, Sylvia, Fernando Galindo-Rueda, and Ana Cinta Gonzalez Cabral. 2019. "Measuring R&D Tax Support: Findings from the New OECD R&D Tax Incentives Database." OECD Science, Technology and Industry Working Paper No. 2019/06. Paris: OECD Publishing. http://dx.doi.org/10.1787/d16e6072-en.

Arrow, Kenneth. 1962. "Economic Welfare and the Allocation of Resources for Invention." In *The Rate and Direction of Inventive Activity*, edited by Richard R. Nelson, 609–25. Princeton, NJ: Princeton University Press.

Balsmeier, Benjamin, Maria Kurakina, Joel Stiebale, and Lee Fleming. 2020. "The Unintended Consequences of R&D Tax Credits: Exploitation, Markups, and Technological Entrenchment." Unpublished manuscript, UC Berkeley, Haas School of Business.

Bartelsman, Eric J., and Roel M. W. J. Beetsma. 2003. "Why Pay More? Corporate Tax Avoidance through Transfer Pricing in OECD Countries." *Journal of Public Economics* 87 (9): 2225–52.

Blandinieres, Florence, Daniela Steinbrenner, and Bernd Weiss. 2020. "Which Design Works? A Meta-regression Analysis of the Impacts of R&D Tax Incentives." Working Paper, Centre for European Economic Research (ZEW), Mannheim.

Bloom, Nicholas, Rachel Griffith, and John Van Reenen. 2002. "Do R&D Tax Credits Work?" *Journal of Public Economics* 85: 1–31.

Bloom, Nicholas, Mark Schankerman, and John Van Reenen. 2013. "Identifying Technology Spillovers and Product Market Rivalry." *Econometrica* 81 (4): 1347–93.

Boehm, Tobias, Tom Karkinsky, Bodo Knoll, and Nadine Riedel. 2015. "The Impact of Corporate Taxes on R&D and Patent Holdings." Working Paper, University of Hohenheim.

Bösenberg, Simon, and Peter Egger. 2017. "R&D Tax Incentives and the Emergence and Trade of Ideas." *Economic Policy* 32 (89): 39–80.

Bradley, Sebastian, Estelle Dauchy, and Leslie Robinson. 2015. "Cross-Country Evidence on the Preliminary Effects of Patent Box Regimes on Patent Activity and Ownership." *National Tax Journal* 68 (4): 1047–72.

Branstetter, Lee G. 2001. "Are Knowledge Spillovers International or Intranational in Scope? Microeconometric Evidence from the US and Japan." *Journal of International Economics* 53 (1): 53–79.

Bräutigam, Rainer, Christoph Spengel, and Frank Steiff. 2017. "Decline of CFC Rules and Rise of Patent Boxes: How the ECJ Affects Tax Competition and Economic Distortions in Europe." *Fiscal Studies* 38 (4): 719–45.

Chang, Andrew C. 2018. "Tax Policy Endogeneity: Evidence from R&D Tax Credits." *Economics of Innovation and New Technology* 27 (8): 809–33.

Ciaramella, Laurie. 2017. "Patent Boxes and the Relocation of Intellectual Property." March 30. https://papers.ssrn.com/sol3/papers.cfm?abstract_id=2943435.

Coe, David T., and Elhanan Helpman. 1995. "International R&D Spillovers." *European Economic Review* 39: 859–87.

Cohen, Linda R., and Roger G. Noll, eds. 1991. *The Technology Pork Barrel.* Washington, DC: Brookings Institution.

Corrado, Carol, Jonathan Haskel, Cecilia Jona-Lasinio, and Bilal Nasim. 2015. "Is International Tax Competition a Zero Sum Game? Evidence from the EU." Presentation to the NBER-CRIW Summer Institute, Cambridge, MA.

Corrado, Carol, Charles Hulten, and Daniel Sichel. 2009. "Intangible Capital and U.S. Economic Growth." *Review of Income and Wealth* 55 (3): 661–85.

Cowx, Mary. 2020. "Investment and Tax Incentive Uncertainty: Evidence from the R&D Tax Credit." Unpublished manuscript, Ohio State University.

d'Andria, Diego, Pontikakis Dimitrios, and Skonieczna Agnieszka. 2018. "Towards a European R&D Incentive? An Assessment of R&D Provisions under a Common Corporate Tax Base." *Economics of Innovation and New Technology* 27 (5–6): 531–50.

Dechezleprêtre, Antoine, Elias Einiö, Ralf Martin, Kieu-Trang Nguyen, and John Van Reenen. 2016. "Do Tax Incentives for Research Increase Firm Innovation? An Rd Design for R&D." NBER Working Paper No. 22405. Cambridge, MA: National Bureau of Economic Research.

Deloitte Consulting. 2014. *Guide to Controlled Foreign Company Regimes.* https://www2.deloitte.com/cy/en/pages/tax/articles/guide-to-controlled-foreign-company-regimes.html.

Dischinger, Matthias, and Nadine Riedel. 2011. "Corporate Taxes and the Location of Intangible Assets within Multinational Firms." *Journal of Public Economics* 95: 691–707.

Dudar, Olena, Christoph Spengel, and Johannes Voget. 2015. "The Impact of Taxes on Bilateral Royalty Flows." ZEW Discussion Paper 15-052.

Eisner, Robert, Steven H. Albert, and Martin A. Sullivan. 1986. "The New Incremental Tax Credit for R&D: Incentive or Disincentive." *National Tax Journal* 37: 171–83.

European Patent Office. 2019. Patstat Database. https://www.epo.org/searching-for-patents/business/patstat.html.

Eurostat. 2020. "Expenditures of Enterprises by Area of Expenditure, NACE Rev. 2 Activity and Size Class." https://ec.europa.eu/eurostat/databrowser/view/inn_cis11_exp/default/table?lang=en.

Evers, Lisa, Helen Miller, and Christoph Spengel. 2015. "Intellectual Property Box Regimes: Effective Tax Rates and Tax Policy Considerations." *International Tax Public Finance* 22: 502–30. http://dx.doi.org/10.1007/s10797-014-9328-x.

EYGM. 2017. *Worldwide R&D Incentives Reference Guide.* https://www.ey.com/Publication/vwLUAssets/EY-worldwide-randd-incentives-reference-guide-2017/$FILE/EY-worldwide-randd-incentives-reference-guide.pdf.

Gaessler, Fabian, Bronwyn H. Hall, and Dietmar Harhoff. 2021. "Should There

Be Lower Taxes on Patent Income?" *Research Policy* 50. https://doi.org/10.1016/j.respol.2020.104129.

Goolsbee, Austan. 1998. "Does Government R&D Policy Mainly Benefit Scientists and Engineers?" *American Economic Review* 88 (2): 298–302.

Griffith, Rachel, Helen Miller, and Martin O'Connell. 2014. "Ownership of Intellectual Property and Corporate Taxation." *Journal of Public Economics* 112: 12–23.

Guceri, Irem, and Li Liu. 2019. "Effectiveness of Fiscal Incentives for R&D: Quasi-Experimental Evidence." *American Economic Journal: Economic Policy* 11 (1): 266–91.

Guellec, Dominique, and Bruno van Pottelsberghe de la Potterie. 2001. "R&D and Productivity Growth: Panel Data Analysis of 16 OECD Countries." *OECD Economic Studies* 33 (2): 103–26.

Guenther, Gary. 2013. *Research Tax Credit: Current Law, Legislation in the 113th Congress, and Policy Issues*. Washington, DC: US Congressional Research Service Report RL31181.

———. 2015. *Research Tax Credit: Current Law and Policy Issues in the 114th Congress*. Washington, DC: US Congressional Research Service Report RL31181.

Hall, Bronwyn H. 1992. "Research and Development at the Firm Level: Does the Source of Financing Matter?" NBER Working Paper No. 4096. Cambridge, MA: National Bureau of Economic Research.

———. 1993. "R&D Tax Policy during the Eighties: Success or Failure?" *Tax Policy and the Economy* 7: 1–36.

Hall, Bronwyn H., Zvi Griliches, and Jerry A. Hausman. 1986. "Patents and R and D: Is There a Lag?" *International Economic Review* 27 (2): 265–83.

Hall, Bronwyn H., and Alessandro Maffioli. 2008. "Evaluating the Impact of Technology Development Funds in Emerging Economies: Evidence from Latin America." *European Journal of Development Research* 20 (2): 172–98.

Hall, Bronwyn H., Jacques Mairesse, and Pierre Mohnen, 2010. "Measuring the Returns to R&D." In *Handbook of the Economics of Innovation*, vol. 2, edited by B. H. Hall and N. Rosenberg, 1034–76. Amsterdam: Elsevier.

Hall, Bronwyn H., and John Van Reenen. 2000. "How Effective Are Fiscal Incentives for R&D? A New Review of the Evidence." *Research Policy* 29: 449–69.

Hall, Robert E. 2001. "The Stock Market and Capital Accumulation." *American Economic Review* 91 (5): 1185–1202.

Hall, Robert E., and Dale W. Jorgenson. 1967. "Tax Policy and Investment Behavior." *American Economic Review* 59 (3): 391–414.

Hines, James R., Jr. 2014. "How Serious Is the Problem of Base Erosion and Profit Shifting?" *Canadian Tax Journal* 62 (2): 443–53.

Holtzman, Yair. 2017. "US Research and Development Tax Credit." *The CPA Journal*, October. https://www.cpajournal.com/2017/10/30/u-s-research-development-tax-credit/.

Jones, Charles I., and John Williams. 1998. "Measuring the Social Return to R&D." *Quarterly Journal of Economics* 113: 1119–35.

Kao, C., M.-H. Chiang, and B. Chen. 1999. "International R&D Spillovers: An Application of Estimation and Inference in Panel Cointegration." *Oxford Bulletin of Economics and Statistics* 61 (S1): 691–709.

Karkinsky, Tom, and Nadine Riedel. 2012. "Corporate Taxation and the Choice of Patent Location within Multinational Firms." *Journal of International Economics* 88: 176–85.

Keller, Wolfgang. 1998. "Are International R&D Spillovers Trade-Related? Analyzing Spillovers among Randomly Matched Trade Partners." *European Economic Review* 42 (8): 1469–81.

Lester, John, and Jacek Warda. 2018. *An International Comparison of Tax Assistance for R&D: 2017 Update and Extension to Patent Boxes.* Calgary, AB: University of Calgary School of Public Policy Research Report 11:13.

Lev, Baruch Itamar. 2018. "Intangibles." https://ssrn.com/abstract=3218586.

Lokshin, Boris, and Pierre Mohnen. 2013. "Do R&D Tax Incentives Lead to Higher Wages for R&D Workers? Evidence from The Netherlands." *Research Policy* 42 (3): 823–30.

Lucking, Brian, Nicholas Bloom, and John Van Reenen. 2019. "Have R&D Spillovers Declined in the 21st Century?" *Fiscal Studies* 40 (4): 561–90.

Mansfield, Edwin. 1984. "How Effective Is the R&D Tax Credit?" *Challenge* 27. 57–61.

———. 1986. "The R&D Tax Credit and Other Technology Policy Issues." *AEA Papers and Proceedings* 76: 190–94.

Mohnen, Pierre, Arthur Vankan, and Bart Verspagen. 2017. "Evaluating the Innovation Box Tax Policy Instrument in the Netherlands, 2007–13." *Oxford Review of Economic Policy* 33 (1): 141–56.

Mulkay, Benoit, and Jacques Mairesse. 2013. "The R&D Tax Credit in France: Assessment and ex ante Evaluation of the 2008 Reform." *Oxford Economic Papers* 65 (3): 746–66.

Mutti, John, and Harry Grubert. 2009. "The Effect of Taxes on Royalties and the Migration of Intangible Assets Abroad." In *International Trade in Services and Intangibles in the Era of Globalization*, edited by M. Reinsdorf and M. J. Slaughter, 111–37. Chicago: University of Chicago Press.

Nelson, Richard R. 1959. "The Simple Economics of Basic Scientific Research." *Journal of Political Economy* 77: 297–306.

OECD. 2015. "Countering Harmful Tax Practices More Effectively, Taking into Account Transparency and Substance." Action 5-2015 Final Report. Paris: OECD Publishing. http://dx.doi.org/10.1787/9789264241190-en.

———. 2019a. "Definition, Interpretation and Calculation of the B Index." https://www.oecd.org/sti/b-index.pdf.

———. 2019b. "Measuring Tax Support for R&D and Innovation." http://www.oecd.org/innovation/rd-tax-stats.htm.

———. 2019c. *R&D Tax Incentive Indicators.* R&D Tax Incentive Database. http://oe.cd/rdtax.

OECD/Eurostat. 2018. *Oslo Manual: Guidelines for Collecting, Reporting, and Using Data on Innovation.* 4th ed. Paris: Eurostat.

Park, Walter G. 1995. "International R&D Spillovers and OECD Economic Growth." *Economic Inquiry* 33 (4): 571–91.

Peri, Giovanni. 2004. "Knowledge Flows and Productivity." *Rivista di Politica Economica* 94 (2): 21–59.

Rao, Nirupama. 2016. "Do Tax Credits Stimulate R&D Spending? The Effect of the R&D Tax Credit in Its First Decade." *Journal of Public Economics* 140: 1–12.

Schwab, Thomas, and Maximilian Todtenhaupt. 2018. "Thinking Outside the Box: The Cross-Border Effect of Tax Cuts on R&D." ZEW Discussion Paper No. 16-073, Mannheim. https://papers.ssrn.com/sol3/papers.cfm?abstract_id=2864304.

Sullivan, Martin. 2015. "An Innovation Box Tax Break: Good Intentions Gone Bad." *Forbes*, June 9. https://www.forbes.com/sites/taxanalysts/2015/06/09/patent-box-tax-break-good-intentions-gone-bad/#79619bd9396e.

Ting, Antony. 2014. "iTax: Apple's International Tax Structure and the Double Non-Taxation Issue." *British Tax Review* 2014 (1): 40–71. https://ssrn.com/abstract=2411297.

US Congress Joint Economic Committee. 2016. *Patent Boxes: A Brief History,*

Recent Developments, and Necessary Considerations. March 10. https://www.jec .senate.gov/public/_cache/files/02a2a18a-1e08-42ce-8c14-72b6138b54dd/031016 -patent-boxes.pdf.

US Congress, Office of Technology Assessment. 1995. *The Effectiveness of Research and Experimentation Tax Credits.* https://ota.fas.org/reports/9558.pdf

US Department of Treasury. 2016. *Research and Experimentation (R&E) Credit.* October 12. https://www.treasury.gov/resource-center/tax-policy/tax-analysis /Documents/RE-Credit.pdf.

van Pottelsberghe de la Potterie, Bruno. 1997. "Issues in Assessing the Effect of Interindustry R&D Spillovers." *Economic Systems Research* 9 (4): 331–56.

Warda, Jacek. 2001. "Measuring the Value of R&D Tax Treatment in OECD Countries." *OECD Science, Technology and Industry Review* 27: 185–211.

Wilson, Daniel J. 2009. "Beggar Thy Neighbor? The In-State, Out-of-State, and Aggregate Effects of R&D Tax Credits." *Review of Economics and Statistics* 91 (2): 431–36.

Wolff, Guntram B., and Volker Reinthaler. 2008. "The Effectiveness of Subsidies Revisited: Accounting for Wage and Employment Effects in Business R&D." *Research Policy* 37 (8): 1403–12.

6

Taxation and Innovation
What Do We Know?

Ufuk Akcigit and Stefanie Stantcheva

6.1 Introduction

There are myriad reasons why we should care about innovation. Innovation is the source of technological progress and the main driver of economic growth in the long run. In recent work, Akcigit, Grigsby, and Nicholas (2017) show that US states with the most innovations also witnessed the fastest growth between 1900 and 2000. Beyond its important role in growth, innovation is also strongly associated with social mobility—especially when it is done by new entrants to the market (Aghion et al. 2018; Akcigit, Grigsby, and Nicholas 2017)—and even with the well-being of people (Aghion et al. 2016).

It is therefore evident why policy makers would try to understand how policies impact innovation and what policy tools can be used to foster it. This issue is particularly pressing in the United States, as business dynamism has been slowing in the last several decades. Recent studies have documented the many faces of this decline: a lower entry rate of new businesses, a slow-down in productivity growth, a falling labor share in output, and rises in

Ufuk Akcigit is the Arnold C. Harberger Professor of Economics at the University of Chicago, a research affiliate of the Centre for Economic Policy Research, and a research associate of the National Bureau of Economic Research.

Stefanie Stantcheva is a professor of economics at Harvard University, a faculty research fellow of the Centre for Economic Policy Research, and a research associate of the National Bureau of Economic Research.

We thank Austan Goolsbee and Ben Jones for very valuable feedback. We also thank the National Science Foundation for financial support. For acknowledgments, sources of research support, and disclosure of the authors' material financial relationships, if any, please see https://www.nber.org/books-and-chapters/innovation-and-public-policy/taxation-and -innovation-what-do-we-know.

market concentration and the corporate profit share. In this context, tax policy can be a powerful tool. Used correctly, it can provide effective incentives for many economic activities, and innovation is no exception. Used inefficiently, it can create heavy deadweight burdens, hurt incentives, and slow down innovation. It is thus critical to innovation to implement the appropriate tax policy.

In this chapter, we will discuss the various roles of tax policy in innovation, and ways in which it could be used to foster technological progress at low fiscal cost. When it comes to innovation, tax policies can be classified into two broad groups: general tax policy (such as the personal or corporate income tax) and targeted tax policies (such as R&D tax credits, local tax incentives for innovating firms, or subsidies for specific types of research).

In the public imagination, innovation is often viewed as a mysterious process whereby wonderful new things are created almost magically. When we think of path-breaking superstar inventors from history, such as Thomas Edison, Alexander Bell, or Nikola Tesla, the picture that comes to mind is one of hardworking and enthusiastic scientists who neglect financial incentives and only strive for intellectual achievement. But innovation is an economic activity and the result of intentional effort and investments. It may certainly have a different time profile and shape of risk and return than other activities. People may also have varying degrees of other motivations—such as social prestige or the love of science—as is the case for other types of economic activities. How strongly innovation responds to economic incentives is ultimately an empirical question.

General taxes are typically set for the purpose of raising revenues and redistributing income; they are typically not set with innovation in mind. Yet they reduce the expected net returns to innovation inputs and can lead to less innovation as an unwelcome by-product. This is an efficiency cost that needs to be taken into account, together with other, more standard margins that are considered when setting tax policy (such as labor supply or tax avoidance). The estimates of these efficiency costs in terms of lost innovation could lead to a reassessment of what the right level of taxes should, and would, be as an input into our optimal tax formulas (Saez and Stantcheva 2018). More specific tax policies targeted to innovations go a step further and can be designed intentionally so as to foster innovation. It is important to understand all the margins along which they can play a role, as innovation is a complex process made of many steps.

In this chapter, we will provide a conceptual framework for thinking about the effects of general and targeted tax policy on innovation. A key consideration is that there are many channels and margins through which innovation will respond to tax policies. We outline them in section 6.2 and summarize them visually in figure 6.1. We then dig into the recent literature that sheds light on each of these channels and response margins. The organization of the chapter is as follows. Each section presents the key issue on the margin under consideration and draws out the implications for tax policy.[1] The literature reviewed is by no means comprehensive. Instead, we focus on work that we have done with coauthors and on extracting the implications for policy design from it. This body of work builds on brand new datasets, such as modern-day data (e.g., European Patent Office data since 1975) or historical long-run data (e.g., the universe of all US inventors since 1836). It also leverages new theoretical and structural methods and models that build up behaviors from the microlevel of the firm all the way to their macro growth implications.

Section 6.3 considers how the quantity and quality of innovation respond to tax policy; section 6.4 focuses on the geographic mobility of innovation and inventors across US states and countries. Section 6.5 focuses on the declining business dynamism in the United States and how specific policies can improve firm entry and productivity. Section 6.6 studies the effects of tax policy on the quality composition of firms, inventors, and teams and how the right design of policy can allow policy makers to foster the most productive firms without wasting public funds on less productive ones. Section 6.7 shows how policy can orient research into different directions, e.g., from applied to basic research, or from dirty technologies to clean ones.

6.2   Through Which Channels Do Tax Policies Shape Innovation?

In this section, we conceptually map the effects of different tax policies on innovation, emphasizing the many channels through which policies can play a role. Each of the channels represented in figure 6.1 will be discussed in light of the existing literature below. To organize the material, the figure gives a one-glance schematic representation of the framework.

The main actors for innovation. Innovation is done by firms or individual inventors. These key agents of innovation are represented at the center of the column. Inventors can be self-employed or work in companies' R&D labs.

Key characteristics of firms and inventors that have to be considered by policy are represented on the diagram. Inventors and firms can be of varying productivity—that is, the efficiency with which they convert R&D and research inputs into innovations. The productivity composition of firms and inventors will shape the impacts of various policies and will be endogenously affected by them. For an individual firm, it is not just its quality overall that matters, but also, more specifically, as emphasized by the literature below, the quality and composition of its research teams. Firms can be at different stages in their life cycle, from early start-ups to mature, large firms. Similarly, inventors can start off as young, inexperienced inventors, and improve their skills through learning and experience over time.

1. When empirical work is presented, the methods are described in some detail in order to allow the reader to better assess the reliability of the estimates.

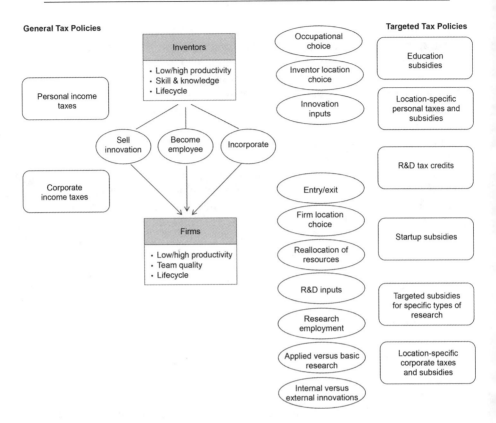

Fig. 6.1   Taxation and innovation: framework

Innovation inputs and actions. Both quality and quantity of innovation require inputs. These inputs are either tangible (e.g., lab space, equipment, material resources) or intangible (e.g., effort, the skill and know-how of workers, the efficiency of management).

As represented by the bubbles in figure 6.1, inventors and firms each have many possible margins on which to optimize, all of which could in principle be responsive to many different policies. Inventors first make an occupational choice: whether to become inventors at all. They also need to decide whether they want to be self-employed or employed by a company. They must choose where to locate geographically. Whether they work for companies or not, they have to select their tangible and intangible inputs. Once a new invention is created, they have to choose whether to sell it to a firm or rather to incorporate and build a business around it. The innovation and the associated flows of income can thus move from the personal to the corporate sector.

Companies have to choose whether to enter a given market, remain in operation, or exit. They also select their geographic location, which could be in multiple places and different for production or research facilities. Companies decide on their innovation and R&D inputs and their research employment. They also choose whether to direct their research operations toward basic or applied innovation (Akcigit, Hanley, and Serrano-Velarde 2021). Basic research is defined as the "systematic study to gain more comprehensive knowledge or understanding of the subject under study without specific applications in mind," and applied research is a "systematic study to gain knowledge or understanding to meet a specific, recognized need."[2] In addition, companies have to decide whether to engage in internal innovations (defined as improvements to existing products) or external innovations (defined as the creation of new products or the overtaking of competitors' products).

General and specific tax policies. The main tax policies that shape innovation can be classified into general tax policies, such as personal income taxes, corporate income taxes, or education subsidies, and more targeted, innovation-specific tax policies, such as R&D tax credits, start-up subsidies, research subsidies for specific types of research and R&D, and location-specific incentives for firms and inventors.

Regarding general tax policy, inventors and firms could in principle be affected by personal and corporate income taxes. For inventors, the personal income tax directly affects the size of their posttax income. For self-employed inventors, the corporate income tax matters if and when they decide to incorporate or not. For employed inventors and firms, any surplus-sharing implies that both the personal and corporate tax shape the payoffs. The extent to which the corporate income tax will affect firms' R&D decisions depends on the share of research inputs that can be expensed; with full expensing, corporate income taxes should have no effect on R&D investment decisions. It also depends on the presence and size of fixed costs, which have to be recouped through future net-of-tax income flows.[3] Firms will also take into account the personal income tax when deciding how many researchers to employ if they have to pay some compensating differential when and where taxes are higher. Education subsidies can shape the choice to acquire the skills needed to become a high-skilled inventor. Corporate and noncorporate inventors can have different responses to tax policy, both because their payoffs may be differently affected by it and because they may have different motives to engage in innovation (which may be why they are in the corporate sector or not to start with).

Turning to the more targeted policies, R&D tax credits can affect the full range of decisions made by firms, and can change the relative payoff to

2. National Science Board, "Science and Engineering Indicators 2018," https://www.nsf.gov /statistics/2018/nsb20181/digest/sections/glossary-and-key-to-acronyms.
3. Given the empirical evidence below, it is likely that there is less than full expensing and/ or fixed costs, as the corporate income tax does matter. It is likely that many R&D inputs are either unobservable (such as the intangible inputs) or hard to measure.

inventors from incorporating and working for companies. Targeted subsidies to start-ups can favor entry, subsidies for specific types of research (e.g., applied or basic) can affect the direction of innovation, and location-specific policies can attract firms and inventors to certain places.

Responses to tax policies. The elasticities of all these different tax and subsidy policies will be a composite of the behavioral elasticities and the technological elasticities. Behavioral elasticities measure how firms and inventors adjust all their margins of action; technological elasticities capture how sensitive innovation outputs—quantity and quality—are to each of these actions. When considering the technological elasticities, one can imagine two polar extremes. At one end is the case of "Newton sitting under the tree"; the apple falls, and innovation happens entirely inelastically. At the other end would be a very mechanical innovation process in which more inputs would automatically translate into more output—for example, if testing many more new chemical combinations results in a scaled-up probability of finding a new material. Similarly, when considering the behavioral elasticities, one can imagine the polar extremes of the "mad genius," who is only doing innovation for the love of science, and the purely profit-driven entrepreneur. Thus, the elasticities of all innovation actions, and hence of the resulting innovation, are empirical questions.

Dynamics. Innovation is an investment-type activity that involves forward-looking behavior, as upfront costs today potentially yield a stream of benefits in the future. Thus, inventors and firms need to form some expectations about the net present value of those returns, which are shaped by the range of aforementioned policies and their predicted changes over time. If firms expect corporate tax rates to increase in the near future, for instance, the net present value of their payoff from innovation would be reduced relative to a scenario in which they expect the corporate tax to decrease. Tax policies are hard to predict, and thus formation of expectations becomes a key issue for agents deciding whether and how much to engage in innovation.

In addition to these forward-looking effects, there can also be lags in the time that it takes innovations to respond to changes in policies. Innovations take time to produce, and the time span between the changes in behavior and the creation of an innovation is also an empirical question. The lags could be different for different policies. For instance, as we will show below, education policies take much longer to work than do R&D tax credits; carbon taxes work faster but at a higher cost than do research subsidies for clean innovation.

Micro to macro: individual and economy-wide responses. The responses to tax policy depend on the level of analysis. At the level of individual firm and inventor, all the response margins just described could in principle occur. Zooming out to the more macro level—for example, localities or states in the United States, or countries in the world—additional effects will be layered on the microlevel effects. For instance, factors can shift between places, leading to a reallocation that may or may not add value overall. To take the example of US states, part of the response seen at the macro, state level could be due to pure business stealing and cross-state spillovers, without a corresponding increase in innovation at the federal level. The same holds for international movement of factors. In addition, at the macro level, the effects of taxes can be augmented or dampened by other features related to tax policy, such as the research infrastructure or amenities, and the formation of innovation hubs. When reading the empirical literature, it is important to bear in mind the level of analysis and to avoid extrapolating without care to other levels.

Measuring innovation. How can we best measure innovation and growth? The literature described in this chapter uses mostly patent data—from the European Patent Office, the US Patent and Trademark Office, the international Patent Cooperation Treaty, and historical patent records—to measure the quantity of innovation. However, some of it instead uses firm growth or R&D spending as a proxy for innovation. It is of course impossible to measure "all" innovation systematically with any of these measures. Take patents, for instance: a share of inventions is not patented. By their very nature, patents will be highly correlated with the quantity of innovation and are thus a prime measure that can shed a lot of light on the issues surrounding innovation, sometimes in conjunction with the other aforementioned measures.[4] To measure the quality of innovation, an often-used metric is the forward citations going to a patent, which have been shown to be a proxy for economic value and to be instructive about the importance of the invention for subsequent innovation (Hall, Jaffe, and Trajtenberg 2005; Jaffe and Trajtenberg 2002). The length of patent claims are also used to measure whether an innovation is incremental or radical (Akcigit and Ates 2021).

6.3 Quantity and Quality of Innovation

Turning to the literature, we start by outlining some recent findings on the effects of general taxation (personal and corporate income taxes) on the quantity and quality of innovation.

The study. The United States has experienced major changes in its tax code throughout the 20th century. Have these tax changes influenced innovation at either the individual or corporate level? This challenging question

---

4. Arundel and Kabla (1998) find that the share of innovations that are patented is very low for low-tech industries such as textiles (8.1 percent), where it is mostly process innovation, and high for high-tech industries such as pharmaceuticals (79.2 percent). Petra Moser believes that historically, the share of innovations patented has been around 50 percent (Eryn Brown, "Do Patents Invent Innovation?," *Knowable Magazine*, March 13, 2018, https://www.knowable magazine.org/article/society/2018/do-patents-invent-innovation). In this Brookings paper summary from 1989, Mansfield reports finding that 60 percent of innovations in the auto industry and 80 percent in the pharmaceutical industry are patented (https://www.brookings .edu/wp-content/uploads/1989/01/1989_bpeamicro_summary.pdf).

has largely gone unanswered because of a lack of long-run systematic data on innovation in the United States and the difficulty of identifying the effects of taxes. Akcigit, Grigsby, and Stantcheva (2018) construct and leverage brand-new datasets from historical data sources to shed light on these questions, namely, a panel of the universe of US inventors since 1920 and their associated patents, citations, and firms, and a historical state-level corporate income tax database. They merge these with data on personal income taxes and other economic outcomes. This unique combination of data allows the authors to systematically study the effects of both personal and corporate income taxation since 1920 on individual inventors—that is, the "micro" level—and on innovation at the "macro," or state level.

The innovation outcomes include, for instance, the quantity of innovation (as captured by the number of patents), the quality of innovation (as measured by patent citations), and the share of patents assigned to companies rather than individuals at both the macro (state) level and micro (individual-inventor) level.

It is challenging to convincingly identify the effects of taxes on the quantity and quality of innovation because when general tax policy changes in a state it may be in response to changes in economic conditions, and it may occur contemporaneously with other policy changes, both of which could also affect innovation outcomes independently. Therefore, the authors approach the question from several angles, which all yield consistent results. First, they control for a detailed set of fixed effects, including state, year, and, at the individual level, inventor fixed effects, plus individual- or state-level time-varying controls; these go a long way toward absorbing unobserved factors that vary by state, by year, or by inventor. In addition, they exploit within-state-year tax differentials between people in different tax brackets (e.g., the top tax bracket versus the median one). This allows them to control for things that vary at the state and year level and to filter out other policy variations or economic circumstances that may occur at the same time in the state. Second, at both the macro and micro level, the authors use an instrumental variable strategy that consists of predicting the total tax burden facing a firm or inventor—which is a composite of state and federal taxes—with the changes in the federal tax rate only, holding the state taxes fixed at some past level. This provides variation that is only driven by federal-level changes, and thus is exogenous to any individual state.

Key findings. The paper finds that higher taxes negatively influence the quantity and the location of innovation, but not the average quality. The state-level elasticities to taxes are large, but they are consistent with the aggregation of the individual inventor-level changes of innovation produced and cross-state mobility in response to taxes.

At the individual inventor level, personal income taxes significantly negatively impact inventors' number of patents and their likelihood of producing a highly cited patent or one that generates substantial value for the firm. Yet, the effects on the quality of the average patent are small. The elasticity of patents to the personal income net-of-tax rate is around 0.8, and the elasticity of citations is around 1. Corporate income taxes only impact the innovation of corporate inventors, but not that of noncorporate inventors. The elasticity of patents of corporate inventors with respect to the net-of-tax corporate rate is 0.49, and that of their citations is 0.46.

Location choices are also affected by taxes. Inventors are significantly less likely to move to states where taxes are higher. The elasticity to the net-of-tax personal rate of the number of inventors residing in a state is between 0.10 and 0.15 for inventors from that state and 1.0 to 1.5 for out-of-state inventors. The elasticities for the corporate tax rate are 0.4 and 2.9, with an average mobility elasticity of 1. Corporate inventors' only take into account the corporate income tax when choosing where to reside, but noncorporate inventors respond to both corporate and personal income taxes. Thus, the aforementioned state-level effects of the corporate tax come predominantly from mobility responses, and such effects are more likely to be zero-sum at the federal level. The effects of the personal income tax come from both mobility and innovation output responses, which are not zero-sum at the federal level.

When it comes to the dynamic effects, innovation responds to general personal and corporate income taxes with a lag: the response starts one year after the tax change and increases for the next three years. Although, as described above, there could also be forward-looking effects, since innovation is an investment-type activity that will potentially yield a stream of returns for a period in the future, no "lead" effects of the tax rates are observed in the data. This could be because, on average, current tax rates may be the best predictor of future tax rates.

Policy implications. Innovation appears to have been responsive to taxation throughout the 20th century. In terms of magnitude, the responses at the individual firm and inventor levels are somewhat larger than other standard margins we typically take into account when setting tax policy, such as labor supply or the overall taxable income elasticity. This means that the efficiency costs of general taxation in terms of innovation should be taken into account in tax evaluation. In addition, policy makers and analysts need to be very careful in extrapolating from state-level responses to federal-level responses. As emphasized, state-level responses are inflated by cross-state spillovers, which are zero-sum effects from the federal point of view. The better approach is to start from the microlevel elasticities and aggregate them up to the federal level.[5]

---

5. To meet standards of rigor, this will require a structural model of how individual-level responses of firms and inventors map onto federal-level outcomes and the incorporation of general equilibrium effects.

6.4   Mobility of Inventors and Firms

Another margin along which both firms and inventors can respond to tax policies is their location choice. Recent evidence shows that there is tax-induced mobility both across US states and across the world's major patenting countries .

*Historical mobility in the United States since 1920.*The historical project described in section 6.3 shows that inventors move in response to state personal income tax rates. The elasticity in the net-of-tax rate of the number of inventors residing in a state is 0.11 for inventors who are from that state and 1.23 for inventors not from that state. Inventors who work for companies are particularly elastic to taxes. Crucially, agglomeration effects appear to matter for location as well: inventors are less sensitive to taxation in a potential destination state when there is already more innovation in that state in their particular field of activity.

International mobility since 1975. There is a heated public debate about whether higher top tax rates in a country will cause a "brain drain" of high-income and high-skill economic agents. In fact, many of the great inventors were international immigrants: Alexander Bell, inventor of the telephone and founder of the Bell Telephone Company; James Kraft, inventor of a pasteurization technique and founder of Kraft Foods Inc.; Ralph Baer, creator of a TV gaming unit that launched the video game industry.

Inventors are much more mobile than other high-skilled individuals. Thus, they carry and transmit their valuable knowledge and expertise to others (as shown in section 6.4), making them essential not only for new knowledge creation, but also for its diffusion. Yet, until recently, little was known about the international mobility of labor in response to taxation, and rigorous evidence was lacking because of a scarcity of international panel data. Akcigit, Baslandze, and Stantcheva (2016) close this gap by using a unique type of international panel data on inventors to study the international migration responses of superstar inventors to top income tax rates for the period from 1977 to 2003; these data come from the European and US patent offices, as well as from the Patent Cooperation Treaty. The authors are able to tackle one major challenge that arises when studying migration responses to taxes, namely, to model the counterfactual payoff that an inventor would get in each potential location.[6]

Their identification of the effects of the top tax rate relies on filtering out all country-year-level variation and exploiting the differential impacts of the top tax rate on inventors at different points in the income distribution within a country-year cell. To implement this strategy, superstar inventors are defined as those in the top 1 percent of the quality distribution, and the authors similarly construct the top 1–5 percent, the top 5–10 percent, and

---

6. This is thanks to a set of detailed controls that come from the patent data, notably measures of an inventor's quality, based on their past citations.

subsequent quality brackets. It is known that inventor quality is strongly correlated with income, and that inventors in the top 1 percent are very high up in the top tax bracket. The probability of being in the top bracket and the fraction of an inventor's income in the top bracket declines as one moves down the quality distribution. Inventors in the top 1 percent and those of somewhat lower quality are comparable enough to be similarly affected by country-year-level policies and economic developments, but only those inventors in the top bracket are directly affected by top taxes. Hence, the lower-quality groups—that is, the top 5–10 percent, the top 10–25 percent, and below the top 25 percent groups—serve as control groups for the top 1 percent group.

The paper finds that superstar inventors' location choices are significantly affected by top tax rates. The elasticity to the net-of-tax rate of the number of domestic superstar inventors is around 0.03, while that of foreign superstar inventors is around 1. These elasticities are larger for inventors who work for multinational companies. On the contrary, inventors are less sensitive to taxes in a country if their company performs a higher share of its research there, suggesting that the location decision is influenced both by the company and by career concerns that may dampen the effects of taxes.

Policy implications. Tax-induced mobility is an issue to take into account, especially when it comes to highly mobile and highly skilled people, such as inventors, who can make major economic contributions to their country of residence. But the right answer may not be to slash general taxes and to engage in relentless tax competition, for example, through preferential tax regimes for foreigners, as has been done in the EU. As argued in Kleven et al. (2020), these are "beggar-thy-neighbor" policies that can reduce overall welfare; international or cross-state tax cooperation is much more fruitful in the long run.

So what can be done? One important margin along which states and countries can act is to provide better amenities and infrastructure for innovation. The studies above consistently show that agglomeration effects significantly dampen the responsiveness to taxes. This occurs for two reasons that can be leveraged. First, agglomeration effects are a proxy for the quality of the research amenities and infrastructure in a place, which are valued by many inventors who choose to live there. Second, inventors and firms directly benefit from being around like-minded, talented innovators. This implies that attracting innovation to a locality in the first place can start a virtuous circle that continues in the long run. Thus, one way of being able to continue using general tax policy for its intended purposes of raising revenues and redistributing income without stifling innovation and causing the outflow of talent would be through the better provision of amenities and infrastructure for innovation.[7]

---

7. In fact, the tax revenues themselves go towards the investment in such amenities.

6.5   Declining Business Dynamism in the United States

As highlighted in the introduction, business dynamism in the United States has been slowing in the last several decades. The key "ten facts" highlighted in the literature (Akcigit and Ates 2021) are that market concentration, average profits, and markups have risen; the labor share has decreased; the labor productivity gap between frontier and laggard firms has increased; entry rates have declined, as has the share of young firms; job reallocation has slowed down; the dispersion of firm growth has increased; and the rise in market concentration and the fall in labor share are positively correlated.

The decline in business dynamism is intrinsically linked to the life cycle of firms. It is thus critical to understand the distinct innovation strategies that firms follow at different stages of their life cycles. Young start-ups and small firms initially explore radical new ideas; for those that survive and grow bigger, innovations tend to become more incremental. Both firms and individuals can be tempted to start erecting barriers against their competitors to prevent entry into their market. They can do this through political connections and lobbying as they gain power, or directly through the intellectual property rights system. This can slow down innovation and influence business dynamism.

Policies can affect firms' innovation very differently based on where they stand in their life cycle. For instance, existing research tax credits help mostly big and profitable firms, as tax credits are only beneficial for firms that make positive profits. Many countries have special policies for start-ups, and others have targeted policies for small businesses. In this section, we consider the effects of various tax policies based on different segments of firms' life cycles, and their implications for business dynamism in the United States.

6.5.1   Start-Ups and Venture Capital

Venture capitalists play a major role in the screening, monitoring, and financing of startups. Akcigit et al. (2019) show that VC-backed start-ups grow faster in their early stages, produce innovations of better quality, and have a higher likelihood of becoming large firms and producing high-quality innovations over time. These effects are stronger if the firms are matched to more experienced venture capitalists. The authors estimate that the existence of venture capital and an efficient match between start-ups and VCs is important for innovation and growth.

When it comes to tax policy, empirically, VC-funded firms are de facto taxed at preferential rates relative to non-VC-funded ones. The authors show that increasing the tax rate on VC-funded firms to harmonize it with the tax rate on non-VC-funded ones would have a significant negative impact on aggregate innovation. Because VCs add a significant value to the start-up and innovation process and do not simply crowd out other firms, the reduction in their activity that would be caused by a higher tax rate is not offset by an equivalent rise in innovation and success of the non-VC-funded firms.

Policy implications. VCs contribute significantly to innovation by fostering high-quality start-ups. Maintaining a low tax burden on VC-funded firms could possibly foster innovation.[8]

6.5.2   Small versus Large Firms

Firms can adopt different innovation strategies. They can engage in external innovation, which creates new products and captures market share from competitors, and they can engage in internal innovation, which improves quality of the product lines that the firm currently owns. Small and large firms typically choose quite different routes when it comes to innovation.

Akcigit and Kerr (2018) explore this key distinction and provide an explanation for why the data show that small firms experience faster growth on average and contribute disproportionately to big and radical innovations. This is not due to different capabilities of firms by assumption, but is rather the result of structural estimation of the model. The authors quantify their model using US data from the Census Bureau for 1982–1997, finding that decreasing returns to external innovation in larger firms are an important departure from the perfect scaling of the Klette and Kortum (2004) framework. This work allows the authors to conclude that the growth impacts of external innovation have exceeded those of internal innovation in the recent US economy, which in turn helps identify some of the special roles that small, innovative firms and new entrants can play in economic growth.

When thinking of total innovation in this context, there are three sources: external innovation by incumbents, internal innovation by incumbents, and (by necessity) external innovation by entrants. While all of them matter, the authors estimate that the key channel for growth is external innovation by incumbent firms. This innovation is done disproportionately by small firms.

Policy implications. Small firms find it more beneficial to engage in external research, which leads them to produce disproportionately more radical, important innovations. Preferential tax rates and tax breaks for small firms can foster this phenomenon further and improve the quality of innovation and the prevalence of breakthrough innovations. In fact, for different reasons, many countries have some sort of preferential tax treatment for small enterprises.

6.5.3   Political Economy

As firms establish themselves in the labor and product market, they may become tempted to keep competitors out. One way to do this is through political connections and lobbying. Akcigit, Baslandze, and Lotti (2018) show that this happens very frequently in Italy and that it reduces the dynamism in the economy, leading to less reallocation of resources, less innova-

---

8. Naturally, in a world without government budget constraints, all firms should be taxed at low rates. The statement here is that given a scarcity of government funds and if the goal is to foster innovation, tax cuts should be given preferentially to VC-funded firms rather than to non-VC-funded firms.

tion, and less entry. Although their empirical analysis uses Italian data, it carries lessons for the United States as well.

To a certain extent, political connections can serve a productive role if they alleviate some bureaucratic and regulatory burdens that cause inefficiencies. But they are also costly and require firms to expand resources to maintain them. Larger firms will find it more profitable to incur these costs and to be politically connected. The authors show that there is a leadership paradox: the leading firms in each industry (i.e., those with the largest market share) absorb the most resources, but are also the least innovative ones, relative to their size. Firms that become connected temporarily enjoy higher employment and sales growth, but lower productivity growth. Over time, industries in which the incumbents are politically connected become more sluggish, with less entry as new entrants are discouraged to try to compete not only in terms of productivity but also in terms of regulatory and bureaucratic burdens. Politically connected incumbents thus have an advantage. Since political connections by incumbents discourage entry, incumbents may decide to preemptively become politically connected to shelter themselves from competition. Politically connected industries will be dominated by older and larger firms and will feature low innovation and productivity growth.

Policy implications. If political connections are predominant and cannot be directly prevented by policy makers, tax policy could take on a corrective role and compensate for the disadvantage that small new entrants face relative to the large, politically connected incumbents. If the frictions are caused by taxes to start with, they could be removed directly, thus also removing the incentive to become politically connected. A more indirect way would be to tax larger incumbents at higher rates to give new entrants a chance to compete.

6.5.4   Declining Business Dynamism and Innovation

Akcigit and Ates (2019) provide a theoretical and quantitative model that is able to explain the ten facts listed above and offer an explanation for what has happened to business dynamism in the United States. The dominant force driving these patterns is a decline in the rate of knowledge diffusion from the frontier, most advanced firms to the laggard ones. This force can explain all ten facts in a way that other explanations cannot. In addition, there is direct evidence for it. For instance, patenting has become more concentrated among firms with many patents. The nature of patents has also changed since the 2000s, with longer claims (indicative of more incremental, rather than radical, innovations) and more self-citations. Overall, the evidence is consistent with a use of intellectual property protection by leading firms to limit knowledge diffusion and entrench their market power.

In the authors' model, in each sector, two firms compete for market leadership. One firm represents "the best," the other "the rest." Prices and markups are a function of the technology gap between firms, as the leading firm can charge up to the level where the nonleading firm with the worse technology can no longer capture a sizable market share. The incentive for leaders to keep innovating is to grow the gap in technology between them and their followers and thus be able to increase prices and markups. Existing followers' incentives to innovate are to catch up with and leapfrog the leader to capture more of the market; similarly, new entrants' incentive is to one day become the market leader.

A key feature of this model, which is clear in the data as well, is that firms make strategic innovation-investment decisions by taking into account where they stand relative to others. When firms are neck and neck and compete very intensely for market leadership, there will be a lot of innovation and business dynamism. But when leaders do very well and open the technology gap between themselves and their followers, prospects for entrants and followers become dim. Then, innovation efforts are reduced and entry declines. Because of this, when the diffusion of knowledge declines, market leaders are protected and establish strong market power. This in turn discourages followers and entrants, slowing innovation in more concentrated sectors. As entry and the threat from competition are diminished, market leaders also slow their innovation efforts. Overall, business dynamism and innovation decline.

Corporate taxes have played a role in this evolution, too, but only a minor one. Corporate tax increases can explain around 10 percent of the decline in business dynamism. This is because lower taxes increase net-of-tax profits and thus only matter for firms that have some market share. They will hence only affect followers and potential entrants in a very muted way, as they are far from taking over the leader and have to discount the potential future gains heavily.

Policy implications. The key lesson from this recent set of papers is that powerful, large incumbents are using their market power to prevent entry and competition by followers. The most direct policy approach to this would be through regulation and competition policy. However, corporate tax policy can play a (second-best) role, too, if it can be designed so as to impose a heavier burden on larger, more mature companies rather than on new entrants. As shown above, this will have only a very small disincentive effect on new entrants (facing the prospect of one day becoming market leaders), but could eat away at part of the advantage the incumbent market leader enjoys.

6.6   The Composition and Quality of Inventors, Firms, and Teams

Firms and inventors are not equally effective at producing innovations. The quantity and quality of innovation in an economy will depend on the composition of firms and inventors, which can also be affected by general and targeted tax policies. In this section, we explain how different policies can play on that margin, considering in turn firms, inventors, and teams within firms.

6.6.1   Firms: Reallocation of Resources between Firms

Not all firms are equally efficient at producing innovation. Whether because of the quality of their ideas, management, or workforce, some firms are excellent at turning research inputs into major innovations, while others are not. Tax policies can affect the selection of firms, their entry and exit, and the reallocation of resources across good and bad firms. Acemoglu et al. (2018) build and estimate a dynamic firm-level innovation model using US Census micro (firm-level) data and patent data. A key finding is that taxing incumbent firms can be very beneficial, in addition to subsidizing R&D. R&D is subsidized to correct for the underinvestment in innovation due to noninternalized spillovers. In the presence of fixed costs, taxing the operations of incumbents encourages less productive firms that are closer to the exit margin to leave the market. This frees up valuable resources—that is, skilled researchers—for more productive firms to hire. On the other hand, when it is not possible to have type-specific R&D subsidies targeted to good versus bad firms, uniform subsidies of R&D alone will not achieve this positive selection because they will benefit both low- and high-productivity firms and encourage low-productivity firms to survive, grow, and absorb scarce resources.

Policy implications. In addition to raising revenues, corporate taxes can serve an efficiency purpose. A sizable, uniform tax on incumbents combined with a uniform R&D subsidy can improve growth and increase welfare. This is an important finding that shows that, despite the distortionary effects of taxes, they can serve an allocative role, by selecting firms that are good enough to survive despite taxes. Corporate income taxes can have a cleansing effect on the economy, freeing up valuable innovation resources for the most productive firms.

6.6.2   Firms: Optimal R&D Policies

Policy makers can do even better with nonuniform policies, by explicitly trying to screen good firms from bad ones. The major obstacle to doing so efficiently is asymmetric information—a key feature in the innovation arena. The innovation literature has extensively addressed how to deal with spillovers, but it has dealt much less with asymmetric information about firms and how to separate productive from nonproductive firms. Yet as a large empirical literature shows, the quality of a firm's organization, management, processes, or ideas—which shape its innovation outcomes, conditional on inputs—is private information and very difficult for outside parties, including the government, to observe. The literature documents the manifestations of asymmetric information in innovation between firms and their shareholders or investors; this problem is even more pronounced between firms and the government. In addition, in the patent and firm data, if one tries to predict the innovation quality of a firm, the prediction is very poor. Seeing which firms are good at innovation and which ones are not is inherently difficult, even using a very large set of observables that is likely a generous overestimate of what the government could realistically condition its policies on.

One way to address the asymmetric information problem is through a strategy adopted by venture capitalist firms, which perform hands-on and thorough screening, and provide staged financing subject to intense monitoring. But this intensive hands-on approach is not easily scalable and thus not applicable when it comes to thinking about large-scale government policies. Instead, what the government can do is to set decentralized tax and subsidy policies that can vary nonlinearly with profits and R&D investments, and in such a way that firms of different productivities will select their customized, uniquely efficient levels of investments and production.

Akcigit, Hanley, and Stantcheva (2016) tackle this problem using a new dynamic mechanism design approach. The key feature of their analysis—and the main impediment to fixing the market distortions typical of innovation, such as nonappropriability and spillovers in a nondistortionary way—is that firms are heterogeneous in their research productivity, and importantly, this research productivity is private information and unobservable by the government. A higher research productivity allows a firm to convert a given set of research inputs into a better innovation output. In addition, while some of the inputs into the R&D process are observable (so-called R&D investment), others are unobservable (R&D effort). The firm's research productivity also evolves stochastically over time. Although the firm has some advance information about its future productivity, it cannot perfectly foresee it. As a result, at the time when the firm invests resources in R&D, the innovation outcome that will result from those investments is yet uncertain.

The authors' main findings are as follows. Asymmetric information can significantly change the optimal policies. From a theoretical perspective, the constrained efficient incentives for R&D trade off a Pigouvian correction for the technology spillover and a correction for the monopoly distortion against the need to screen good firms from bad ones. How much R&D should optimally be subsidized depends critically on a key parameter, namely the complementarity of R&D investment to R&D effort (i.e., the complementarity between observable and unobservable innovation inputs) relative to the complementarity of R&D investment to the firm's research productivity. The more R&D investment is complementary to firm research productivity, the more rents a firm can extract if R&D investment is subsidized. This puts a brake on how well the government can set the Pigouvian correction and compensate for the monopoly distortion. Optimal screening in this case requires dampening the first-best corrective policies. On the other hand, if R&D investments are more complementary to the firm's unobservable R&D effort, they stimulate the firm to put in more of the unobservable input, which is unambiguously good and would make R&D subsidies optimally larger. Other key determinants of the magnitudes and age patterns of the optimal policies are the persistence of firms' research productivity shocks and the strength of spillovers.

The data show that R&D investments are highly complementary to a firm's research productivity: highly productive firms are disproportionately good at transforming R&D inputs into innovation. Given that this implies that higher-productivity firms have a comparative advantage at innovation, it is better to incentivize R&D investments less for the lower-productivity firms, as this makes mimicking them more attractive for high-productivity firms.

Policy implications. It is possible to very closely implement the optimal allocations with simple nonlinear or linear policies that feature lower marginal corporate income taxes for more profitable firms and lower marginal subsidies at higher R&D investment levels. The policies can be simplified even further without much loss, as the most important quantitative feature turns out to be the nonlinearity in the R&D subsidy. Thus, making the profit tax linear only generates a small welfare loss. The intuition is that a constant profit tax that is set at a too generous level for low-profit firms and at about the right level for high-profit firms does reasonably well, since the loss from giving low-profit firms a too generous tax is quantitatively small, given that they make low profits to start with. Therefore, linear corporate income taxes such as the ones we see around the world can be very close to optimal for innovating firms if combined with the right nonlinear R&D subsidy.

6.6.3   Inventors and Education Policies

When it comes to the composition and quality of individual inventors, innovation policies have an important interaction effect with education policy through the occupational choices of inventors, and, hence, the supply of high-skilled researchers. Akcigit, Pearce, and Prato (2019) point out that education policy and general or targeted tax policies for innovation will address different frictions in the innovation chain. In their setting, inventors of varying abilities and with different career preferences take time to build their human capital and face financial constraints in acquiring education. As a result, in the short run, targeted policies such as R&D policies may not be as effective as expected; they may face the bottleneck of insufficient supply of research talent due to lack of education capacity or credit constraints. In the long run, these policies may have limited effectiveness if they are not coupled with education policies. This new interplay can explain why innovation models typically predict much larger effects of R&D policies than those that are observed in the data.

Policy implications. How do different policies influence aggregate innovation and economic growth? The authors find that the impact of R&D subsidies can be strengthened when combined with higher-education policy that sorts talented but credit-constrained individuals into research. In addition, the role of education policy is increased in societies or times when financial constraints on the acquisition of education are more stringent. Education subsidies are particularly critical and effective in unequal societies where many individuals face financial constraints preventing them from efficiently acquiring education. In these cases, R&D policies alone are highly ineffective.

There is, of course, a critical timing issue. In the short run, only R&D policies can be effective, as education policies act with longer lags. R&D policies stimulate the purchase of more research capital and equipment, making researchers more productive almost upon impact. However, the expansion of educational slots takes some time and surpasses R&D after six years. Educational subsidies, on the other hand, take the longest to transmit to the growth rate but gradually become the most effective policy tool in the long run.

6.6.4 Teams and Knowledge Diffusion

Inventors do not work alone: most patents are the result of collaborative work and are produced by teams of inventors of different talents and skill levels. In addition, inventors learn from each to produce better innovations. When an inventor interacts with other, more knowledgeable inventors, they improve their own knowledge and subsequently produce higher-quality innovations.

Akcigit et al. (forthcoming) provide a model and empirical analysis that capture these key features observed in their data. In their framework, inventors can learn (i.e., improve their productivity) in two ways. They can meet others and interact with them, and they can learn on their own, through learning-by-doing, formal education, experience, or individual discovery. Given their realized productivity after learning, inventors form teams. Some inventors who are highly productive and knowledgeable become "team leaders" and work with less-skilled team members to produce innovations. Better team leaders will be able to hire larger teams and produce better innovations. The quality of innovation, and thus of technological progress, will depend on the quality of teams in the economy. The authors estimate the model using new European Patent Office data for inventors across many years and countries and find that interactions with others are quantitatively very important for improving inventors' productivity, and hence for economic growth. Interactions can occur at the level of the firm, at the levelof the technological field (in a given area), or at different geographic levels. In addition, there is a strong complementarity between access to external knowledge and learning from others: if others around oneself learn more from outside sources and then interact more, one will also end up interacting with more knowledgeable people and learning more.

Therefore, when thinking of the effects of tax policies, one has to consider, on the one hand, their implications for team formation and team composition, and on the other hand, their implications for interactions, learning, and knowledge diffusion among inventors.

Policy implications. In line with the mobility results discussed above, policies that attract many inventors to a given area can foster interactions and thus learning. As discussed above, preferential local tax regimes can achieve this goal, but at the cost of penalizing other areas in a zero-sum way. Better amenities can achieve the goal more efficiently, without ruthless tax competition. On the other hand, the imposition of large employer payroll taxes or firing taxes, which are particularly heavy in many European countries, can reduce labor market fluidity and prevent inventors from moving to the team most suited to them. Education subsidies increase the quality of the pool of inventors and make it more worthwhile for inventors to interact with others and to learn from them.

6.7   Applied versus Basic Innovation and Choice of Technologies

Innovations come in different shapes and sizes. Companies and inventors can choose to orient their research in different directions, and their choices here too can be shaped by tax policy.

6.7.1   Applied and Basic Research

A major distinction, as described in section 6.2, is between basic and applied research. Akcigit, Hanley, and Serrano-Velarde (2021) refer to "Pasteur's quadrant" for illustration of the different types of research. At one extreme lies pure, basic research, as done most often by the public sector in academic institutions and universities. At the other extreme lies purely applied research, destined for immediate commercial use. In between exists a mix of basic and applied, captured in the authors' paper by the private sector's basic research—research that is ultimately driven by a profit motive and with the hope of being one day applicable, but without immediate, intentional commercial implications.

Without government intervention, there is a stark misallocation of research effort. The authors find that 68 perent of the spillovers from basic research are not internalized. Once these different types of research are taken into account, it appears that the bigger problem is not the insufficient investment in research overall, but rather the wrong allocation of research efforts between basic and applied innovation. There is too little investment in basic research—yet there can be too much investment in applied research in the face of competition between firms, if there is strategic complementarity between basic and applied research (i.e., the returns to applied research increase the level of basic research).

The authors also shed light on the debate about the worrying decline in research productivity in the US economy. They highlight the strong complementarity between public and private research efforts. When there is more investment by public entities in predominantly basic research, private research investment both becomes more productive and increases.

Policy implications. Which policies can address the inefficient allocation of research efforts? A uniform research subsidy to private firms—which subsidizes all of their research at the same rate—carries a large fiscal cost in this context. Although it will stimulate investment in basic research, it will generate even greater overinvestment in applied research. Subsidizing applied and basic research at different rates can reduce fiscal costs without compromising investment in innovation. The authors find in their model that the optimal subsidy rate for basic research is almost five times as high as that for applied research. Clearly, distinguishing between applied and basic research inputs could be difficult, which means that it's important to allow for some misclassification by firms, which will be tempted to relabel applied research as basic research. But even with substantial levels of misreporting of research types, a higher subsidy for basic research remains very effective. Going forward, finding a feasible way to differentiate between basic and applied research is essential to better innovation tax policies.

In addition, subsidies and funding for public research could also indirectly foster investment in private research, as public research is highly complementary to private research.

6.7.2 Innovation in Green Technologies

Tax policies can orient research toward different directions when it comes to the environment and the development of clean technologies. Given how pressing and critical an issue climate change is, tax policy tools for innovation in these areas have to be very carefully considered and deployed.

Acemoglu et al. (2016) provide a clear theoretical and quantitative framework to think about tax policy for innovation in clean technologies. Goods can be produced using either a "dirty" (polluting) technology or a "clean" (less-polluting, environmentally friendly) technology. Producers choose which technologies to employ based on their costs, which in turn depend on how efficient the technologies are, and are also based on public policies, such as production taxes, that vary by technology type. For instance, carbon taxes or taxes on other polluting particles or greenhouse gases would imply a higher tax on the dirty technology. In addition to picking their production technology, private firms can also choose to do research to improve either the clean or dirty technology. Research and innovation decisions are shaped by public tax policies and the current state of technology. If the clean technology is very far behind the dirty technology in terms of efficiency, research in it that produces only incremental improvements is unlikely to yield immediate benefits to producers and is thus not profitable in the short run. However, sustained research efforts and cumulative incremental improvements may eventually render the clean technology competitive and profitable.

Taxing pollutants, for example, through carbon taxes, can redirect research toward clean technologies. Subsidizing clean research can also achieve this goal. But as long as the dirty technology remains much cheaper than the clean one, carbon taxes will reduce pollution but at a high efficiency cost in terms of foregone consumption. A research subsidy can redirect research successfully, even when combined with a low carbon tax initially, until the clean technology becomes able to compete with the dirty one. Research subsidies in this model can be optimal even if there is no underinvestment in research overall; they are used to counteract the negative externalities of pollution for the environment.

Policy implications. Both carbon taxes (as well as taxes on other pollutants) and research subsidies for clean technology can be used to direct innovation to clean technologies. However, carbon taxes are very costly initially when the clean technology is still inefficient relative to the dirty technology. Thus, initially, carbon taxes are a more cost-effective tool to correct for the direct externality of pollution from carbon or other pollutants, but research subsidies are more cost effective for guiding research toward clean technologies. A mix of policies that stimulate investment in green technologies at lower fiscal cost than other policies can be described as follows: policy initially focuses heavily on the research subsidy, which declines over time; carbon taxes are backloaded initially (and increase over time as the clean technology becomes more efficient), but eventually also decline as pollution is reduced thanks to the use of cleaner technology.

6.8   Conclusion

Tax policies offer a wide array of tools commonly used by governments to influence the economy. In this chapter, we reviewed the many margins through which tax policies can affect innovation, the main driver of economic growth in the long run. These margins include the impact of tax policy on (1) the quantity and quality of innovation; (2) the geographic mobility of innovation and inventors across US states and countries; (3) the decline in business dynamism in the United States, firm entry, and productivity; (4) the quality of firms, inventors, and teams; and (5) the direction of research efforts (e.g., toward applied versus basic research, or toward dirty versus clean technologies). We gave ideas drawn from research on how the right design of policy can allow policy makers to foster the most productive firms without wasting public funds on less productive ones.

The interplay between tax and innovation is arguably among the most policy-relevant and underexplored areas in endogenous growth and public finance. The scarcity of empirical studies has been due to the lack of data at the microeconomic level needed to estimate the strength of tax responses of firms and inventors. However, our computational powers are increasing at a time when many countries are making their firm- and individual-level microdata sets available to researchers. In addition, thanks to optical character recognition techniques, more and more large-scale historical records are being digitized for use in economic research. These are all very exciting developments that can potentially foster this important and growing area of research.

References

Acemoglu, D., U. Akcigit, H. Alp, N. Bloom, and W. R. Kerr. 2018. "Innovation, Reallocation and Growth." *American Economic Review* 198 (11): 3450–91.

Acemoglu, D., U. Akcigit, D. Hanley, and W. Kerr. 2016. "Transition to Clean Technology." *Journal of Political Economy* 124 (1): 52–104.

Aghion, P., U. Akcigit, A. Bergeaud, R. Blundell, and D. Hémous. 2018. "Innovation and Top Income Inequality." *Review of Economic Studies* 86 (1): 1–45.

Aghion, P., U. Akcigit, A. Deaton, and A. Roulet. 2016. "Creative Destruction and Subjective Well-Being." *American Economic Review* 106 (12): 3869–97.

Akcigit, U., and S. T. Ates. 2019. "What Happened to US Business Dynamism?" NBER Working Paper No. 25756. Cambridge, MA: National Bureau of Economic Research.

———. 2021. "Ten Facts on Declining Business Dynamism and Lessons from Endogenous Growth Theory." *American Economic Journal: Macroeconomics* 13 (1): 257–98.

Akcigit, U., S. Baslandze, and F. Lotti. 2018. "Connecting to Power: Political Connections, Innovation, and Firm Dynamics." NBER Working Paper No. 25136. Cambridge, MA: National Bureau of Economic Research.

Akcigit, U., S. Baslandze, and S. Stantcheva. 2016. "Taxation and the International Mobility of Inventors." *American Economic Review* 106 (10): 2930–81.

Akcigit, U., S. Caicedo, E. Miguelez, S. Stantcheva, and V. Sterzi. 2018. "Dancing with the Stars: Innovation through Interactions." NBER Working Paper No. 24466. Cambridge, MA: National Bureau of Economic Research.

Akcigit, U., E. Dinlersoz, J. Greenwood, and V. Penciakova. 2019. "Synergizing Ventures." NBER Working Paper No. 26196. Cambridge, MA: National Bureau of Economic Research.

Akcigit, U., J. Grigsby, and T. Nicholas. 2017. "The Rise of American Ingenuity: Innovation and Inventors of the Golden Age." NBER Working Paper No. 23047. Cambridge, MA: National Bureau of Economic Research.

Akcigit, U., J. Grigsby, T. Nicholas, and S. Stantcheva. Forthcoming. "Taxation and Innovation in the 20th Century." *Quarterly Journal of Economics.*

Akcigit, U., D. Hanley, and N. Serrano-Velarde. 2021. "Back to Basics: Basic Research Spillovers, Innovation Policy and Growth." *Review of Economic Studies* 88 (1): 1–43.

Akcigit, U., D. Hanley, and S. Stantcheva. 2016. "Optimal Taxation and R&D Policies." NBER Working Paper No. 22908. Cambridge, MA: National Bureau of Economic Research.

Akcigit, U., and W. R. Kerr. 2018. "Growth through Heterogeneous Innovations." *Journal of Political Economy* 126 (4): 1374–1443.

Akcigit, U., J. Pearce, and M. Prato. 2019. "Tapping into Talent: Coupling Education and Innovation Policies for Economic Growth." Working paper, University of Chicago.

Arundel, A., and I. Kabla. 1998. "What Percentage of Innovations Are Patented? Empirical Estimates for European Firms." *Research Policy* 27 (2): 127–41.

Hall, B., A. Jaffe, and M. Trajtenberg. 2005. "Market Value and Patent Citations: A First Look." *RAND Journal of Economics* 36 (1638).

Jaffe, A., and M. Trajtenberg. 2002. *Citations and Innovations: A Window on the Knowledge*. Cambridge, MA: MIT Press.

Klette, T. J., and S. Kortum. 2004. "Innovating Firms and Aggregate Innovation." *Journal of Political Economy* 112 (5): 986–1018.

Kleven, H., C. Landais, M. Muñoz, and S. Stantcheva. 2020. "Taxation and Migration: Evidence and Policy Implications." *Journal of Economic Perspectives* 34 (2): 119–42.

Saez, E., and S. Stantcheva. 2018. "A Simpler Theory of Optimal Capital Taxation." *Journal of Public Economics* 162: 120–42.

Government Incentives
for Entrepreneurship

Josh Lerner

7.1 Introduction

In the dozen years since the global financial crisis, there has been a surge of interest on the part of governments in promoting entrepreneurial activity, largely by providing financing (Bai et al. 2020). This chapter explores these policies, focusing on financial incentives to entrepreneurs and the intermediaries who fund them. (Other chapters in this volume discuss related policies to create a general business environment conducive to entrepreneurship and innovation, such as through the tax code, cluster development, and labor force reforms.)

The motivation for these efforts is clear: the well-documented relationships between economic growth, innovation, entrepreneurship, and venture capital. Yet despite good intentions, many of these public initiatives have ended in disappointment. To cite several examples from the past decade:

- The US Department of Energy's (DOE) clean energy initiative was created in 2005 but remained unfunded until 2009, when it received financing as part of the American Recovery and Reinvestment (also known

Josh Lerner is the Jacob H. Schiff Professor of Investment Banking at Harvard Business School and a research associate and codirector of the Productivity, Innovation, and Entrepreneurship Program at the National Bureau of Economic Research.

Parts of this chapter were adapted from Ivashina and Lerner (2019) and Lerner (2009, 2012). I thank Ben Jones and Ralph Lerner for helpful comments, Susan Woodward of Sand Hill Econometrics for access to data, and Harvard Business School's Division of Research for financial support. I have received compensation from advising institutional investors in private capital funds and private capital groups, and from governments for designing policies relevant to private capital. All errors and omissions are my own. For acknowledgments, sources of research support, and disclosure of the author's material financial relationships, if any, please see https://www.nber.org/books-and-chapters/innovation-and-public-policy/government-incentives-entrepreneurship.

as the Stimulus) Act.[1] The program was to provide loan guarantees and direct grants to risky but potentially rewarding energy projects that may otherwise have been too risky to attract private investment. More than $34 billion was spent in less than four years, which was almost $2 billion more than the total private VC investment in the field. The proposed investments were controversial at the time. As one organization protesting the program noted, "DOE has minimal experience administering a loan guarantee program, and its one test case ended with taxpayers paying a heavy price. In the late 1970s and early 1980s, DOE offered billions in loan guarantees for the development of synthetic fuels. Due in large part to poor administration and market changes, the federal government was forced to pay billions to cover the losses" ("Oppose Wasteful $10 Billion Increase," 2010). These worries proved prescient. The enormous scale of the public investment appears to have crowded out and replaced most private spending in this area, as VCs waited on the sidelines to see where the public funds would go. Moreover, in the wake of extensive industry lobbying, the investment decisions of government administrators led to a number of bankruptcies (e.g., Solyndra, A123 Systems, Beacon Power).[2] Rather than being stimulated, cleantech has fallen from 14.9 percent of venture investments in 2009 to 1.5 percent of capital deployed in the first nine months of 2019.[3]

- The Saudi government has spent many tens of billions of dollars seeking to promote venture capital activity in the kingdom.[4] These have included a wide variety of regulatory reforms (creating, for instance, a second-tier market for entrepreneurial listings and facilitating the business registration process), the establishment of venture funds and regional hubs (often in conjunction with new universities), and global venture capital investments. In the last regard, the most notable was a

1. See, for instance, Gold (2009), Kao (2013), Kirsner (2009), Mullaney (2009), and Sposito (2009).
2. Evaluating the return from these start-up investments is very difficult. As far as I can tell, the numerous evaluations of these programs by government agencies and academics have not attempted to compute one. Much of the difficulty stems from the fact that payments were made under a variety of programs (e.g., the 1705 Loan Guarantee Program and the Advanced Technology Vehicle Manufacturing Loan Program), and payments to start-ups were mingled with those to established entities like Goldman Sachs and NRG Energy, where the bankruptcy risk was presumably much lower (though the rationale for public funding may have been so as well) (Lipton and Krauss 2011). But given that public funding went to some of the most spectacular start-up bankruptcies in the sector, and that even independent venture capital investments in this sector between the beginning of 2008 and the third quarter of 2019 have yielded (according to Sand Hill Econometrics) an annualized loss of –2.6 percent (before accounting for fees), it is hard to be optimistic about the performance of the investments in entrepreneurial firms as part of this initiative.
3. Based on the author's analysis of data from Sand Hill Econometrics.
4. This paragraph is based on Seoudi and Mahmoud (2016), Sindi (2015), and assorted press accounts.

commitment of $45 billion by the Saudi Public Investment Fund—a Saudi sovereign wealth fund whose stated mission is to be "the engine behind economic diversity in the KSA" (Kingdom of Saudi Arabia 2019)—to the SoftBank Vision Fund. Yet the level of venture capital in the kingdom has remained very modest. According to the consulting firm MAGNiTT (2020), only $50 million of venture capital was raised by Saudi firms in 2018, and $67 million in 2019. The 2018 value represented 0.006 percent of gross domestic product, a level one-sixtieth of that of Israel and akin to that of the lowest nations tracked on this measure by the Organisation for Economic Co-operation and Development (e.g., Italy, the Russian Federation, and Slovenia) (OECD 2019).

- The Chinese government, after a series of adept moves to promote venture capital over two decades, made a major commitment in the middle part of the 2010s to promoting venture capital.[5] Under the Government Guidance Fund program, over $231 billion was invested in government-sponsored venture funds in 2015 alone, largely by Chinese government bodies and state-owned enterprises. By way of context, this amount was more than five times the total amount committed to venture funds worldwide by all other investors in 2015. The government claimed it had raised $1.8 trillion for these funds by the end of 2018.[6] The result appears to have been a massive bubble, followed by a quick collapse and slowdown. Between the fourth quarter of 2016 and the fourth quarter of 2018, fundraising dropped by nearly 90 percent, a trend that has continued into 2019. As a result, Chinese companies have fallen from a peak of 45 percent of venture capital invested worldwide to 15 percent in the second quarter of 2019 (Rowley 2019). The prediction of Gary Rieschel of Qiming Venture Partners (Shen 2016) is looking increasingly prescient: "They have a fantasy that if they give everyone money they'll create entrepreneurs. What it will result in is catastrophic losses for the government."

In this chapter, I argue that these disappointing outcomes have not simply been a matter of bad luck—for instance, the choice by the Obama administration to target its subsidies to entrepreneurial firms to A123 Systems and Solyndra rather than to more viable cleantech firms that would have avoided bankruptcy. Instead, the unfortunate outcomes have reflected the fundamental structural issues that make it difficult for governments to launch successful efforts to promote entrepreneurship over sustained periods. I highlight several critical challenges, and outline two principles that might render these efforts more effective.

5. This paragraph is based in part on Feng (2018), Oster and Chen (2016), and Yang (2019).
6. Based on the author's compilation of Preqin data (https://www.preqin.com/).

7.2 The Motivation

Public bodies have been motivated to undertake these efforts by the perceived relationship between entrepreneurial activity on the one hand and employment opportunities, innovation, and economic growth on the other. The reader by this point in the volume should be convinced of the importance of innovation to economic growth. But the role that entrepreneurship in general and venture capital in particular play in promoting innovation has been much less thoroughly discussed so far.

Initially, economists generally overlooked the creative power of new firms: they suspected that the bulk of innovations would stem from large industrialized concerns. For instance, Joseph Schumpeter (1942), one of the pioneers of the serious study of entrepreneurship, posited that large firms had an inherent advantage in innovation relative to smaller enterprises.

These initial beliefs have not stood the test of time. Rather, today they look like the intellectual by-product of an era that saw large firms and their industrial laboratories (such as IBM and AT&T) replace the independent inventors who accounted for a substantial part of innovative activity in the late 19th and early 20th centuries.

In today's world, Schumpeter's hypothesis of large-firm superiority does not accord with casual observation. In numerous industries, such as medical devices, communication technologies, semiconductors, and software, leadership is in the hands of relatively young firms whose growth was largely financed by venture capitalists and public equity markets. (Think, for example, of Amazon, Boston Scientific, Facebook, and Google.) Even in industries where established firms have retained dominant positions, such as finance, small firms have developed an increasing share of the new ideas, and then licensed or sold them to larger concerns. Large firms are if anything cutting back their investments in basic science. (See the evidence in Arora, Belenzon, and Patacconi 2015.)

This pattern of new ventures playing a key role in stimulating innovation has been especially pronounced in the past two decades. The two arenas that have seen perhaps the most potentially revolutionary technological innovation—biotechnology and the internet—were driven by smaller entrants. Neither established drug companies nor computer software manufacturers were pioneers in developing these technologies. Small firms did not invent the key genetic-engineering techniques or internet protocols. Rather, the enabling technologies were developed with government funds at academic institutions and research laboratories. It was the small entrants, however, who first seized on the commercial opportunities. Even in areas where large firms have traditionally dominated, such as energy research, start-up firms appear to be playing an increasing role.

Not only do Schumpeter's arguments fail the test of experience, but systematic studies have generated little support for his belief in the innovative advantage of large firms. Over the years, economists have tried repeatedly to measure the relationship between firm size and innovation. While this literature is substantial, it is remarkably inconclusive. I will not inflict on the reader a detailed review of the hundreds, if not thousands, of papers on this subject, but it is worth highlighting that they give very little support to the claim that large firms are more innovative.[7] Much of this work has related measures of innovative discoveries—for example, R&D expenditures, patents, or inventions—to firm size. Initial studies were undertaken using the largest manufacturing firms; more recent works have employed larger samples and detailed data (e.g., studies employing data on firms' specific lines of business). Despite the improved methodology of recent studies, the results have remained inconclusive: the studies seem as likely to find a negative as a positive relationship, and even when a positive relationship between firms' size and innovation has been found, it has had little economic significance. For instance, one study concluded that a doubling of firm size increased the ratio of R&D to sales by only 0.2 percent (Cohen, Levin, and Mowery 1987).

Whatever may be the relationship between a firm's size and its innovations, one of the relatively few things that researchers can agree on is the critical role played by new firms, or entrants, in many industries. The role of start-ups in emerging industries has been highlighted not just in many case studies, but also in systematic research. For instance, a study by Acs and Audretsch (1988) examined which firms developed some of the most important innovations of the 20th century.[8] The authors documented the relative contribution of large and small firms. Small firms contributed almost half the innovations they examined. But they found that the contribution of small firms was not central in all industries. It was greatest in immature industries in which market power was relatively unconcentrated. These findings suggest that entrepreneurs and small firms play a key role in observing where new technologies can meet customers' needs and respond rapidly to them. Whether owing to poor incentives, inefficient internal capital markets, or other causes, larger firms do not appear to fare well in this regard.

Recent studies have also pointed to the special advantage in innovation enjoyed by young entrepreneurs backed by venture capital firms. Considerable evidence shows that venture capitalists play an important role in encouraging innovation. The types of firms they finance—whether young start-ups hungry for capital or growing firms that need to restructure—pose numerous risks and uncertainties that discourage other investors.

Where, then, does this advantage come from? The financing of young firms is a risky business. A lack of information makes it difficult to assess the potential of these firms and permits opportunistic behavior by entrepreneurs after financing arrives. To address these information problems,

---

7. The interested reader can turn to surveys by Azoulay and Lerner (2012) and Cohen (2010).
8. Similar studies include Aron and Lazear (1990) and Prusa and Schmitz (1994).

venture investors employ a variety of mechanisms that seem to be critical in boosting innovation.

The first of these devices is the screening process that venture capitalists use to select investment opportunities. This process is typically far more efficient than that used by other funders of innovation, such as corporate research and development laboratories and government grant makers. In addition to conducting careful interviews and financial analysis, venture capitalists usually make investments with other investors. One venture firm will originate the deal and look to bring in other venture firms. Involving other firms provides a second opinion on the opportunity. There is usually no clear-cut evidence that an investment will yield attractive returns. Having other investors approve the deal limits the likelihood of funding bad deals. The result of this detailed analysis is, of course, many rejections: only about 0.5 to 1 percent of business plans are funded (Kaplan and Stromberg 2004). Inevitably, many good ideas are rejected as part of the assessment process.

When venture capitalists invest, they hold not common stock but rather preferred stock (Kaplan and Stromberg 2003). The significance of this distinction is that if the company is liquidated or otherwise returns money to the shareholders, preferred stock is paid before the common stock that entrepreneurs, as well as other, less privileged investors, hold. Moreover, venture capitalists add numerous restrictive covenants and provisions to the preferred stock. They may be able, for instance, to block future financings if they are dissatisfied with the valuation, to replace the entrepreneur, and to have a set number of representatives on (or even control of) the board of directors. In this way, if something unexpected happens (which is the rule rather than the exception with entrepreneurial firms), the venture investor can assert control. These terms vary with the financing round, with the most onerous terms reserved for the earliest rounds.

The staging of investments also improves the efficiency of venture capital funding (Gompers 1995; Neher 1999). In large corporations, research and development budgets are typically set at the beginning of a project, with few interim reviews planned. This pattern contrasts with the venture capital process: once they make a decision to invest, venture capitalists frequently disburse funds in stages. The refinancing of these firms, termed "rounds" of financing, is conditional on achieving certain technical or market milestones. Proceeding in this fashion allows the venture capitalist to gather more information before providing additional funding, thus helping investors separate investments that are likely to be successful from those that are likely to fail. Managers of venture-backed firms have to return repeatedly to their financiers for additional capital, which allows venture capitalists to ensure that their money is not being squandered on unprofitable projects. Thus, an innovative idea continues to be funded only if its promoters continue to execute well.

Finally, venture capitalists provide intensive oversight of the firms they invest in. Survey evidence (Gompers et al. 2020) suggests that over 25 percent of venture capitalists interact with the entrepreneurs that they are funding multiple times per week, and an additional one-third interact once a week. These interactions can have profound impacts. One intriguing study by Bernstein, Giroud, and Townsend (2016) supports these claims, showing that when an airline adds a direct flight between the city of a venture capitalist and one of his or her existing portfolio firms (which presumably facilitates face-to-face interactions), the firm is likely to experience a boost in innovative and financial performance.

With support from venture capitalists, start-ups can better invest in the research, market development, marketing, and strategizing they require to attain the scale necessary to go public. The importance of this backing can be illustrated in stylized facts, such as that of the ten most valuable companies in the world as of mid-2020, fully seven (five based in the United States and two in China) were originally venture backed (based on an analysis of Compustat data and various venture capital databases and media reports).

The positive impact of venture capital is also corroborated in large-sample research. Especially relevant is the finding of Kortum and Lerner (2000) that even after addressing the concern that venture capital investments are highly targeted, venture funding does have a strong positive impact on innovation. The estimated coefficients vary according to the techniques employed, but on average a dollar of venture capital appears to be *three to four* times more potent in stimulating patenting than a dollar of traditional corporate R&D. While venture capital has historically been small relative to corporate research, it is responsible for a much greater share of US commercial innovations.

7.3   The Challenges

Given the apparently strong relationship between entrepreneurship, innovation, and growth, it is not surprising that governments worldwide have sought to promote new ventures. But as the examples in the introduction suggest, many public efforts have gone astray.

In particular, in this section, I highlight three aspects of the nature of entrepreneurial ventures that pose substantial challenges to government policy makers.

7.3.1   The Geographic Dilemma

The first challenge is the tight geographical focus of entrepreneurial businesses. Entrepreneurial businesses are often clustered geographically (Glaeser, Kerr, and Ponzetto 2010), venture-backed businesses even more so (Chen et al. 2010). These patterns characterize such businesses around the world.

The highly skewed distribution of venture capital investment can be illustrated by a tabulation of Pitchbook data between 2015 and 2017 by Florida and Hathaway (2018). The authors concluded that the top ten urban areas for venture financing (six in the United States and two in China, as well as in London and Bangalore) accounted for 62 percent of venture disbursements worldwide, while the top 25 urban areas accounted for 75 percent of all disbursements.

This disbursement is not accidental, but rather reflects the nature of investment performance. The Sand Hill Econometrics index of gross (pre-fee) returns from venture capital investments between 1980 and 2019 highlights a substantial discrepancy between Silicon Valley and other US regions. Northern California transactions reported an annualized return of 25.6 percent, substantially more than other regions such as New England (14.3 percent), mid-Atlantic (15.4 percent), and non-California Pacific states (13.5 percent).[9] While accurate regional return data are not available worldwide, undoubtedly this pattern would repeat itself elsewhere.

Yet many efforts to boost high-potential entrepreneurship end up directing far too much funding to unpromising areas in an effort to "share the wealth." Much of the impact is diluted as funds that could be very helpful in a core area end up where they are not useful.

The Small Business Innovation Research (SBIR) program, the largest public venture program in the United States, provides an illustration of this problem. The effect of a fairness policy was shown in my work (Lerner 1999) comparing the performance of program recipients with that of matching firms: awardees grew considerably faster than companies in the same locations and industries that did not receive awards. In the ten years after receipt of SBIR funding, the workforce of the average award recipient in a high-tech region grew by 47, a doubling in size. The workforces of other awardees— those located in regions *not* characterized by high-tech activity—grew by only 13 employees. Though the recipients of SBIR awards grew considerably faster than a sample of matched firms, the superior performance, as measured by growth in employment (as well as sales and other measures), was confined to awardees in areas that already had private venture activity. Many other examples can be offered from the Americas, Asia, and Europe, where the pressure for fairness has led to the diversion of substantial funds for entrepreneurial investments with little chance of success.

These issues are particularly relevant for science-based entrepreneurship. Economic activity linked to disruptive new technologies seems to evolve in a very concentrated pattern (Bloom et al. 2020). Potential explanations for these patterns include the dependence on close ties with academia (many of these initial hubs are near academic centers), agglomeration effects that encourage firms to bunch together, and labor market dynamics. Whatever

9. Based on the author's compilation of Sand Hill Econometrics data.

the causes, the effect has been to render government efforts to encourage science-based ventures in peripheral locations very difficult.

Thus, in the name of geographic "diversity," the SBIR program funded firms with inferior prospects. Underneath these patterns lie some intense political pressures and conflicting interests. For one thing, congressmen and their staffers have pressured program managers to award funding to companies in their states. As a result, in almost every recent fiscal year, firms in all 50 states (and indeed in every one of the 435 congressional districts) have received at least one SBIR award. These patterns are far from unique: pressures for "fair" distribution of subsidies (Weingast, Shepsle, and Johnsen 1981) often lower the social and private returns from these government initiatives.

7.3.2   The Timing Dynamic

Another issue stems from the boom-bust cycles that frequently characterize entrepreneurial markets. The venture market is extraordinarily uneven, moving from cycles of feast to famine and back again. In some periods, far too many firms can get access to financing, while in others, worthy companies languish unfunded.

Funds operating in periods with little competition often eventually experience very good returns, a pattern that may reflect the fact that the funds operating during these years can invest in the most promising firms at relatively modest valuations. Over time, however, these high returns attract the interest of institutional investors. What starts as a trickle of funds ends as a torrent. The competition for deals rises, as does the pricing of these transactions. Ultimately, the expansion proves to be unsustainable, and returns fall. Then the cycle repeats itself all over again.

These cycles have led to considerable drama in the venture industry. Each industry downturn produces melodramatic claims that the venture industry is fundamentally broken, with too many investors competing for a limited supply of deals. For instance, in the dark days after the NASDAQ crash of 2000–2002, Steve Dow of the venerable firm Sevin Rosen indicated that his group was unlikely to raise a new fund. "The traditional venture model seems to us to be broken," he noted. "Too much money had flooded the venture business and too many companies were being given financing in every conceivable sector" (Helft 2006). (More typically, the conclusion of the complaining venture capitalist is that everyone should exit the market except for the market observer and his best friends.)

This song has been repeated almost verbatim in every market downturn. "Dramatic inflows of cash weaken the 'fragile ecosystem' of the venture capital industry by forcing some to 'shovel' money into deals. . . . The answer is to discourage more money from coming in and to suppress what [gets invested]," preached the *Venture Capital Journal* in 1993 (Deger 1993). The same periodical bemoaned in 1980, "The rate of disbursements from venture investors to developing businesses continues to be extraordinary. . . . [A] major limiting factor in expansion will be the availability of qualified venture investment managers. Direct experience is so critical to venture investment disciplines" ("Special Report," 1980). (With the benefit of hindsight, the *Journal* was exactly wrong in both cases. The typical funds raised in the years of these two articles had a return of 26.1 percent and 21.6 percent, respectively, which remain among the two best vintage years for venture funds ever.)

Despite all the hype and drama, these boom-and-bust patterns are important, and the interest that these cycles have attracted is justified. It is natural to wonder why pensions and others seem to put most of their money to work almost inevitably at exactly the wrong time. Why don't venture groups pull back from investing in market peaks, rather than continuing to dance the dance? While much remains uncertain about these cycles of boom and bust, several drivers of the patterns have been documented.

At least some of the deterioration of performance stems from the phenomenon of "money chasing deals." As more money flows into their funds from institutional and individual investors, venture capitalists' willingness to pay more for deals increases: a doubling of inflows into venture funds led to between a 7 percent and 21 percent increase in valuation levels for otherwise identical deals. These results do not reflect improvements in the venture investment environment; when we look at the ultimate success of venture-backed firms, the success rates do not differ significantly between investments made during periods of relatively low inflows and valuations, and those of the boom years. But the findings, while suggesting how these cycles work, do not explain why they come about.

Part of the decline in venture activity stems from new funds. During hot venture markets, many inexperienced groups raise capital. In many cases, these funds are raised from inexperienced investors, who are attracted by the excitement surrounding venture funds or by funds-of-funds, which target these investors. Often, they cannot get into top-tier funds and instead reach out to less experienced funds, not appreciating the differences across groups.

Part of the deterioration in performance around booms reflects the changes in the venture funds. Established groups often take advantage of these hot markets to increase their capital under management aggressively. (This decision is likely to be driven by the typical compensation that venture funds enjoy, which is largely driven by fees from capital under management.) As venture groups grow in size, they tend to increase the capital that each partner is responsible for and to broaden the range of industries in which they invest. These changes are often associated with deteriorating performance.

Whatever the precise mechanisms behind these cycles, their impact on innovation is most worrisome. Skeptical observers of the venture scene frequently argue that these cycles can lead to the neglect of promising companies. For instance, during the deep venture trough of the 1970s—in 1975, no venture capital funds at all were raised in the United States—many companies seeking to develop pioneering personal-computing hardware and software languished unfunded. Ultimately, these technologies emerged with revolutionary impact in the 1980s, but their emergence may have been accelerated had the venture market not been in such a deep funk during the 1970s.

Townsend (2015), in an intriguing analysis of the technology-market collapse of 2000–2003, looks at the probability that firms failed to get refinanced through no fault of their own. He examines the probability that firms in sectors unrelated to IT during the collapse period got another financing round, and how this varied with their lead venture firm's exposure to the internet sector. He compares non-IT firms whose backers invested heavily in internet companies during the years leading up to the peak of the bubble with those whose backers invested little in the internet sector during that time. (Based on all observable characteristics, these firms are otherwise identical.) The unlucky ones with internet-exposed backers were far less likely to raise another financing round. The analysis suggests that these unlucky firms—even though their technologies had nothing to do with the internet, telecommunications, or software—experienced a 26 percent larger drop in the probability that they would raise additional funding than did those backed by funds without a heavy exposure to the internet. If a potential entrepreneur realizes that even if he does everything right, his business may fail because he was unlucky in choosing a financier, his enthusiasm for the new venture may fade. He might well conclude that if he is going to be gambling, a trip to Vegas is a less costly and painful alternative.

It might be thought that this termination of new ventures is not a big deal. After all, the personal-computing technology that may have languished unfunded during the 1970s ultimately saw the light of day in the next decade. But in addition to the delays inherent in this disruptive process, there is also the question of its impact on incentives.

Nor is the overfunding of firms during booms necessarily a good thing. While it can stimulate creativity (Ewens, Nanda, and Rhodes-Kropf 2018), it can also lead to wasteful duplication, as multiple companies pursue the same opportunity, with each follower often being ever more marginal. Often, the initial market leader's staff is poached by the me-too followers, disrupting the progress of the firm with the best chance of success. Moreover, once the overfunding subsides, the firms that still survive struggle to attract funding, as the sector often takes on a poisonous atmosphere that deters venture investors. Numerous examples of such crazed duplication can be offered: the recent plethora of social networking companies, the frenzy surrounding B2B and B2C internet companies in the late 1990s, and the surge in funding disk-drive companies in the early 1980s. In each case, a surge of activity was followed by a reaction, when venture capitalists, suffering from poor returns, recoiled from the industry. As a result, these periods were incredibly disruptive to all firms within the affected industries.

In many cases, however, political leaders interpret these surges in activity as signals that it is appropriate to intervene with new subsidies, even as the marginal returns from public money decline. The public funds can have the effect of adding "fuel to the fire" of an overheated market. The decision of the Chinese government to "double down" on subsidizing venture activity after the boom in the first half of the 2010s is a dramatic example.

7.3.3   The Human Dimension

The final disengagement reflects the nature of people who often are associated with the greatest entrepreneurial success. Government officials may have many valuable talents and play incredibly important roles, but the skill sets associated with successfully identifying and funding entrepreneurial businesses are very different from those encountered in their typical daily work. The ambiguity, complexity, and specialization associated with such ventures make these tasks quite challenging.

In many instances, officials may be manifestly inadequate to the task of selecting and managing entrepreneurial or innovative firms. Many examples can be offered of government leaders who did not think carefully about realistic market opportunities, the nature of the entrepreneurs and intermediaries being financed, and how the subsidies they offered would affect behavior. Well-intentioned officials can make rules that prove to be very harmful to those they mean to help, whether they are rules that affect the ability of firms to accept outside financing, to offshore routine coding work, or to respond to shifts in customer demands.

But beyond public incompetence, much of economists' attention has been focused on a darker problem that affects these and similar programs: the theory of "regulatory capture." This hypothesis suggests that entities, whether part of government or industry, will organize to capture the direct and indirect subsidies that the public sector hands out.[10] Yet public subsidies are often prone to political capture problems, where well-connected individuals end up with the bulk of the benefits, and those geared toward entrepreneurial firms are no exception (Akcigit, Baslandze, and Lotti 2018). These issues are exacerbated by the fact that the most creative entrepreneurs are often outsiders; for instance, an extensive literature has documented the disproportionate representation of immigrants in US entrepreneurship, both in general and among high-potential enterprises (Kerr and Kerr 2017; see Fairlie and Lofstrom 2015 for a more general review).

These capture problems are often exacerbated by opaque and poorly

10. The articulation of this model in the economics literature is frequently attributed to Olson (1965); its formal modeling is attributed to Becker (1983) and Peltzman (1976).

defined processes. While selecting the most promising new ventures is unlikely to ever be easy, making the process opaque is unlikely to help. For instance, the Department of Energy had little transparency about the criteria used to select the awards to cleantech firms discussed in the introduction. Reflecting this lack of clarity, firms responded by hiring lobbyists to seek awards. More than half of the cleantech companies in the portfolio of New Enterprise Associates, a large US venture firm, hired lobbyists to attempt to influence the rewards. The emphasis on influence activities was exacerbated by the huge size of the individual awards: rather than scattering the funds over a variety of contenders, the Obama administration sought to pick winners. This is a classic situation where a public program targeted an area that was already interesting to private investors and actually ended up introducing counterproductive distortions.

7.4   The Search for Solutions

How can these seeming disconnects be addressed? In the final part of the chapter, I discuss two potential policy reforms—independence and reliance on matching funds—that could address them.

7.4.1   The Need for Independence

One way to address the incentive issues described above is for policy makers to emulate central bankers and seek to insulate entrepreneurial policy making from day-to-day political pressures. A long list of economists has extolled the need to separate monetary policy form political pressures, lest the temptation to "do the wrong thing" prior to an election be too strong. Establishing an organization to implement new venture policies in which the leadership has the independence from day-to-day political pressures can similarly lead to longer-term decisions that can address some of the challenges delineated above. Such a step may also make it easier to terminate a program when it is no longer needed.

Similar independent governance has been successfully implemented in other investment arenas. For instance, consider the experience of the Canadian Pension Plan (CPP).[11] The plan was established in 1966 as a layer of retirement savings sitting between the Old Age Security System (similar to Social Security in the United States) and individual savings. It collected mandated contributions from employers and workers, and offered benefits that were a set percentage of wages, paid by the contributions of previous years and the returns from the plan's investments.

For the first 30 years of CPP's existence, expenses rose as benefits like inflation indexing were added. Funds were invested in nonnegotiable Canadian-

---

11. This vignette is drawn from Canadian Pension Plan Investment Board (various years); Hardymon, Leamon, and Lerner (2009); and Lerner, Rhodes-Kropf, and Burbank (2013).

government fixed-income bonds and also loaned to the provinces at sub-market interest rates for projects such as building schools and roads. These projects may have benefited Canadian society, but not surprisingly they did little for CPP's bottom line. Furthermore, an aging population was working against CPP. The government realized that rescuing CPP meant either drastic cuts in benefits or sharp increases in contribution rates.

Similar problems have been shown to beset many US pensions, especially those with heavy political representation on their board (Andonov, Hochberg, and Rauh 2018). But unlike in the United States, where governments have almost universally kicked pension problems "down the road," between 1995 and 1997, the federal and provincial Canadian governments managed to craft a solution.

The CPP Investment Board was established in 1997 in response to these challenges. One crucial part of the reforms adopted by the Canadian government was a dramatic restructuring of the plan's governance. It adopted a structure that former CEO Mark Wiseman referred to as "turducken," except instead of a series of stuffed poultry, it featured "a partnership model inside a Crown corporation inside a pension plan" (Lerner, Rhodes-Kropf, and Burbank 2013). In order to limit political influence, the CPPIB governance was set up as a 12-member board notionally appointed by the federal and provincial governments, with appointments based entirely on business acumen, not political connections. The board of directors in turn appointed the CEO, with no right of veto from any government. The organization's mandate was set as investing "solely for the benefit of CPP members" to achieve the best long-term, risk-weighted returns for the plan's beneficiaries, regardless of government policy objectives. To further insulate CPPIB from political influence, any changes to its charter required approval by an amending process more stringent than that of the Canadian constitution itself. Small experiments along these lines have been reasonably successful in the entrepreneurial promotion business, such as the New Zealand Venture Investment Funds program,[12] and it is my hope that these can be expanded.

Another advantage of independence is more flexibility in setting pay. Setting competitive compensation is even harder for public institutions in Western democracies, where the media may be overeager to engage in sensationalism. The architects of the modern CPPIB created a structure that allowed the public pension unique freedoms, including the ability to set salaries and bonuses completely outside the Canadian civil service scale. With multimillion-dollar bonuses—as well as the ability to live in Toronto, work in a congenial setting, and contribute to the betterment of the nation—CPPIB attracted a high-caliber investment team, many of them Canadians, eager to move home after a stint on Wall Street.

---

12. For a detailed history and analysis of the program, see Lerner, Moore, and Shepherd (2005).

But implementing this scheme has been challenging. The fund was bitterly criticized for proposing to pay bonuses totaling $7 million to four top executives for 2008–9, after the fund had lost almost 19 percent of its value during the financial crisis. CPPIB's rationale that the pay packages were based on long-term performance fell on deaf ears, whether due to its complexity or the political feeding frenzy. The board ultimately adjusted its compensation policy downward. Perhaps unsurprisingly, eventually much of CPPIB's leadership team left for jobs elsewhere.

A similar cautionary tale emerges from the experience of In-Q-Tel, a nonprofit VC firm that was established in 1999 to give the US Central Intelligence Agency greater access to cutting-edge technologies.[13] The agency's scientific leaders realized that the most sophisticated technologies were being developed not within government laboratories, but rather in Silicon Valley start-ups. In-Q-Tel was designed to address this problem by allowing the government to access some of the key innovations of these firms. Using a variety of venture-like tools, the organization invested modest stakes in emerging companies, often in conjunction with independent venture firms.

The CIA realized it needed a special kind of team to run In-Q-Tel: individuals who were at once conversant with the world of high-technology start-ups and with a ponderous, security-conscious government bureaucracy. To maximize the chance of getting the right people, the CIA set up In-Q-Tel as an independent, not-for-profit entity, which shielded it from civil service rules that might discourage many recruits. In order to attract these staff members—and to avoid a revolving door through which people left as soon as they had the requisite experience—the CIA designed a compensation scheme quite different from that of typical government jobs. The package included a flat salary, a bonus based on how well In-Q-Tel met government needs, and an employee investment program, which took a prespecified portion of each employee's salary and invested alongside In-Q-Tel in the young firms in its portfolio.

After In-Q-Tel had operated for a few years, the *New York Post* decided to turn its attention to the organization.[14] Describing the undertaking as "an astonishing tale of taxpayer-financed intrigue on capitalism's street of dreams," journalists homed in on the compensation scheme; one article charged that In-Q-Tel employees were "speculat[ing] with taxpayer money for their own personal benefit." Needless to say, there was no discussion of the challenges of recruiting investment staff conversant with Silicon Valley, or the likelihood that many In-Q-Tel professionals could make far more in the private sector. This arrangement, the *Post* intoned, was "almost identical to the so-called 'Raptor' partnerships through which top officials at Enron

13. This account is based on Book et al. (2005), Business Executives for National Security (2001), and numerous press accounts.
14. These quotes are drawn from one of several pieces on In-Q-Tel done by Byron (2005).

Corp were able to cash in personally on investment activities of the very company that employed them." Whether it was the criticism of the compensation levels—which while attractive by government standards, were far below those of independent venture capitalists—the distractions associated with frequent congressional investigations, or the media scrutiny, In-Q-Tel has struggled to hold on to its investment staff, despite a creative attempt to establish attractive incentives.

While independence does not necessarily guarantee effective policy making, it can increase the likelihood that decisions avoid political fads, relying instead on rules-based approaches and experimental evidence. All too often, in the rush to boost entrepreneurship, policy makers allow no provision for the evaluation of programs. In an ideal world, the future of initiatives should be determined by their success or failure in meeting their goals, rather than considerations such as the vehemence with which supporters argue for their continuation. Independent governance can facilitate better decisions.

Turning again to the SBIR program, there are many examples where analysis could be enormously helpful. A striking study by Howell (2017) suggests while the initial Phase I awards made up only 20 percent of the total of $2.8 billion in awards in fiscal year 2017 (US Small Business Administration 2018), essentially all of the program's positive benefits resulted from those initial grants. Similarly, both Howell's analysis and my own suggest the troublesome impact of the companies that have managed to capture a disproportionate number of awards. These "SBIR mills" commercialize far fewer projects than the firms that receive just one SBIR grant (or a handful of grants). They often have staffs in Washington that focus only on identifying opportunities for subsidy applications. These problems have proven difficult to eliminate, as "mill" staffers tend to be active, wily lobbyists.

An added benefit of such efforts has to do with time frames. Democracies worldwide are shaped by the ebb and flow of election cycles. This inevitably leads to a short-run orientation. And even leaders in office for life are often anxious to display progress and look for quick fixes. But building a venture capital industry is a long-run investment, which takes many years until tangible effects are realized. To cite one example, historians date the birth of the modern US venture capital industry to 1978, a full 20 years after the enactment of the SBIC program. This is not a process that can be accomplished overnight.

As a result, an entrepreneurship or venture capital initiative requires a long-run commitment on the part of public officials. The one certainty is that there will be few immediate returns. If programs are abandoned after a few months or years, they are highly unlikely to bring any benefits. There has to be a commitment to be undaunted by initial failures—for example, the low rate of return that early publicly subsidized investments or funds garner—and instead to fine-tune programs in the face of such discouragements. An independent governance structure can limit these distorting effects.

At the same time, there may be times when a program has lived its useful life and is no longer needed. One nomination might be the Small Business Investment Company (SBIC) program in the United States, which subsidized the formation of venture funds. The US industry is today many orders of magnitude bigger, and the need for the program much less compelling. And many of the firms receiving SBIC funding have been marginal ones that cannot attract private funds. Yet SBIC recipients have vehemently argued for expanding the program, not terminating it.

7.4.2   Matching Funds

Far too often, decisions about fund allocation are distorted by a lack of understanding of how the market works or by political rather than economic considerations. By requiring that matching funds be raised from the private sector, the dangers of uninformed decisions and political interference can be greatly reduced.

We have already alluded to examples of well-intentioned but uninformed leaders making boneheaded decisions, as well as political capture leading to unfortunate decisions, such as to allocate much of the funding to regions where there is little chance of success. Yet another distortion is when policy makers make decisions based on "buzz," or incomplete information. One study determined that 49 of the 50 US states started major programs to promote the biotechnology industry, in hopes of creating a cluster of activity (Feldman and Francis 2003). In fact, only a handful of these states had the base of scientific resources and the supporting infrastructure (e.g., lawyers versed in biotechnology patent law and financing practice) to support a successful cluster, so the bulk of the funds was wasted. When these programs did support a promising firm, in many cases it rapidly moved to a region more conducive to biotechnology entrepreneurship.[15]

The vast majority of efforts by the public sector to target particular industries seem to have been far from successful. If dozens of PhDs poring for years over econometrics models with mountains of historical data have been unable to show how to target industries, how can the typical government leader identify good prospects in a compressed time period and with limited information?

But there is a way to address this problem, at least partially. The most direct way is to insist on matching funds. If venture funds or entrepreneurial firms need to raise money from outside sources, organizations that will ultimately not be commercially viable will be kept off the playing field. In order to ensure that these matching funds send a powerful signal, the matching should involve a substantial amount of capital (ideally, one-half the funding or more should come from the private sector). These stipulations can

15. See, for instance, the saga of Cleveland's biotechnology initiative, as related in Fogarty and Sinha (1999).

limit the temptation to impose geographic diversity requirements that direct funds into nonviable areas.

The power of matching funds was clearly demonstrated in what has been considered the gold standard of public venture capital initiatives. In June 1992, the Israeli government established Yozma Venture Capital Ltd., a $100 million fund wholly owned by the public sector (for more details, see Avnimelech, Kenney, and Teubal 2004; OECD 2003; Senor and Singer 2009; and Trajtenberg 2002). At the time, a single venture fund, Athena Venture Partners, was active in the nation. While there were certainly well-trained engineers in Israel working on promising technologies, entrepreneurs (and would-be company founders) were suspicious of venture investors. This reluctance was based in part on their interactions with the pioneering venture capitalists, as well as on their general skepticism about selling equity to unaffiliated parties. Instead, they preferred to rely on bank debt for financing. The only problem, of course, was that such financing was rarely available for young, risky ventures.

The key goal of Yozma was to bring foreign venture capitalists' investment expertise and networks of contacts to Israel. The need for this assistance was highlighted by the failure of the nation's earlier efforts to promote high-technology entrepreneurship. One assessment concluded that fully 60 percent of the entrepreneurs in prior programs had been successful in meeting their technical goals but nonetheless failed because the entrepreneurs were unable to market their products or raise capital for further development. Foreign expertise was seen as key to overcoming this problem.

Accordingly, Yozma actively discouraged Israeli financiers from participating in its programs. Rather, the focus was on getting foreign venture investors to commit capital to Israeli entrepreneurs. The government provided matching funds to investors, typically $8 million of a $20 million fund. The venture fund was given the right to buy back the government stake within the first five years for the initial value plus a preset interest rate of roughly 5 to 7 percent. Thus, the design of Yozma meant that the government provided an added incentive to the venture fund if the investments proved successful. Moreover, learning from the nation's misadventures during earlier programs to stimulate the venture industry—when cumbersome application procedures and burdensome reporting requirements discouraged participation—the administration of the program was deliberately made simple.

The Yozma program delivered beyond the wildest dreams of the founders. Ten groups took advantage of the offer, mostly from the United States, Western Europe, and Japan. Many of the original Yozma funds, including Gemini and Walden Ventures, earned spectacular returns and served as precursors to larger, follow-on funds. Moreover, many of the local partners recruited by the overseas venture capitalists were able to spin off and establish their own firms, which global venture capitalists were eager to fund because of their impressive track records. (A Yozma "alumni club" allows groups to learn from each other's experiences while making these transitions.) One decade after the program's inception, the ten original Yozma groups were managing Israeli funds totaling $2.9 billion, and the Israeli venture market had expanded to include 60 groups managing approximately $10 billion (Erlich 2007). The magnitude of this success is also suggested by the fact that the ratio of venture investment to GDP is consistently higher in Israel than in any other nation.

As powerful an idea as matching funds is, the devil is in the details. In the Government Guidance Fund initiative in China, the central government imposed matching fund requirements as well. In a number of the top cities, the government funds were matched with capital from legitimate investors. In many second- and third-tier cities (where many of the funds were set up), however, the requirements for matching funds were relaxed. Much of the capital came not from informed private-sector actors, but rather from provincial and state governments eager to boost the local economy, or else from state-owned enterprises under these officials' control. Thus, the informative quality of the matching funds was much reduced.

One concern about a requirement of matching funds is that there are sectors and regions where private funding is very scarce. In these cases, a requirement that firms raise matching venture funding may lead to very little public funding at all. It may be possible to resolve this "chicken or egg" problem by targeting earlier-stage, more informal investors such as individual angel investors. Some governments, for instance, have not only matched the funding provided by these investors, but subsidized the groups to hire an executive director to ensure that their activities run more smoothly. In other cases, however, it may make sense for government to back up even further and focus on "table-setting" activities that create a conducive environment for entrepreneurs and their potential investors, rather than directly financing companies or investors.

7.5   Final Thoughts

Many of the same policies that have driven governments to promote innovation in general have led to a public policy focus on entrepreneurship. The bulk of these efforts have been well intentioned. But the substantial challenges associated with the promotion of entrepreneurial businesses have meant that the success rate is not as great as many policy makers hoped or expected.

At the same time, the numerous efforts around the globe suggest some guiding principles for maximizing the success of these funds. In particular, I highlight here two ideas. Rather than distributing the public funds willy-nilly, a requirement for matching funds can ensure market validation for the ideas. And placing the body under the aegis of an independent body can help buffer these long-run initiatives from the ebbs and flows of political fashion.

References

Acs, Zoltan J., and David B. Audretsch. 1988. "Innovation in Large and Small Firms: An Empirical Analysis." *American Economic Review* 78: 678–90.

Akcigit, Ufuk, Salomé Baslandze, and Francesca Lotti. 2018. "Connecting to Power: Political Connections, Innovation, and Firm Dynamics." NBER Working Paper No. 25136. Cambridge, MA: National Bureau of Economic Research.

Andonov, Aleksandar, Yael Hochberg, and Joshua Rauh. 2018. "Political Representation and Governance: Evidence from the Investment Decisions of Public Pension Funds." *Journal of Finance* 73: 2041–86.

Aron, Debra J., and Edward P. Lazear. 1990. "The Introduction of New Products." *American Economic Review Papers and Proceedings* 80: 421–26.

Arora, Ashish, Sharon Belenzon, and Andrea Patacconi. 2015. "Killing the Golden Goose? The Decline of Science in Corporate R&D, 1980–2007." NBER Working Paper No. 20902. Cambridge, MA: National Bureau of Economic Research.

Avnimelech, Gil, Martin Kenney, and Morris Teubal. 2004. "Building Venture Capital Industries: Understanding the U.S. and Israeli Experiences." BRIE Working Paper No. 160.

Azoulay, Pierre, and Josh Lerner. 2012. "Technological Innovation and Organizations." In *The Handbook of Organizational Economics*, edited by Robert Gibbons and John Roberts, 575–603. Princeton, NJ: Princeton University Press.

Bai, Jessica, Shai Bernstein, Abhishek Dev, and Josh Lerner. 2020. "Public Entrepreneurial Finance around the World." NBER Working Paper No. 28744. Cambridge, MA: National Bureau of Economic Research.

Becker, Gary S. 1983. "A Theory of Competition among Pressure Groups for Political Influence." *Quarterly Journal of Economics* 98: 371–400.

Bernstein, Shai, Xavier Giroud, and Richard R. Townsend. 2016. "The Impact of Venture Capital Monitoring." *Journal of Finance* 71: 1591–1622.

Bloom, Nicholas, Tarek Hassan, Aakash Kalyani, Josh Lerner, and Ahmed Tahoun. 2020. "The Geography of New Technologies." August 13. https://ssrn.com/abstract=3671016.

Book, Kevin, Felda Hardymon, Ann Leamon, and Josh Lerner. 2005. "In-Q-Tel." Harvard Business School Case No. 9-804-146.

Business Executives for National Security. 2001. *Accelerating the Acquisition and Implementation of New Technologies for Intelligence: The Report of the Independent Panel on the Central Intelligence Agency In-Q-Tel Venture.* Washington, DC: BENS.

Byron, Christopher. 2005. "Penny Stock Spies." *New York Post*, April 25.

Canadian Pension Plan Investment Board. Various years. *Annual Reports.* Toronto: CPPIB.

Chen, Henry, Paul Gompers, Anna Kovner, and Josh Lerner. 2010. "Buy Local? The Geography of Venture Capital." *Journal of Urban Economics* 67: 90–110.

Cohen, Wesley M. 2010. "Fifty Years of Empirical Studies of Innovative Activity and Performance." In *Handbook of Economics of Innovation*, vol. 1, edited by Bronwyn H. Hall and Nathan Rosenberg, 129–213. Amsterdam: North-Holland.

Cohen, Wesley M., Richard C. Levin, and David C. Mowery. 1987. "Firm Size and R&D Intensity: A Re-examination." *Journal of Industrial Economics* 35: 543–63.

Deger, Renee. 1993. "Disbursements on the Rise: Sharp Gains Raise Yellow Flag to Some Venture Capitalists." *Venture Capital Journal* 33 (December): 29.

Erlich, Yigdal. 2007. "The Yozma Group: Policy and Success Factors." Unpublished presentation.

Ewens, Michael, Ramana Nanda, and Matthew Rhodes-Kropf. 2018. "Cost of Experimentation and the Evolution of Venture Capital." *Journal of Financial Economics* 128: 422–42.

Fairlie, Robert W., and Magnus Lofstrom. 2015. "Immigration and Entrepreneurship." In *Handbook of the Economics of International Migration*, edited by Barry R. Chiswick and Paul W. Miller, 877–911. Amsterdam: North-Holland.

Feldman, Maryann P., and Johanna L. Francis. 2003. "Fortune Favors the Prepared Region: The Case of Entrepreneurship and the Capitol Region Biotechnology Cluster." *European Planning Studies* 11: 765–88.

Feng, Emily. 2018. "China's State-Owned Venture Capital Funds Battle to Make an Impact." *Financial Times*, December 23. https://www.ft.com/content/4fa2caaa -f9f0-11e8-af46-2022a0b02a6c.

Florida, Richard, and Ian Hathaway. 2018. *The Rise of the Startup City*. Washington, DC: Center for American Entrepreneurship.

Fogarty, Michael, and Amit Sinha. 1999. "Why Older Industrial Regions Can't Generalize from Route 128 and Silicon Valley: University-Industry Relationships and Regional Innovation Systems." In *Industrializing Knowledge*, edited by Lewis M. Branscomb, 473–509. Cambridge, MA: MIT Press.

Glaeser, Edward L., William R. Kerr, and Giacomo A. M Ponzetto. 2010. "Clusters of Entrepreneurship." *Journal of Urban Economics* 67: 150–68.

Gold, David M. 2009. "Cleantech Stimulus Not Very Stimulating." *GreenGold Blog*, September 29. http://www.greengoldblog.com/2009/09/cleantech-stimulus-not -very-stimulating.html.

Gompers, Paul. 1995. "Optimal Investment, Monitoring, and the Staging of Venture Capital." *Journal of Finance* 50: 1461–90.

Gompers, Paul, Will Gornall, Steven Kaplan, and Ilya Strebulaev. 2020. "How Do Venture Capitalists Make Decisions?" *Journal of Financial Economics* 135: 169–90.

Hardymon, Felda, Ann Leamon, and Josh Lerner. 2009. "Canada Pension Plan Investment Board." Harvard Business School Case no. 809-073.

Helft, Miguel. 2006. "A Kink in Venture Capital's Gold Chain." *New York Times*, October 7. https://www.nytimes.com/2006/10/07/business/07venture.html.

Howell, Sabrina T. 2017. "Financing Innovation: Evidence from R&D Grants." *American Economic Review* 107: 1136–64.

Ivashina, Victoria, and Josh Lerner. 2019. *Patent Capital: The Challenges and Promises of Long-Term Investing*. Princeton, NJ: Princeton University Press.

Kao, Hilary. 2013. "Beyond Solyndra: Examining the Department of Energy's Loan Guarantee Program." *William and Mary Environmental Law and Policy Review* 37: 425–509.

Kaplan, Steven N., and Per Stromberg. 2003. "Financial Contracting Theory Meets the Real World: An Empirical Analysis of Venture Capital Contracts." *Review of Economic Studies* 70: 281–315.

———. 2004. "Characteristics, Contracts, and Actions: Evidence from Venture Capitalist Analyses." *Journal of Finance* 109: 2173–206.

Kerr, Sari P., and William R. Kerr. 2017. "Immigrant Entrepreneurship." In *Measuring Entrepreneurial Businesses: Current Knowledge and Challenges*, edited by John Haltiwanger, Erik Hurst, Javier Miranda, and Antoinette Schoar, 187–249. Chicago: University of Chicago Press.

Kingdom of Saudi Arabia. 2019. *Vision 2030*. https://vision2030.gov.sa/en /programs/PIF.

Kirsner, Scott. 2009. "Does Lobbying Always Pay?" *Innovation Economy Blog*, August 6. http://www.boston.com/business/technology/innoeco/2009/08/does_lobbying _always_pay.html.

Kortum, Sam, and Josh Lerner. 2000. "Assessing the Impact of Venture Capital on Innovation." *RAND Journal of Economics* 31: 674–92.

Lerner, Josh. 1999. "The Government as Venture Capitalist: The Long-Run Effects of the SBIR Program." *Journal of Business* 72: 285–318.

———. 2009. *Boulevard of Broken Dreams: Why Public Efforts to Boost Entrepreneurship and Venture Capital Have Failed—and What to Do about It*. Princeton, NJ: Princeton University Press.

———. 2012. *The Architecture of Innovation*. Boston: Harvard Business Press.

Lerner, Josh, David Moore, and Stuart Shepherd. 2005. *A Study of New Zealand's Venture Capital Market and Implications for Public Policy: A Report to the Ministry of Research Science and Technology*. Auckland: LECG.

Lerner, Josh, Matthew Rhodes-Kropf, and Nathaniel Burbank. 2013. "Canada Pension Plan Investment Board: October 2012." Harvard Business School Case no. 813-103.

Lipton, Eric, and Clifford Krauss. 2011. "A Gold Rush of Subsidies in Clean Energy Search." *New York Times*, November 12. http://www.nytimes.com/2011/11/12/business/energy-environment/a-cornucopia-of-help-for-renewable-energy.html?_r=1&nl=todaysheadlines&emc=tha2.

MAGNiTT. 2020. *Q3 2020 MENA Venture Investment Summary*. Dubai: MAGNiTT.

Mullaney, Tim. 2009. "Lobbyists Are First Winners in Obama's Clean-Technology Push." *Bloomberg Business News*, March 25. http://www.bloomberg.com/apps/news?pid=20601109&sid=aNH.vsK2D.lQ&refer=home.

Neher, Darwin V. 1999. "Staged Financing: An Agency Perspective." *Review of Economic Studies* 66: 255–74.

OECD. 2003. "Venture Capital Policy Review: Israel." STI Working Paper No. 2003/3. Paris: Organisation for Economic Co-operation and Development.

———. 2019. *Financing SMEs and Entrepreneurs 2018: An OECD Scoreboard*. Paris: Organisation for Economic Co-operation and Development.

Olson, Mancur. 1965. *The Logic of Collective Action*. Cambridge, MA: Harvard University Press.

"Oppose Wasteful $10 Billion Increase for DOE Nuclear Loan Guarantee Program." 2010. *Letter from Taxpayers for Common Sense*, December 10. http://www.taxpayer.net/search_by_tag.php?action=view&proj_id=4063&tag=loan%20guarantees&type=Project.

Oster, Shai, and Lulu Yilun Chen. 2016. "Inside China's Historic $338 Billion Tech Startup Experiment." *Bloomberg Business News*, March 8. https://www.bloomberg.com/news/articles/2016-03-08/china-state-backed-venture-funds-tripled-to-338-billion-in-2015.

Peltzman, Sam. 1976. "Towards a More General Theory of Regulation." *Journal of Law and Economics* 19: 211–40.

Prusa, Thomas J., and James A. Schmitz Jr. 1994. "Can Companies Maintain Their Initial Innovation Thrust? A Study of the PC Software Industry." *Review of Economics and Statistics* 76: 523–40.

Rowley, Jason. 2019. "Chinese Startups Net Smallest Share of Global VC Investment in Years." *Crunchbase News*, July 18. https://news.crunchbase.com/news/chinese-startups-net-smallest-share-of-global-vc-investment-in-years/.

Schumpeter, Joseph. 1942. *Capitalism, Socialism, and Democracy*. New York: Harper & Brothers.

Senor, Dan, and Saul Singer. 2009. *Start-Up Nation: The Story of Israel's Economic Miracle*. New York: Twelve.

Seoudi, Iman, and Salma Mahmoud. 2016. "Public Policy for Venture Capital: A

Comparative Study of Emirates, Saudi Arabia and Egypt." *Review of Business and Finance Studies* 7: 19–42.

Shen, Lucinda. 2016. "China Is the Biggest Venture Capital Firm in the World." *Fortune*, March 9. https://fortune.com/2016/03/09/investors-venture-capital-china/.

Sindi, Hayat. 2015. "Building the Entrepreneurial Ecosystem in Saudi Arabia and the Middle East." In *Social Entrepreneurship in the Middle East*, vol. 2, edited by Dima Jamali and Alessandro Lanteri, 63–88. London: Palgrave Macmillan.

"Special Report: Capital Transfusion Renewal." 1980. *Venture Capital Journal* 20 (July): 6–8.

Sposito, Sean. 2009. "A123 Gets $249m in Stimulus Funding." *Boston Globe*, August 6. http://archive.boston.com/business/articles/2009/08/06/a123systems_receives_249m_in_stimulus_funds/.

Townsend, Richard. 2015. "The Propagation of Financial Shocks: The Case of Venture Capital." *Management Science* 61: 2782–2802.

Trajtenberg, Manuel. 2002. "Government Support for Commercial R&D: Lessons from the Israeli Experience." In *Innovation Policy and the Economy*, vol. 2, edited by Adam Jaffe, Josh Lerner, and Scott Stern, 79–134. Cambridge, MA: MIT Press.

US Small Business Administration. 2018. *FY 2017 SBIR/STTR Annual Report*. Washington, DC: US Small Business Administration.

Weingast, Barry R., Kenneth A. Shepsle, and Christopher Johnsen. 1981. "The Political Economy of Benefits and Costs: A Neoclassical Approach to Distributive Politics." *Journal of Political Economy* 89: 642–64.

Yang, Jing. 2019. "China's Venture Capital Boom Is Over, Leaving Investors High and Dry." *Wall Street Journal*, November 15. https://www.morningstar.com/news/dow-jones/201911144209/chinas-venture-capital-boom-is-over-leaving-investors-high-and-dry.

Contributors

Ufuk Akcigit
Department of Economics
University of Chicago
1126 East 59th Street
Chicago, IL 60637

Pierre Azoulay
MIT Sloan School of Management
100 Main Street
Cambridge, MA 02142

Austan Goolsbee
Booth School of Business
University of Chicago
5807 S. Woodlawn Avenue
Chicago, IL 60637

Bronwyn H. Hall
Department of Economics
University of California
Berkeley, CA 94720

Benjamin F. Jones
Department of Management and
    Strategy
Kellogg School of Management
Northwestern University
2211 Campus Drive
Evanston, IL 60208

Sari Pekkala Kerr
Wellesley College
106 Central Street
Wellesley, MA 02481

William R. Kerr
Harvard Business School
Soldiers Field
Boston, MA 02163

Josh Lerner
Harvard Business School
Soldiers Field
Boston, MA 02163

Danielle Li
MIT Sloan School of Management
100 Main Street
Cambridge, MA 02142

Stefanie Stantcheva
Department of Economics
Harvard University
Cambridge, MA 02138

Lawrence H. Summers
Harvard Kennedy School of
 Government
79 JFK Street
Cambridge, MA 02138

John Van Reenen
London School of Economics
Houghton Street
London WC2A 2AE, United
 Kingdom

Author Index

Subject Index

spillovers, 3–4, 14–15; imitative, 43; intertemporal, 44–45; negative, duplication
and, 45; positive, 14; user, 43–44
start-ups: small vs. large firms, 201; US tax
treatment of, 179–82; venture capital and,
200–201
start-up visas, 100–101; international web-
sites on, 110; US modifications to, 108–9;
US proposals for, 107–8. *See also* entrepreneur visas
stealing, business, 45
STEM workers: immigration and, 71–72;
policies for increasing, 68–69
student visas, 99

talent, pool of potential, 5
targeted, innovation-specific tax policies,
193–94
taxation: framework for innovation and,
192f; mobility of inventors and firms and,
198–99
tax credits, incremental, 177–78
taxes: corporate, 203; general, 190
tax policies: categories of, 193; comparing
different incentives and, 159–61; design
issues for, 154–56; general, 193, 195–97;
innovation and, 7–9, 189–90; questions
for, 151–52; responses to, 194; targeted,
innovation-specific, 193–94; ways, shape
innovation, 191–95

teams: composition and quality of, 203–7;
knowledge diffusion and, 207–8
temporary visas, 91

undergraduates, increasing number of, 68
United States (US): declining business
dynamics in, 200–203; history and current status of R&D tax credit in, 169–75;
immigration system of, summary, 90–93;
mobility of inventors and firms in, 198–
99; potential reforms within existing
immigration system of, 93–100; ratio of
researchers in, 64, 64t; tax treatment of
start-ups in, 179–80
universities, expanding, 68–71
user spillovers, 43–44. *See also* spillovers
venture capital funding, staging of investments and efficiency of, 218
venture capitalists, 200, 216–19; preferred
stock and, 218
venture capital (VC)–backed start-ups,
200–201
visas, 6; for entrepreneurs, 100–107; for
inventors, 90–100; Optional Practical
Training, 6, 99; start-up, 100–101, 107–
10; student, 99–100; temporary, 91. *See
also* H-1B visas

Yozma Venture Capital Ltd., 230–31